FROM

DROUGHT to DROUGHT

An Archaeological record
of life patterns as developed by the
Gallina Indians of north central New Mexico
(A.D. 1050 to 1300)

CANJILON MOUNTAIN

Hunting and Gathering Sites

By

Florence Hawley Ellis

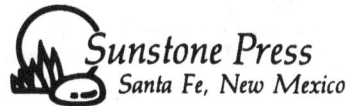

Sunstone Press
Santa Fe, New Mexico

DEDICATED TO TWO FELLOW WORKERS,
ALLEN AND GEORGEANNA FAUX,

Library of Congress Cataloging in Publication Data:

Ellis, Florence Hawley
    From Drought to Drought: an archaeological record of life patterns as devloped by
the Gallina Indians of north central New Mexico / by Florence Hawley Ellis.
        p.   cm.
    Bibliography: v. 1, p.
    Includes index.
    Contents: v. 1. Canjilon Mountain: hunting and gathering sites.
    1. Indians of North America — New Mexico — Antiquities.   2. Excavations (Ar-
chaeology) — New Mexico.   3. New Mexico-Antiquities.   I. Florence Hawley Ellis
Museum of Anthropology.   II. Title.   III. Title: Gallina Indians of north central New
Mexico (A.D. 1050 to 1300)
E78.N65E38 1988
978.9'52 — dc19   88-16898
                                                          CIP
ISBN: 0-86534-120-6 (v. 1) : $14.95

Published in 1988 by SUNSTONE PRESS
            Post Office Box 2321
            Santa Fe, NM 87504-2321 / USA

Table of Contents

List of Illustrations

Dulce Springs, Site III

Preface

A Word of Explanation and 500 Words of Thanks

Our three and a fraction short seasons of work in the Gallina hunting-gathering camps on Canjilon Mountain were done before our one early and several later seasons at Rattlesnake Point (where our excavations are continuing) and five in the Gallina villages of the south Llaves area, but as nothing like those Canjilon sites previously had been known, we delayed their final analysis until we should have had considerable experience with ruins illustrating Gallina home life. The several but usually short reports of other archaeologists who worked in the Gallina area at different times clearly indicated that the culture had been far from static. There still were numerous new discoveries to be made, as found by our workers who consisted of six to seven experienced crew chiefs plus thirty-five to sixty enrollees per season in the Ghost Ranch Seminar on Southwestern Archaeology.

By intent, publication of data from the village site studies was to have preceded that on the mountain sites, for this is as the analyses were handled, but chance has set the date for this volume a bit ahead of the others and designated it Volume I. Our summary chapter reflects the whole.

We are deeply appreciative of those faithful crew chiefs, whose required annual reports on the specific sites they supervised provide the bases on which our studies depend. Without the details for which they are responsible day by day, no overall picture could have emerged.

James Bain (deceased 1987)	Peter McKenna
David Bardé	Mary Lu Moore
Gordon Bronitsky	Gordon Page
Bruce Campbell	William Perret
John Hayden	Mary Purdy
Frances Kenney	Darlene Shibley (deceased 1985)

Two deaths, two retirements, and some withdrawals cut into this unit, and several persons, Jim Shibley, Bill McNatt, Cheryl Muceus, Chip Hatch, Andrea Ellis Dodge, Brian Blanchard, Pat and Fred Trusell have been added for one or more sessions, so that the supervisory personnel usually stays at six, plus myself as overall supervisor. We also are most grateful to Fred Trusell whose newly learned instrument surveying provided Bill Perret with a partner for the Butts Site mapping. Jim Shibley's delicate manipulation of the Ranch backhoe when needed for occasional trenching and the moving of excess surface debris almost could be likened to a caterer slicing a wedding cake!

We want to thank Jim Hall, director of Ghost Ranch when this work was done, not only for prying out and moving a multitude of boulders, but also for Ranch backing in this project of interpreting and describing how peoples with backgrounds very different from our own met and handled problems seven centuries ago in the same region where Anglos and Spanish Americans have struggled to make a living — and periodically given up — in the last 300 years.

And we must express our appreciation of the museum staff members who aided in getting out this volume: Darlene Shibley, Lesley Poling-Kempes, and Cheryl Muceus who labored over cataloging, finding specimens as needed, and the typing of manuscripts and charts, and Andrea Ellis Dodge who has typed, designed the book, seen to the technicalities, and pieced the volume together like a fine patchwork quilt. Ryan Bricco and Andrea Ellis Dodge traced into final form the drawings originally made by Ellis and the several crew chiefs. Dodge and Janice Baker labored patiently once and again over "final" proof corrections, Dodge and Lou Baker worked on the production of camera ready text, and Katherine Murdock did the drawing for the cover. Finally, there were Dick Bice and those others of the Albuquerque Archaeological Society whose cooperation and expert professional aid through technicalities made it possible to put out our projected three volumes.

And where would all this have gotten us had it not been for the blessing of Horace Butts (since deceased) of Albuquerque, original owner of the south Llaves area lands on which we worked, and similarly of the new purchasers, Charmaine and William Crawford of Roswell, New Mexico. Thanks to the generosity of past and current owners, the finds all are in the FHE Museum of Anthropology at Ghost Ranch, together with those from the mountain camps on loan from Maxwell Museum of Anthropology at the University of New Mexico through which our original permit for excavations was made, and those exciting items we later uncovered at Rattlesnake Point, under permit from the U.S. Forest Service.

Our museum's Gallina Room presently houses one of the largest existent exhibits of artifacts and pottery representing this relatively little-known culture, and more is being added annually.

Let us be your host!

Florence Hawley Ellis
Executive Curator and Director of Excavations,
Florence Hawley Ellis Museum of Anthropology
Ghost Ranch, Abiquiu, N.M.

GENERAL LOCATION MAP

Turkey Spring

Site I—LA:10641
Site II—LA:10643

• Turkey Spring

• Santa Fe
• Albuquerque

CANJILON RANGER DISTRICT
CARSON NATIONAL FOREST
NEW MEXICO

1969

Scale

1 ½ 0 1 2 3 4 5 Miles

LEGEND

━ ━ ━ ━ Ranger District Boundary

━━━━ National Forest Land

MAP 1

9

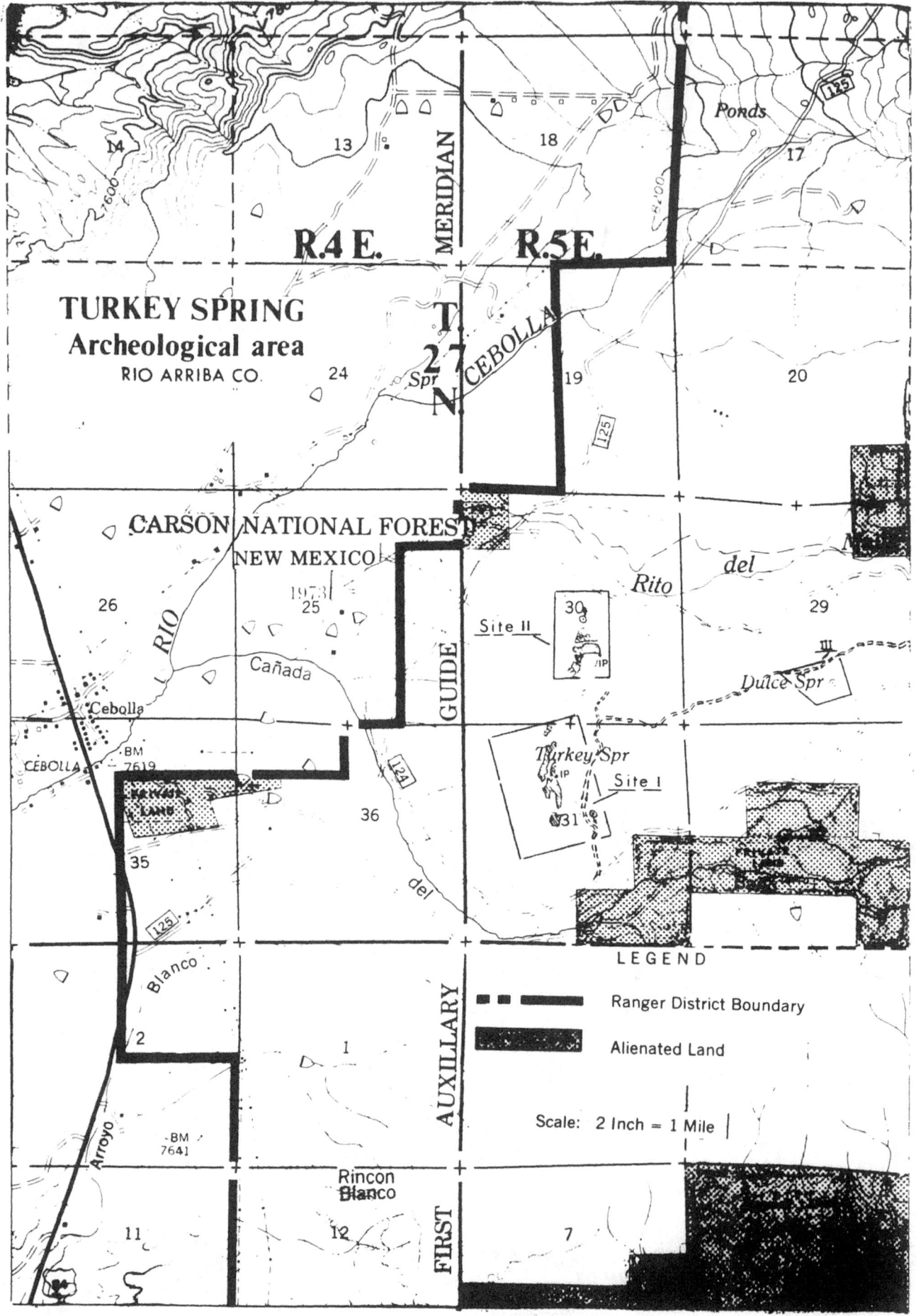

Loation of specific Gallina hunting-gathering sites on the slopes of Canjilon Mountain

TURKEY SPRING
Archeological area
RIO ARRIBA CO.

R.4 E. | R.5E.

MERIDIAN

T. 27 N.

CEBOLLA

CARSON NATIONAL FOREST
NEW MEXICO

Ponds

Rito del

Site II

30

III

Dulce Spr

Turkey Spr

Site I

31

LEGEND

- - - Ranger District Boundary

▬▬▬ Alienated Land

Scale: 2 Inch = 1 Mile

Rincon
Blanco

Blanco

Arroyo

MAP 2

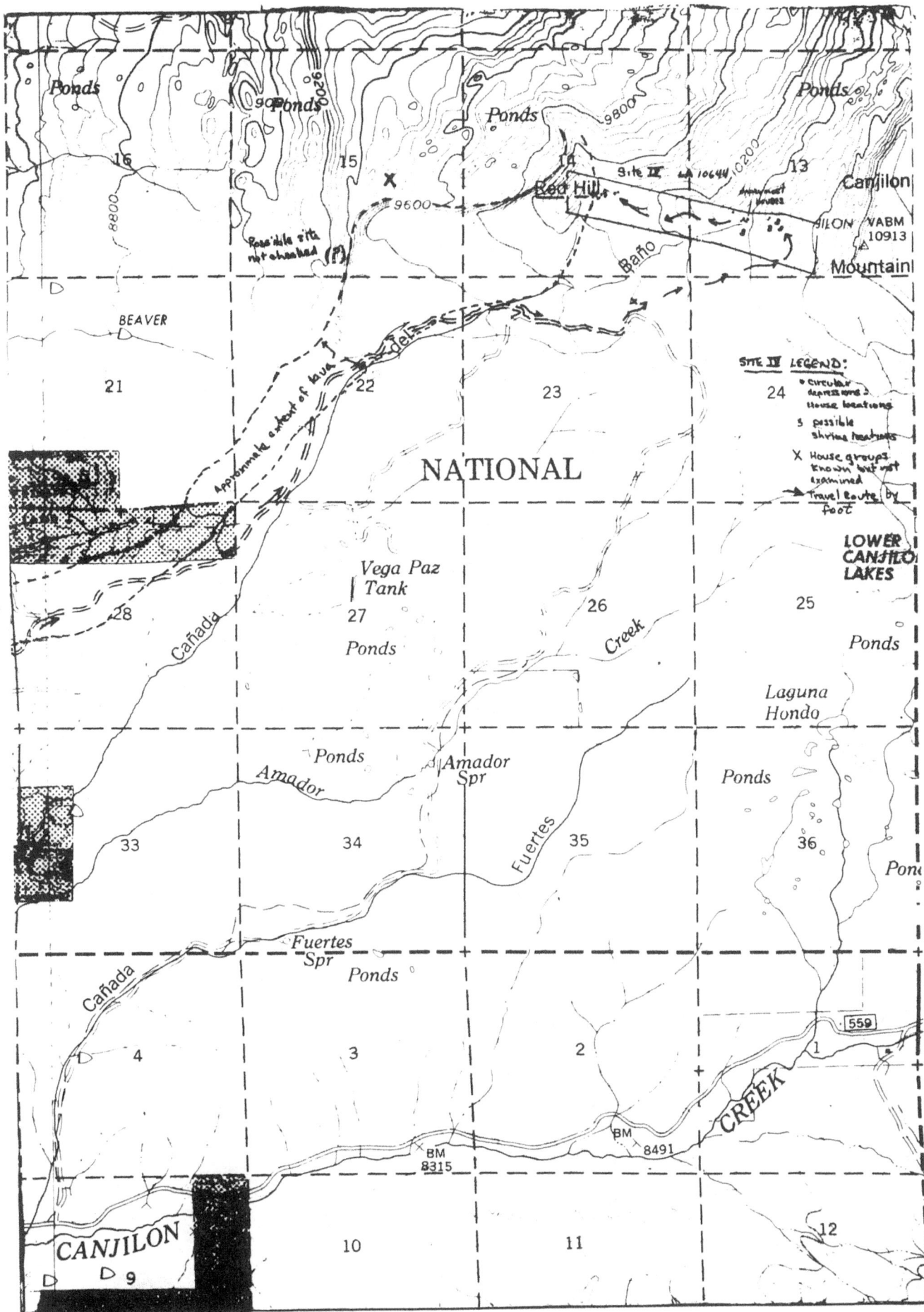

Ponds

Ponds

Ponds

Ponds

9800

9600

10200

16

15

14

Site IV   LA 10644

13   Canjilon

Red Hill

Monument knolls

CANJILON VABM
10913

Mountain

9800

Baño

X

9600

Possible site
not checked (?)

BEAVER

del

SITE IV LEGEND:

o circular
depressions:
house locations

s possible
shrine locations

X House groups
known but not
examined

Travel route by
foot

21

22

23

24

Approximate extent of lava

NATIONAL

LOWER
CANJILON
LAKES

Cañada

28

Vega Paz
Tank

Ponds

26

Creek

25

Ponds

27

Laguna
Hondo

Ponds

Amador

Ponds

Amador
Spr

Ponds

33

34

Fuertes

35

36

Pon

Fuertes
Spr

Ponds

Cañada

559

4

3

2

1

CREEK

BM
8491

BM
8315

CANJILON

9

10

11

12

TURKEY SPRING
ARCHEOLOGICAL
SITE No.:
I
LA No.: 10641

LEGEND

surface features

⊙ house, storage unit, etc.
◖ cave, lrg.
◁ " , small
⊙ ?
↘ roasting pit
basalt slope
  volcanic flow
timbered areas

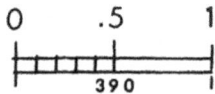

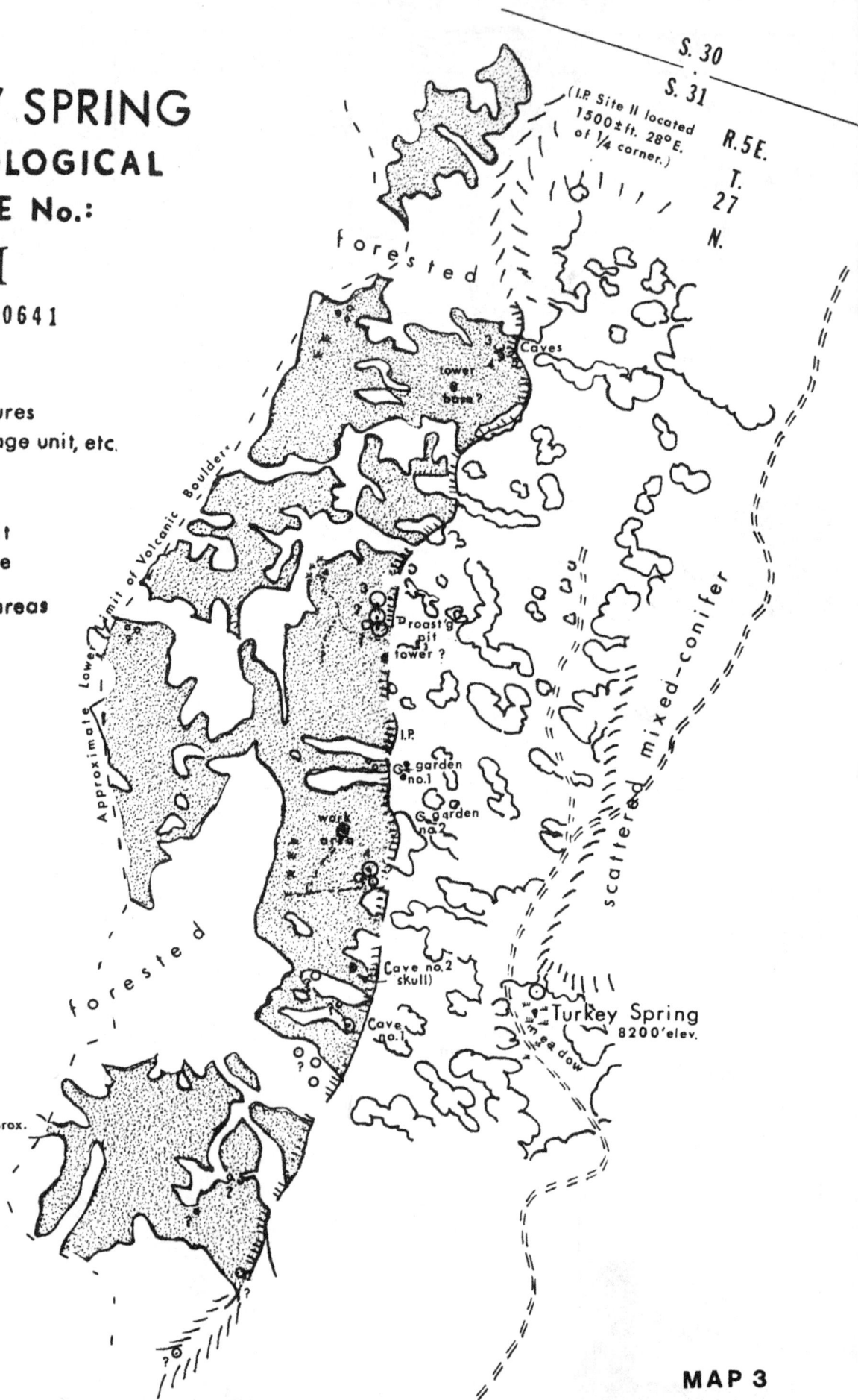

N

0   .5   1
        390
scale
1 in = 390 ft. approx.
jsh 11/73

forested

S. 30
S. 31
R. 5 E.
T. 27 N.

(I.P. Site II located
1500±ft. 28°E.
of 1/4 corner.)

Caves
tower
& base?

scattered mixed-conifer

roast'g pit
tower?

I.P.

garden no.1

garden no.2

work area

Cave no.2 (skull)

Cave no.1

Turkey Spring
8200' elev.

meadow

Approximate Lower Limit of Volcanic Boulder

forested

?

MAP 3

Turkey Spring Site I (LA 10641),
location of structures

12

INTRODUCTION

The Canjilon Mountain Hunting-Gathering Sites as One Expression of Gallina Culture

At the time of our first Gallina work in 1971 and the three summer seasons following, we realized that we could not legitimately evaluate the significance of our new and unusual finds because too little had been published to provide an adequate background on Gallina culture *per se*. Most of the publications had been short, covering specific features of certain sites and the others so generalized that one tended to feel a bit uncertain as to their data base. Certainly no one previously had excavated and studied sites representing concentrated periods of hunting and gathering activities for any of the prehistoric Pueblo groups, though various archaeologists had surmised that at times some of those peoples had been temporarily forced to such extremes during periods of extended food shortages. There is little question that Gallina culture is ancestral to that of today's Jemez Pueblo people living on the Rio Jemez, a major tributary of the Middle Rio Grande, but to date the Gallina remains one of the least known prehistoric cultures of the Pueblo Southwest.

In consequence, we decided that we would not publish on our Canjilon finds until we ourselves had covered several seasons of work on Gallina home sites and patterns of daily life in one of the most heavily occupied Gallina districts. For this we chose the Llaves area on the drainage of the now commonly dry Rio Gallina and north to Rattlesnake Ridge. Some seasons of work had been done on the latter by University of New Mexico students under direction of Dr. Frank Hibben, but the resulting reports were of no more than magazine length and left many questions. More recent studies by Mackey and Holbrook have filled some gaps but left other problems. A few small excavations by other archaeologists have added bits and pieces, largely but not entirely since 1930.

With this problem in mind, we began what at time of publication adds up to 16 seasons of two-week intensive excavation in the Llaves and Rattlesnake districts by registrants for the Ghost Ranch Archaeological Seminar, their numbers varying between 40 and 60 per season. Study of the resultant data and artifacts was done later, at home by the six or more crew chiefs who supervise the field work under my general direction, each responsible for an annual report, as well as my writing an overall report. These studies and notes provide the basis for future work, for the reports turned in to the U.S. Forest Service on each site under their jurisdiction, and our papers intended for publication.

At first we thought that our initial publication should be on our Llaves and Rattlesnake sites from which we have obtained considerable new data on Gallina culture. These were Gallina home towns. Second thought, however, suggested that it would be better to follow the same chronology in publication as in our work, with the Canjilon hunting-gathering sites to appear as Volume I in a three monograph compilation. Where necessary, we would permit ourselves the benefit of later insights with explanations and discussion. This, then, is our intent, and to aid in understanding, we have included regional culture outlines of the Gallina ancestral line.

Gallina Ancestry

One of the problems periodically brought to the attention of archaeologists specializing in the northern Rio Grande country has been that of Gallina origin. Although it still is known only in a sketchy manner, pertinent data have been accumulating. The history of any people adds considerably to our understanding of their culture.

Recently Gooding (1980:6-11), in writing of the Basketmaker III sites excavated a short distance south of the city of Durango, Colorado, prefaced his discussion with a background definition of the Durango district and its prehistory. The specific importance of this to us lies in the fact that the Rosa Phase in the Gobernador long has been recognized as directly ancestral to Gallina culture, and Gooding makes a strong point for the Rosa Phase having developed from the Basketmaker III La Plata Phase which in turn had developed from the Eastern Basketmaker II culture of the Durango district of southwestern Colorado.

The Durango district fills the space between the La Plata and the Piedra districts, both north of the San Juan River. It is bounded by the drainages of the Animas, Florida, and Los Pinos Rivers, all on the north side of the San Juan. The Gobernador lies directly to the south, across the river.

In the Durango district evidence is plentiful for occupation from 200 or 300 B.C. into the 4th century A.D. by the Eastern branch of the Basketmaker II people. Their groups, living along the edge of mountain valleys where game was abundant, were first described by Morris (1939; Morris and Burgh 1954) when he pointed to their physical and cultural differences from the contemporary Western Basketmaker II people and culture of northeastern Arizona, with which Kidder and Guernsey (1919; Guernsey and Kidder 1921; Guernsey 1931) earlier had acquainted us. In their discussion and conjectures, Morris and Burgh (1954:80-86) call attention to the numerous parallels between Eastern Basketmaker culture and that of the early Mogollon of southwestern New Mexico and southeastern Arizona, a number of which can be found as holdovers into the later Gallina culture. Early contacts or small migrations up what now is the New Mexico-Arizona line were easily possible, and some Mogollon sites actually have been found north of Gallup, New Mexico.

In the Durango district Basketmaker II occupation continued into the 4th century A.D., but by the 6th century Basketmaker III sites, as Gooding notes, were reaching florescence. Villages varied somewhat architecturally, but everywhere preference was shown for open country which made the new major dependence on agriculture possible. The frost sensitivity of beans, introduced in the A.D. 700s and an important food resource because of their high protein content, probably was of considerable concern. The wide valleys provided longer frost-free growing seasons. But at about A.D. 800, when Basketmaker III culture was changing toward that of Pueblo I, the Animas Valley ceased to be a place of permanent abode for anyone.

As Gooding (1980:10) reminds us, the end of occupation of the entire Durango district came with a severe local drought between A.D. 800 and 809. The people, no doubt discouraged by four drought spells within 110 years (A.D. 690-710, around 750, 770-779, and worse in 800-809), apparently abandoned their Durango settlements in a mass exit, though not necessarily within a single year. Where to?

In the nearby Mesa Verde district the weather had remained relatively cool and damp and the count of archaeological sites of what we know as Piedra Phase (A.D. 750-990) shows a tremendous increase above that for the preceding phase, so we can make an educated guess that many Durangans had moved in. Many other Durango households migrated into the area east of Bloomfield and Aztec, New Mexico, in what we now know as the Navajo Reservoir district, where entire villages sprang up. Some went eastward into the Piedra district along the Pine and upper San Juan Rivers. The Gobernador drainage, which had very little occupation before A.D. 800, lay just across the San Juan from the Durango district but nevertheless was cool and damp enough to invite settlement. At least five 9th-century sites were established.

What did the migrants take along? Let us go back a bit, for we will see that some of the traits of the later Gallina culture have a long history.

In contrast to the Western Basketmaker II peoples for whom no constructed homes are known, the knowledge and abilities of the Eastern Basketmaker II people included grading and terracing dwelling sites, the edges sometimes reinforced with embankments of stone. Houses consisted of one approximately circular room with a slightly sunken saucer-like floor in or on which there was a shallow heating pit to hold hot coals brought in from an outside hearth where cooking was done. Some houses had an adjoining smaller room, probably for storage. A few small-to-large storage cists were dug into the floor and some beehive-dome storage compartments were constructed above ground in the main room. The sloping house walls of horizontally laid pieces of tree trunks chinked with clay may have tapered inward and upward into a domed roof, probably cribbed, with no post supports required (Morris and Burgh 1954:75, 84-85).

These Eastern Basketmaker II people were primarily hunters and gatherers but secondarily agriculturists, with corn and squash for small crops. They collected seeds of amaranth, tansy mustard, wild vetch, sunflower, burreed, and the rootstocks of reed grass. *Yucca baccata* and *Yucca glauca* were macerated for ties or stripped for fiber. Bulrushes provided material for mats and bags (Jones and Fonner in Morris and Burgh 1954:94-105). According to Morris (1954:76), neither they nor the Western Basketmakers had any fired or "true" pottery, but in 1963 Dittert, Eddy, and Dickey reported unfired vegetal-tempered pottery and a few rare sherds of a "fired and polished brown ware with a sand temper," Los Pinos Brown, for some Basketmaker II sites of Los Pinos Phase (A.D. 1-400) in the Navajo Reservoir district. There has been a surmise that its finish and color (which involves type of firing) and that of the closely related Sambrito Brown of Basketmaker III both may fit into the Mogollon background Morris had hypothesized. In other words, we seem to have a combination of Basketmaker III architecture and pottery as two reasons to argue that influence spreading from a migration of some Mogollon people northward up the present Arizona-New Mexico line at A.D. 300, or a bit later. This may account for the appearance of Basketmaker II in the eastern portion of the Four Corners area (Morris and Burgh 1953:83-85).

Other crafts with which we can credit the Eastern Basketmaker II people were many types of coiled basketry, twined matting, and twisted cordage of vegetable fiber, human and animal hair, and leather, some of which was hide-wrapped or feather-wrapped. They braided cords and headbands and made aprons consisting of a belt and flap. Finely twined bags ranged from small to large. We have no evidence for sandals other than those of yucca leaves though the Western Basketmakers excelled in production of yucca fiber sandals with decorative designs. Seed beads, stone beads, bone tubes, and shell beads and pendents show interest in personal decoration and also adequate production of some things so that the excess might be used in trade with persons bringing shells from the Gulf of Lower California.

Although they had no hafted axes or mauls, they fashioned corner- and side-notched points for the darts used with their atlatls (spear throwers), made flake knives, scrappers, drills, "horseshoe-shaped" (one-open-end) metates, one- and two-hand manos, stone pipes, rubbing and polishing stones, bone awls, notched animal ribs for cleaning yucca fiber, flakers, antler wrenches, and other less important items. Cooking of stews probably was managed, as by other peoples, by placing the ingredients and water in a tightly coiled basket, dropping heated rocks into it, and a bit later removing the cooled rocks to replace them with more heated rocks. Thus the housewife labored, hour by patient hour.

Now let us step up to the next period.

The Durango Basketmaker III people, who were to abandon their original area for the Mesa Verde, Piedra district, Navajo Reservoir, and the Gobernador at about A.D. 800 because of heavy localized drought, had developed or adopted a number of cultural innovations.

The bow and arrow supplanted the atlatl and dart. The production of gray ware and Black-on-white ware, characteristic in various local types throughout most of the San Juan area, was begun. We also have the Basketmaker III Sambrito Brown vessels from the Upper Navajo Reservoir. In both the gray and the brown wares were two-lugged canteens with much the shape of the two-to-four-lugged canteens produced four centuries later, as we were to find in the Turkey Spring and Dulce Springs mountain sites. The Basketmaker III shouldered brown vessels are sisters in profile to the occasional gray culinary vessels we found at Turkey Spring and wondered whether they should classify as cook pots or small storage jars.

The Basketmaker II surface houses with their horizontally laid, mud-chinked log-section walls now were supplanted by pithouses.

In the 1920s and 1930s when Morris (1939:24-47; 67-75) was working on archaeology of the La Plata district which, as we have said, directly adjoins the western edge of the Durango district and forms a wedge separating it from the Mesa Verde district by a few miles, he unraveled the basic sequence of house and village types for the eastern Four Corners area. This included Basketmaker III in the Chaco. Early Basketmaker III houses were individual pit structures with bases dug a meter or less into the ground and a flat roof supported by four vertical posts set at the edges of the floor excavation or somewhat in from the corners. The walls which sloped from roof to a line back from the edge of the pit were constructed of slender poles covered with reeds, brush, or grass, and then topped with mud. The flat roof was used for additional living-working space, and entrance was through a roof hatchway. Small storage pits were made both inside and outside the structure.

Many areas favored a clever engineering design in which a ventilator opening put through the house wall behind the fire pit led into a short tunnel and shaft and so up to the surface. This let in cool fresh air which was diverted from becoming a direct draft onto the fire pit by a deflector block of stone, clay, or jacal, but still helped the warm smoke to rise and disappear out the smoke-hole hatchway directly over the fire pit.[*] In early Chaco sites, the ventilator shaft was replaced by a vestibule room with an aboveground opening at the far end. That opening may have served primarily for entrance and the room itself for storage, but the supply of fresh air still was available.

In some districts, especially as seen in the early sites of Mesa Verde and Chaco Canyon, a sipapu, the symbolic small jar-shaped opening through which man communicated with Earth Mother, was dug into the floor on the opposite side of the fire pit. (Sipapus are not commonly found in the Durango district.) Orientation of sipapu, fire pit, deflector, and ventilator was actually or approximately north-south. We can be sure of ritual activities being carried on by families in their own homes at this period, though the people of Shabik'eshchee Village in Chaco Canyon also constructed a large kiva which would have accommodated all the inhabitants of the site for what probably were periodic major religious celebrations, possibly solstice and/or rain-fertility rites.

The later Basketmaker III complex in the La Plata district (classified by some as Pueblo I), a local counterpart of the Sambrito Phase in the Navajo Reservoir area, was represented by a similar underground chamber intended for domiciliary use but also for ceremonial activities. The main distinction of this stage consists in storage arrangements now having been concentrated into a single or double row of approximately rectangular surface storerooms constructed of adobe or jacal in an arc behind the pithouse. A few of those in the front row were made larger than others and equipped with fire pits and metates, household requirements. This, says Morris (1939:27), marked the beginning of

---

[*]   I was amused in recently seeing this basic design written up as a newspaper recommendation for an efficient root cellar in which the owner also might live if he chose.

totally secular housing which left the pit structure out in front as a "proto-kiva," a chamber dedicated to religious affairs though still showing by its equipment that it was occupied. Orientation was north-south. In certain sites the proto-kiva was considerably larger than other habitations. The sipapu is found in some pithouses and some proto-kivas of the La Plata and adjoining Mesa Verde districts but not in others.

Archaeologists have suggested that the family which lived in the proto-kiva must have been in charge of religious activities held there. Today's Jemez people, who never have seen a site of this type, still describe it from tradition: "In the early days the people of a village built a house for their most important fetish, and the priest and his family who must protect and do everything necessary for it had to live in that house."

At the same time a few sites consisting of a deep pithouse surrounded at a little distance by a stockade began to appear in the Durango district, both the crescentic and stockaded sites being present by the A.D. 750s (Morris and Burgh 1954:85).

This brings us to the opening of the 9th century and the dissemination of Durango communities already noted.

The precise dating of sites and group movements is a real problem, primarily because relatively few structures yield datable wood or charcoal, and dating by pottery complexes can only provide a time period defined by rather broad limits. One must add that of the many ruins found, only a sampling could be examined because of time and cost. In some areas a fair number are lost to the creation of artificial lakes and other modernizations.

The establishment of early Rosa Phase sites (early Pueblo I: roughly A.D. 700-750) in the Navajo Reservoir area may have resulted from the drought of A.D. 690-710, more severe in the Durango district than in Mesa Verde or the Gobernador. If it was brought about by the drought of the early 800s, the rounded dates given for Reservoir occupation should be set a bit later. Sites centered around a deep but simple circular pithouse with a backdrop of surface storerooms without fire pits, some of which may have been seasonally occupied. Random placement of extra surface structures and random scattering of trash was typical. Outside fire hearths, deep storage pits, and "undercut cooking ovens" (of jar shape) were common, but in the Reservoir area the stockade which surrounded many Rosa Phase Gobernador sites was not often seen until a later date.

The Piedra Phase sites which succeeded those of Rosa Phase in the Reservoir area "were composed of an association of pithouses, surface structures, exterior pits, occasional refuse areas, and a few stockades" (Eddy 1966:493). The two largest yet excavated contained examples of the great "Shabik'eshchee type inter-community kivas" but nothing of the smaller religious society type or the proto-kiva. Most of the homes were of the category referred to by Eddy as the "elaborate pithouse" developed after A.D. 750, deeper and larger than the earlier pithouses. They contained "a wide range of floor and wall architectural details, including ventilator, fire basin, partition wall, and ash pit, warming pit or deflector. All had benches and partition walls ... " (Eddy 1966:363)

Some of these domestic pithouses in the smaller sites did have sipapus, from which archaeologists have surmised that "family and clan ceremonies"[*] were held in homes in those villages, whereas major religious events took place in the intercommunity kivas (Eddy 1966:377). This tells us that the visible sipapu continued to be known to these people, relatives at not too great a distance from the late Rosa-into-Gallina population, but it provides no evidence of the small or religious society kivas. Roberts (1930), excavating sites of this phase at Stollsteimer Mesa in the Piedra district, reported lines of surface rooms in front of which were depressions he believed were borrow-pits for clay to use in house construction, but others have thought that these pits probably were badly eroded small kivas.

Gobernador Canyon which drains into the San Juan River from the southeast, the drainages of the Francis and La Jara Creeks which run parallel courses and reach the San Juan (now actually the Navajo Reservoir) a short distance farther to the northeast, and Canyon Largo which after a long and less precipitous drop finds the San Juan River at Blanco, New Mexico, a short distance east of Bloomfield, all run westward from the Continental Divide. These and the drainage of Pine River on the north side of the San Juan River apparently were taken over by people of the Rosa Phase in upriver moves designed to get around the problem of headward cutting by streams and in the hope of finding more precipitation at higher altitudes.

Our special concern, of course, is with the groups which made the first settlements in the Gobernador, bringing with them, presumably from Durango, the concept of a large and deep pit structure, sometimes backed with a line of small storerooms but characteristically enclosed at a distance with a stockade, one of the most distinctive traits of the Gobernador Rosa Phase (dated broadly as Pueblo I: A.D. 700-900) to which E. T. Hall introduced us in 1944.

---

[*] · This should have read "family and religious society ceremonies." Although in pueblos where clans exist they may own ceremonies and ritual items pertaining to them, in none of the pueblos do clans put on ceremonies. That is done by religious societies. Confusion has arisen because in some cases (best known among the Hopi) the society leader must come from a specific clan and he "owns" clan ceremonies and ritual equipment. But other membership in the associated religious society which performs the ceremony is entirely unrelated to clanship. The Tewa do not have clans, though the Indians have borrowed the term and applied it to religious societies, a problem similarly existent in some other Pueblo groups. Where "clans" in the anthropological sense) actually are reported among other Tanoan-speaking Pueblos, they probably are a late adoption from neighboring groups. (For fuller discussion, see Ellis 1964.) Another matter of Pueblo ethnography often overlooked by archaeologists is that although membership in a Pueblo religious society is for life, a person may be a member of more than one such society. Further, an estimation of the number of religious societies in a pueblo, made on the basis of number of kivas found, must not be considered exact because more than one society may have used the same meeting place, as sometimes was true in the historic period.

The early Gobenador pithouses (Hall 1944a:85-89) were circular, 2 meters or more in depth and 6-12 meters in diameter. One can describe them in general terms, but the Rosa Phase here was far from thoroughly standardized. This should be expected for the living pattern of a people who had only recently changed their major economy to agriculture, with its requirements of relative sedentism, and who, even more recently, had been forced to find and move into a new area, rebuilding homes and reestablishing fields.

The Gobernador pithouse usually had a bench cut from the earth around three quarters of its interior circumference. This aided in minimizing the tendency of walls to collapse inward and at the same time provided space where household items could be set above floor level and, hence, out of the way. At each end of this bench a small rounded bin often was found. A break in the bench (a few houses had an unbroken bench and a few had no bench) characteristically was left on the east side of the room to permit excavation of a ventilator shaft through the bottom of the wall and upward to the surface. Entrance was from the roof hatchway through which a ladder led at a slant to the floor. Carefully worked stone hatch-covers provided protection during wet weather. The ventilator shaft occasionally, but rarely, had two openings into the room.

A circular fire pit, lined either with clay or with slabs of stone, occupied the center of the floor, sometimes with an attached or nearby small ash pit. A few builders placed an adobe deflector, slightly crescentic in shape, between the fire pit and the ventilator shaft opening to prevent drafts from blowing directly onto the fire. In the more elaborate houses a low clay wall, perhaps 20 cm wide and somewhat greater in height, was extended from the bench-end bins to the edges of the fire pit. This arrangement, which separated the house floor into two sections, was similarly coming into use elsewhere in the Anasazi area. Archaeological interpretation usually postulates women concentrating their duties of food preparation within the small enclosed section and the men using the larger section. From what little evidence we have, it would be more accurate to suggest that the area between fire place and ventilator opening, where one sometimes still finds a metate, quite certainly was the kitchen and storage area and that indoor life otherwise was concentrated on the opposite side of the low partition wall. Occasionally, small pits and bins were dug into the floor. Bins customarily had ventilator holes which could be opened to let in air and discourage the tendency toward mold. Through these the women also could reach for the daily supply of shelled corn. Clay plugs were made to fill the holes and deter encroachment by mice or other rodents.

The roof rested on four supports, two on the west side of the room and two toward the south end, frequently rising through the low partition wall.

Outside the houses of the early period were a few isolated storehouses, but later a single or even a double crescentic row of small surface-level storehouses was common. These customarily were built with a log support set into the two opposite ends of a shallow pit floor. Log joists were laid over the supports and topped with adobe to provide a raised floor to keep foodstuffs dryer than otherwise would have been possible in an area of heavy winter snows. Walls of the storage structures were of adobe turtlebacks (loaf-like rolls of clay laid perpendicular to the long direction of the wall), coursed adobe

(adobe laid in horizontal layers), or jacal in which the uprights were reeds. A small underground storage pit often was constructed near the house, its intended purpose unknown today. Our suggestion is that this pit could have been intended to provide a slightly moist atmosphere in which to store basketry materials collected in summer for use during the less busy winter period, an hypothesis equally applicable to similar small outside storage pits near some Gallina Phase houses.

Roofed shades often were built to protect an outside work area where corn grinding and other food preparation, including cooking, was done in warm weather. A large jar-shaped storage cist (145 cm deep and 112 cm at maximum width) of the type common in the following Gallina Phase was found dug beneath one such shade, the lower 60 cm all excavated into soft sandstone. Three restorable utility vessels lay in the bottom of the cist. Another vessel, left in the work area, contained ground pigment, and still another held a pendant and a fragment of ground stalactite.

The stockade constructed by people of Rosa Phase in the Gobernador and even occasionally elsewhere enclosed the one or two pithouses, storage structures, and outside work area, if any, which comprised a family establishment. Within the stockade, also, were randomly scattered small deposits of trash.

The Gobernador stockade was built of posts up to 18 cm in diameter and perhaps 2 meters high set into the ground at intervals of 10 to 25 cm. Small branches of brush apparently were interlaced between or lashed to the uprights as indicated by charred remains left when everything of the complex was burned by the owners at departure. As no entrances through stockades could be defined, it may be that the wall was scaled by ladders (Hall 1944a:28). Although the stockades commonly have been suggested to have been a measure of defense, we propose that they may have been pens for the protection of flocks of turkeys.

How do we know the Gobernador people were turkey farmers?

> Of over 275 bird bones, all were portions of turkey, showing great range in size, except for two ulna from the Little Brown Crane and one metacarpal of a Canadian Goose (Hall 1944a:78).

The same type of stockade enclosure, long known as a "coyote fence," has been built by natives of New Mexico to protect chickens and other livestock into our own century. A major development in Anasazi territory about A.D. 700 was the wrapping of split turkey-feathers (the soft short type) onto a length of twisted yucca warp cordage and then weaving across it with plain yucca cord at intervals. As turkeys could not be raised easily in all areas (we quote early Spanish commentary), some pueblos made the raising of these birds a specialty. The fluffy and warm turkey-feather blankets made an excellent trade item. Also, turkey feathers were, and still are, important as an attachment on prayer sticks.

We should add that, yes, we are quite aware of the flying ability of turkeys; they could have sailed over a stockade 6 feet high. But we have not forgotten the old system of "clipping the feathers on one wing," handled in our past with a pair of heavy scissors but also accomplishable with the sharp fresh obsidian and chert blades our subjects were accustomed to use for anything from trimming hair to slicing meat. Moreover, though turkeys may range in the daytime, wild turkeys are difficult to drive away from a habitation around which some food can be picked up (as Park Service personnel living at Mesa Verde describe in exasperation). The Gobernador problem would not have been nearly so much that of keeping turkeys *in* as keeping coyotes and other predators *out* of the stockade. Coyotes are not likely to leap 6-foot fences.

Throughout historic native Mexico the outlining of a family's establishment with a "coyote fence" of upright posts of juniper or other wood set close together and with support added by long thin branches attached horizontally by withes at two or more heights on the fence, has been common. Inside the fence are the structures, equipment, and animals belonging to that household. When the family sponsors a religious ritual, guests and officials come to the compound. The fence posts and cross-pieces, if covered with clay, duplicate the widespread types of house walls known as "wattle and daub" or "jacal," used throughout the Southwest and Latin America. In Mexico, upright stalks of fleshy cacti planted to produce such a wall are not unusual; in southern Arizona and northern Mexico stems of the slender but tough *ocatillo* still are set into a trench where they take root and provide a wall for house, shed, or yard. Such a wall may be somewhat transparent, but it permits both ventilation and relative privacy.

When the Rosa Phase people moved into the Gobernador area, the family dogs came with them. Hall (1944a:74-78) reports that the majority of mammal bones found in the trash mounds of their pithouses represented three types of dogs: the large Basketmaker dog, a smaller dog with slender nose, and the small and short-nosed dog sometimes referred to as the "Techichi." The bones prove that some reached old age, but the number of other animals which died or were killed in youth has led to the suggestion that although a few may have been kept as pets or for breeding, the dog could have been used in part for food, even as we know was true in Hopi Pueblo villages as late as this century. Also, with one or more dog skulls found accompanying each of Hall's Rosa burials, as similarly with some in the Navajo Reservoir, we cannot help but recall that in parts of prehistoric and early historic Mexico a dog was believed to lead the spirit of the dead into the afterworld.

We know that dog hair was the closest Pueblo weavers could come to wool before Spanish introduction of domestic sheep. Some very fine dog hair belts from the Four Corners country are exhibited at the Mesa Verde National Park Museum, and certainly the dogs themselves and dog hair textiles must have been valuable trade goods. Of course little of such material would have lasted through centuries of the inroads of insects and occasional moisture, even in cave sites.

Some fragmentary remains of bones from mule or white-tail deer, a few from jackrabbits, and a meager representation of pronghorn antelope, gopher, and badger complete the category for mammalian bones in Gobernador middens. We are forced to one of two conclusions. Either the people were primarily dependent on vegetable crops, wild or cultivated, or they hunted at a distance and brought "jerky" (thin slices of dried meat) back to their permanent residences for consumption. Considering the evidence for periodic concentration on hunting as illustrated in our Gallina Phase mountain campsites, the latter possibility must be taken seriously.

The evidence for plant foods used by the occupants of Hall's sites (1944a:79-81) consists of goosefoot (Chenopodium) seeds, pigweed (Amaranthus) seeds, piñon nuts, rushes or reeds, unidentified leaves, and the cultigens, corn, kidney beans (cultivated from late Basketmaker times to the present), possibly a tepary bean, and squash or pumpkin. There also was evidence (impressions in clay as well as on the exterior of pottery vessels) for coiled basketry and "plaited basketry" with rigid warp and flexible weft.

Further evidence of basketry came from the multitude of pot sherds recorded by Hall which showed impressions of basketry coils on bases and lower sides of pottery vessels. Rio Grande Tewa Pueblo potters, up to 15 or 20 years ago, often used a low bowl or tray-shaped basket as the *puki* into which the pressed-out base of a vessel was set while the maker continued to add coil after coil of clay to build the body. The modern potter usually protects the surface of her vessel from permanent basketry imprints with a coating of sifted fine white sand or ground volcanic tuff in the *puki*. Use of a *puki* permits turning the vessel to see that the sides are rising in a even curve. As the clay of the vessel dries and shrinks it would naturally pull away from the basket, but without the layer of fine sand impressions on the lower body of a jar or bowl would remain. Certainly such texturizing would have been at least as attractive and as useful in preventing the vessel from slipping through one's hands as the common surface-scoring probably produced with a dried corncob, a type of finish frequently found on Rosa and Gallina Utility wares. Nevertheless, an attempt was made to eliminate the basketry impressions on many vessels by smoothing them over or covering them with a thin surface layer of clay.

In her special study on Rosa Phase textiles in the Gobernador (Hall 1944a:43-45) Kent speaks of 20 complete vessels and 400 sherds (4 percent of the total number) from one site and some from another, all showing basketry imprints. This is important to us because little other evidence of what apparently was an elaborate and flourishing craft has survived. From the impressions Kent could recognize three somewhat differing basket shapes: trays with broad bases and almost straight sides, shallow bowls with curving sides, and deep bowls with sides curving somewhat. The baskets ranged in diameter from 3.8 to 50 cm at the rim, and from 1.5 to 24 cm high.

From some of the clearest imprints on vessel bases it is possible to see that the weaving technique of the majority was that succinctly described by Weltfish as "coiling, with non-interlocking stitch, on a two-rod and bundle triangular foundation." This is the type most typical for Basketmaker culture but also for the later Pueblo stages even into the historic period in the Rio Grande. Material used for rods probably consisted of willow or cottonwood twigs and the "bundle," says Kent, may have been of yucca fiber. As seen on the "working surface" (the "front side" on which the maker initiates most of his work) count for stitches was from 3 to 5 per cm, which would be comparable to those of good-to-excellent baskets of the historic period. Some even show mending.

That this basketry continued in popularity into the Gallina Phase is seen in Mera's report on 12th-century remnants of two coiled baskets showing two-rod-and-bundle foundation from the 13th-century Largo area, and four other less well-made fragments showing single rod and possible bundle foundation, with 6 to 7 coils per inch, sewed with noninterlocking stitches averaging 9 to 10 stitches to the inch horizontally.

Basketry was a much older craft than pottery in both the Anasazi and the Mogollon areas, and in comparison to the sophistication in basketry development, pottery-making was a new and only partly conquered field.

Rosa Phase pottery consisted of undecorated Rosa Smoothed in its two subtypes, the earlier Rosa Brown and the later Rosa Gray ware. Both were made of rather sandy soft clay containing "small opaque or glittering inclusions, and occasionally large white pebbles," a description similarly appropriate to the following Gallina Black-on-white ware. Rosa Brown and Rosa Gray both show that their basal portion was pressed into or fashioned in a basketry *puki*, as already explained, without any lining of fine sand being provided. Thus the clay took the shape and impressions of the basket while the vessel base was left in it to set and partially dry before the top of the vessel was added. The basket would have continued to provide some stability while the upper portion of the long-necked jars and, less commonly, of pitchers and utility bowls was added. Hall points out that the clay coils which formed the vessel were overlapped on the inside rather than the outside because of the base actually being fashioned inside the basket and pushed against it. This is an interesting commentary in that the great majority of vessels of prehistoric Pueblo peoples show the opposite or clapboard type of outside overlap, and we rarely find evidence of bases having been pressed into rather than merely set onto a basket *puki*. The inside coil-overlap technique is used today by Tewa potters of the Upper Rio Grande. As the Jemez largely lost their pottery techniques during the 17th- to 18th-century migrations of the Pueblo Rebellion period and later had to relearn the craft, their present techniques would tell us little.

The final surface finish of the upper exterior of Rosa Utility ware usually was random heavy, but generally vertical, scoring. Jar interiors show the same finish but done horizontally. Leaving neck coils visible was not unusual and a single rim fillet is found on some.

Rosa Black-on-white ware shows a 10-to-1 ratio of bowls to jars. The clay was not appreciably different from that of the undecorated ware. Surfaces seem to have been floated rather than slipped. Basket prints often appear on bases; rims usually are rounded. Black carbon paint made from plant juice is four times as commonly found as that containing iron oxide. Designs are simple and identifiable as of the Pueblo I style, though some of the later specimens described as "Transitional Decorated" forecast Gallina Black-on-white decoration styles.

As Hall comments, the Rosa Phase potters seem to have been in an experimental stage without standardized traditions and were making timid imitations of types of vessels traded in from both north and south. We can add that pottery seems never to have been a really strong point with the Rosa or the Largo-Gallina Phases; baskets, in contrast, were.

Stone work, a requisite to life, included the expectable necessities. In the category of pecked and ground stone were 23 metates from one site and fragments of 12 from another, all whole specimens being of the one-open-end type common in Pueblo I, though 3 had two use-surfaces apiece. The most abundant manos were of the two-hand type, wedge-shaped in cross section, but some two-hand manos had rectangular cross sections. There also were some one-hand manos, a stone bowl and fragments of 2 others, a few mauls, an "axe-sharpener," and a few objects of unclear usage. Hall found no stone axes, those undoubtedly having been carried by their owners to new homes.

Among the pecked and polished items were a number of circular slabs for covering storage jars. There also were 16 "plaster polishers" of varying stones with highly smoothed surfaces, 8 to 15 cm in length, which "sometimes had secondary use as choppers," 25 rubbing stones of quartzite, 6 polishing pebbles, 11 flat sandstone tablets worn on the edges, and 11 round river pebbles of quartzite and granite showing marks of use.

Under chipped implements excavated we find listed 19 quartzite choppers ranging from 6.5 to 19 cm in length, 26 quartzite core scrapers, 77 flake scrapers of which 90 percent were quartzite, 23 side scrapers of quartzite or chert, 6 quartzite notched side-scrapers, 8 thumbnail or snubnosed scrapers of assorted materials, and 6 quartzite planoconvex scrapers. Quite obviously, these people worked with hides, but one may wonder if some of the "scrapers" were not knives.

The small projectile points, described as "stemmed, side and base notched, and side notched," from 2 to 3.4 cm in length are listed as 50 percent obsidian, 20 percent chert, 20 percent chalcedony, 5 percent basalt, and 5 percent jasper. In Hall's Figure 31 photograph of points and Figure 32 photograph of "Knives and Specialized Forms" we can recognize the types we have defined for our Gallina hunting-gathering mountain sites, but the specimens seem to be exceedingly few in number.

Among unusual objects was a tablet which, when tried, worked effectively on a pine board as a plane, and three 10 to 12.5 cm long quartzite wedges, each showing evidence of considerable use at both ends. We long have wondered why so few, including ourselves, ever reported wedges from prehistoric sites, for to obtain the planks found here and there in ruins, wedges of stone or of hard wood must have been used to split slabs lengthwise from a tree trunk.

Under inorganic materials for Gobernador sites were found pure hematite lumps, limonite lumps, one vessel filled with limonite, lumps of diatomaceous earth resembling chalk, unworked powdery lumps of turquoise, sulphur crystals cached in a floor pit, and a cube of graphite. We are reminded of the small bowl found hidden away at Turkey

Spring I with remains of gypsum burned and then dissolved in water, still identifiable on its interior.

For miscellaneous objects, Hall lists 3 olivella shells pierced for stringing, 1 bone bead, a fossil oyster shell, a perforated jaw-bone, a lump of hematite worn on several faces and left in a vessel containing ground pigment, crystalline nodules worn on one face, a ground stalactite with all faces polished, a calcite crystal, a piece of feldspar worn on more than one face, a piece of unworked quartz, and a stone pipe of fine-grained reddish sandstone.

The majority of these unusual items probably would have pertained to ritualistic procedures, the pigments possibly used for personal decoration during dancing or while laying out the designs of "ground altars." Pieces of mineral today are employed in psychotherapeutic treatments by Pueblo medicine men and probably were then. Almost all of those found in the Rosa Phase sites are paralleled in our finds representing the Largo-Gallina Phase.

With this background we can better comprehend the interrelated patterns we have been finding for the Pueblo III Gallina Phase. We still are without any specific excavations of late Gobernador Rosa Phase which should show some Pueblo I Piedra Phase characteristics. We are equally without anything excavated to illustrate what we might designate as early Gallina Phase but which officially has been termed "Bancos Phase." Its pottery, Bancos Black-on-white (A.D. 950-1050), succeeded the Piedra Black-on-white ware characteristic of Piedra Phase sites in the nearby Piedra district north of the San Juan River. The time gap of these two postulated phases certainly must be filled in by fieldwork. Nevertheless, in comparing the Gobernador Rosa Phase data with that already known for the A.D. 1050-1300 Gallina Phase, the parallels are so clearly seen that one well may wonder what distinguishing traits or patterns intervening phases could show.

The Gallina Phase of Gallina Culture and its 13th-Century Modifications

The "Largo-Gallina" or Gallina Phase (approximately A.D. 1050-1300) on which our own work sponsored by Ghost Ranch has concentrated hitherto was known only from scattered excavations on which little data other than that pertaining to architecture had been published. What of the artifact complexes so important to daily living?

No detailed study has been available on the stone implements of the Gallina area, although photographs and descriptions of a few are found. It is clear the Gobernador stone complex was closely related to that of our mountain camps. Parallels run from the type of metate to our "possible floor polisher" which Hall would have classified as one of his wall plaster polishers. But, as we have no evidence of wall plaster and little of clay floors in those mountain camps, the function of this artifact may have been something quite different such as a "tanning stone." We have not found a parallel for this one in the home sites of the Llaves area where we have been excavating since our three and a fraction seasons on the Canjilon camps. The choppers and the specific but varied types of points are duplicated in both the Gobernador and the Gallina phases. We have a single core scraper and some snubnosed, end, and flake scrapers, but many of the implements we first classified as "scrapers" were moved into the category of knives after examination under magnification. Classification is difficult because many of the shapes could have served either purpose. Only a careful analysis of type, by evidence of use — if visible — can answer the functional problem.

Hall mentions neither lunate cutting-curves nor burins for his Rosa Phase, but we must remember that Southwestern studies on the details of stone work largely evolved after the period of his study.

And pottery?

That from our three closely related and mutually contemporaneous mountain camps apparently is the largest collection of Gallina whole or restorable vessels recovered from any Gallina site or closely unified geographic unit. Where do we turn for comparisons? The fact that we have found so little evidence of pointed bottoms for jars brings a quick question: could we be dealing with Rosa rather than Gallina Phase in those mountain campsites?

The answer is "No." The shapes of our vessels, though related to shapes shown for Rosa Phase and for the preceding Sambrito Phase (Basketmaker III) certainly are a long way from duplicating them. The widemouthed cook pot, so important in our mountain campsites and for the Gallina Phase in general, does not appear at all among Hall's collection of Rosa Phase shapes shown in his Figure 23. Shoulders apparently disappeared from cooking vessels between the time of Rosa Phase and the 13th-century period represented by pottery of Gallina Phase in the Llaves and Turkey Spring areas. The only exception is an occasional holdover such as seen in our three or four vessels already likened to Hall's small- to medium-size shouldered storage jars.

The tendency toward modified neck corrugations on some jars, usually Plain Utility but sometimes Black-on-white, remained from Rosa through Gallina Phases, probably because these made a vessel easier to hold firmly. The big narrow-necked water canteen which Hall shows for Rosa Phase is, overall, similar to ours, but its base is quite flat in contrast to the tapering underbody so consistent for ours. From the photograph one cannot say whether the lugs were merely to aid in handling or pierced for suspension.

The bases of all the Rosa Phase vessels Hall illustrates are either flat or very rounded, as one would expect for vessels with their lower parts fashioned in baskets. A few of our vessels have flat bottoms and many are rounded, but none of Hall's Rosa vessels carries the tapered underbody we so commonly find on our Gallina vessels, even though these bases do not culminate in a point. Other pointed bases consist merely of a central extrusion added to a rounded base. Tapered underbodies and points both would have served the function of helping to hold a cooking vessel upright when set into a bed of ash in the fire pit.

27

Of our four Gallina Black-on-white vessels from the campsites, one shows an individualistic, rambling, wide-line design atypical for any period. The simple designs on two bowl interiors are of characteristic Gallina parallel-line type with, in one, a double triangle motif at center bottom. This bowl is almost a duplicate of that pictured at the lower left in Hibben's Figure 46 (1949). Our Gallina Black-on-white canteen has a relatively complex pattern definitely not of Rosa Phase. Although its accuracy in brush work leaves something to be desired, as in so many Gallina painted vessels, this canteen is a Pueblo III product in sophisticated shape, with its four turned-up canteen lugs and painted pattern of triangles filled with dots and enclosed by a line ending with the "ceremonial break." Simply stated: The design of this canteen is just too complex for Rosa Phase.

The paint on our Gallina Black-on-white jar (see cover of this volume) from one of our Canjilon sites is faded, but the design is individualistic and interesting with its outlines filled by Gallina-favored wide hatching. Workmanship was better than on many vessels, but one still wonders: why was the average Gallina potter such a poor draftsman?

Rosa Phase baskets from the Gobernador and Gallina Phase baskets from the Llaves district, both known largely from imprints on the exterior of pottery vessel underbodies, appear to have been similar in materials and in proportions of coil and stitch sizes. Further evidence of Gallina basketmaking is seen in the numerous bone awls with a very slender sharp point found in our Llaves sites. Whether made by men or women (men having been the fabricators of baskets in the historic New Mexico pueblos but women at Hopi) some of the Llaves baskets would have been fine by anyone's standards. None, as far as we know from imprints, was poor.

We can say in general that stone work changed less than pottery between the Rosa and Gallina Phases. Basketry, of which we know too little to do much about conclusions, appears to have remained much the same through the two phases. Basketry, worked skins, turkey feathers and their side products well may have composed much of Gallina's offerings in trade to the outer world. Not so for their pottery. But when one thinks through the evidence for trade types of pottery in any of the Pueblo districts, not a great deal other than the most outstanding in color and design, such as the handsome St. Johns Polychrome, ever became widespread exchange items. One major consideration in trade, of course, would have been the value of a vessel versus its weight and fragility in comparison with the value of lightweight unbreakable items such as feathers, fur or feather blankets, skins, and baskets. We know that desirable local stone, such as Jemez Mountain obsidian and Pedernal chert, was widely traded, whether raw or, more probably, as preforms. Our people, living nearby and using this material for their own flaked implements, presumably were among the traders. And the exchange? Quite possibly food.

On the derivation of Gallina architecture, there is now much more to be said than a few years back. It derives, as all agree, from that of Rosa Phase in the Gobernador and Navajo Reservoir areas. This in turn derives from the architecture of Eastern Basketmaker III in the Durango area, as we have outlined in the historical sequence with which we began our present summary and commentary. It is easy enough to follow the thinking of the builders during this succession. Shelter, yes, for the family and its perishable foods, including foods for immediate use set away in indoor bins or cists and jars sometimes topped with stone or even with clay. Add a few exterior, small surface structures and later double or triple their number, built near the house to hold foods for out-of-season use during the hard winter and early spring periods. This also provided a small "bank account" for years when frosts might last too late or come too early or the spotty rainfall of the Southwest might skip certain valleys or even entire districts.

The general movement of Rosa Phase people up the Gobernador and the neighboring Largo drainage all the way to the Continental Divide, on both sides of which we find the Largo-Gallina Phase represented by pithouses and surface structures, fairly certainly resulted from a combination of a series of difficult drought years with the need for more arable land. We know from tree-ring studies that during this period many years produced subaverage growth for pines and hence probably for crops. Higher altitudes would have offered a promise of cooler and damper weather, and space along the Divide was plentiful.

The earliest tree-ring dates we have for the Gallina Phase are 1059r, 1064r, 1087c, again 1087c, 1089+r, and 1090+v, all from Bg 20, Tower 1, of Rattlesnake Point (Robinson and Warren 1971:11). This tower had been constructed on the spine of a high ridge. Close to the tower were two pithouses and at a little distance a third. We cannot prove that the first two pithouses were contemporaneous with the tower, though it seems likely. We cannot even prove positively that these dates, derived from beams taken from the tower when it was first excavated, give the approximate time of the tower's construction, but in this case that seems very likely. One more wood specimen with a date in the 1050s was found when we re-excavated that tower to its bedrock base in 1983-1984.

Only conifers are used for tree-ring dating in the Southwest because these have been found to best reflect the variations in the temperature-moisture combination primarily responsible for annual growth as seen in ring diameter. Trees add each year's increment of growth directly under the outer bark. The use of a "c" after the date of the outermost ring still present on a specimen indicates that this date was found to be continuous around the full circumference of a complete cross section from a tree trunk or branch. If continuous, that ring could have been the last grown by the tree, even though no bark remains to prove it. A "B" indicates that bark is present; the cutting date of the tree is that of its last ring present. The addition of an "r" after the date of the last ring present on the specimen indicates that this ring is continuous around the available circumference, but less than a full cross section was sent to the laboratory. At least a small possibility that a full section might have shown some evidence of later growth must be recognized. The addition of "v" means that in the subjective judgment of the specialist doing the dating, one or more rings may be missing near the end of the ring series, but their presence or absence cannot be determined because that ring record does not extend far enough to provide an adequate check. The symbol "vv" means that the specialist cannot determine approximately how many rings have been eroded, burned, decayed, or trimmed from the exterior of this log or branch. The addition of a "+" indicates one or more rings may be missing near the end of the ring series whose presence or absence cannot be determined because the specimen does not extend far enough to provide an adequate check.

We thus know that some of the dates quoted actually may have been the cutting dates of those trees and, if not, that the dates obtained are close to cutting dates, except when marked as "vv." Moreover, it seems to have been a common prehistoric custom to cut and stockpile timber when construction was contemplated, even as in our own times. Timbers also sometimes were reused. However, with 14 dates obtained on the wood from Tower 1, all but one (for which the last ring still present was far from the original log exterior) falling between 1038vv and 1090+v, it becomes clear that Gallina men probably were on this ridge and cutting trees for this tower at least from about A.D. 1060 on. The tower, we would guess, may have been built around A.D. 1090 to 1100.

The third pithouse, only a little more distant than the other two, was trenched to its floor by our group in 1976. On that floor lay a charred piece of wood which dated 1209+B, which would place its date of cutting early in the 1200s. This pithouse, then, had been built during the first part of the 13th century, or wood cut at that time had been taken into the house to make repairs or to be burned.

If Gobernador domiciles were pithouses, the early Gallina homes probably would have been similar. Many still unexcavated pithouses as well as those dug by Mera, Mackey, Dick, and others are known.

We do not know when Gallina surface houses, which overlapped pithouses in period, first were constructed. These "unit type" surface houses can be described as, at the beginning, nothing more than a pithouse built above ground, with thick walls of largely unworked stones set in mud mortar. The interior of the wall was smooth and neatly plastered with clay. Behind the fire pit was a deflector which had been changed from the Rosa Phase type, merely a short free-standing wall, to a U-shape usable as a heating or even small roasting pit with a high curved back reflecting warmth from hot coals or ashes placed in its enclosed basin-shaped base.

There was also a ventilator shaft which should have gone up through the house wall but in some cases may have merely pierced it. By the Gallina Phase, the orientation of these features had shifted from east-west, as found in the early Gobernador, to north-south. Because orientation usually is found to have been consistent within an area, a change probably would reflect influence from some other area being taken very seriously.

Long surface bins reaching from east and west walls toward the deflector now made the division of the room into a kitchen-storage area versus main living-and-sleeping space on the opposite side of the fire pit. A rather high bench usually edged all or a part of the floor. The antechamber, as we have referred to the area south of the bins, also may have served for considerable storage and as a prehistoric "broom closet"; in many, a small grinding bin sufficient for a single metate occupied one end. Occasional moderate-sized floor pits and small bins in the bench provided additional storage for immediate needs.

Bags full of dried meat or other foods may have been hung from the unusually high ceilings, somewhat comparable to those in the Chaco Canyon pueblos. Small jacal surface structures commonly were built at a little distance or onto the exterior of a house for more extended storage. Trash and ash were deposited in small, thin, random piles. Long occupation of structures is not indicated. Movement probably resulted largely from the hope of catching the spotty rainfall a few miles distant. Roof timbering and all usable equipment were taken from the old structure, presumably for use in the new domicile, which suggests that moves usually covered only short distances.

We are much in need of more information on Gallina towers, of which but few have been excavated and even fewer hitherto reported in any detail. Their construction continued through the later years of Gallina Phase but certainly not at every site. If we think in terms of using towers plus high open spots or the roofs of houses constructed in such locations for signal stations in this area of mountain ridges and crests, it is not difficult to imagine what can almost be pictured as a line of telegraph stations. The thick walls and better-than-usual masonry of Gallina towers undoubtedly were intended to support height, the most distinctive characteristic of towers anywhere. Even the tallest Gallina tower on which we presently have data shows no evidence of a second floor, and it seems (from the few and somewhat undetailed descriptions existent) that entrance was gained by a ladder up the outside and another which descended into the interior. If towers averaged less floor space than domiciles (Mackey and Green 1979: Figure 6), a tower of one floor surely could not have given shelter to all the people from even one of the Gallina extended villages. Persons hiding in a tower could be easily worsted by a food/water blockade, just as the Spaniards of Santa Fe, crowded into the thick-walled Governor's Palace at the start of the 1680 Pueblo Rebellion, were brought to quick surrender by the Indians cutting off the irrigation ditch which carried their drinking water.

To anyone familiar with the Chaco, the hypothetical but close date on Rattlesnake Tower 1 immediately places its construction in the middle of the period of great Chaco culture when Chacoans were using a combination of towers and high open places to provide locations for a signal system stretching some 200 miles (Hayes and Windes 1975:149-156; Lister and Lister 1981: see index). The system was perpetuated into historic times in the Rio Grande area, as briefly mentioned in early Spanish documents (Hackett 1942: cxliii and cxliv) and explained to us (Ellis 1956) by elders of Zia, Santa Ana, and Jemez Pueblos when relating some of their early historic problems. One, two, or three fires were built on specific high points, the number of fires indicating the seriousness of the danger. Jemez and Zia could signal to each other; Zia and Santa Ana had similar communication. Santa Ana also could signal to San Felipe or Sandia, which could send a signal south to Isleta or north to San Felipe. San Felipe could signal to Santo Domingo, and Santo Domingo to Cochiti. All Middle Rio Grande pueblos, including those which later disappeared, thus were covered. I asked for an example and was given the following story from oral tradition.

When the Spaniards returned in 1692, after having been forced to flee from New Mexico by the Pueblo Rebellion of 1680, the Pueblo people believed they were pushing the natives for full acceptance of Catholicism and total abandonment of the old religion.

The Indians feared refusal might lead to loss of their lands. To resolve the stalemate, Santa Ana tradition relates that the Spaniards resorted to a ruse, persuading some of the men of Cochiti Pueblo to organize a big hunt in which all able-bodied men of Zia, Santa Ana, and Jemez would participate. When the hunters were out of sight over the mesa to the northwest, the Spaniards struck at the home communities. One of the old Indians hastily sent a young boy to the high signal spot on top of Santa Ana Mesa to signal for help, but the lad was confused and lighted only two brush fires instead of the appropriate three. The hunters saw the smoke from a distance, wondered at its significance, and returned but without haste, quite unprepared to find their women weeping and all the children in the custody of the Spaniards. The captives, so they were told, were to be taken to Mexico to learn Catholicism and Spanish culture. None ever were seen again. The story of their loss has perpetuated the memory of the old signal system even today.

In Acoma, even now, the tribal war captain and aides are provided with a male cook and must live in special upper-story quarters maintained for this purpose on the high mesa of Acoma, though the individuals themselves maintain ceremonial-period homes on Acoma Mesa and year-round homes in one of the Acoma farm villages. Enemy invasions certainly are not expected today, but the old system holds, an example of Pueblo conservatism. In the historic Pueblo period every village had its war captain and his lieutenants whose duties were to keep constant watch, whether for outside enemies, witches, or misbehaving tribal members, as well as to place offerings at specific shrines on the peripheries of a tribe's territory. Watch stations could be low stone-walled enclosures on ridges, peaks or roofs in the village itself. When a religious society goes into retreat in its own society house today, the war captain or an assistant (in conservative villages) still posts himself on its roof as protector for the full retreat period. The roof of even a low tower would have provided an advantageous position.

Some towers, but not all of the few known, did have living quarters on the ground floor. In the Bg 88 complex, two pithouses were associated with the tower, one connected by a trench-type covered tunnel and the other showing several feet of unfinished tunnel leading toward the tower (Green, Danfelser, and Vivian 1958; Green 1979, Figure 3). Both of those pithouses had the usual interior features of dwellings and a little more floor space than the tower itself which, in this example, was said by Hibben (Pendleton 1952) to be entirely without living arrangements. We would interpret this complex as possibly providing quarters for war captain and assistants, even though not on the tower floor. The nearby pithouse could have been the residence for a family or guards assigned to Tower 1 at Rattlesnake Point, though our own re-excavation in the base of this structure, not reached by the previous archaeologists, did show some dwelling-type features. (See Vol. III of this series for details.)

When Redondo Tower was constructed in the Carricito Community (Green 1964) a short distance from Rattlesnake Point, it was given a lined fire pit and a ventilator shaft, presumably with intent that someone dwell in or at least temporarily occupy the original floor. These could have been guard/signalmen.

Later Redondo Tower would have the original floor features sealed over and partitions put in to provide storage compartments. How much later? Wood from a unit house constructed against the south wall of Tower 1 at Rattlesnake, possibly for occupation by the family which was renovating the old tower into a storeroom, yielded 16 dates, all in the A.D. 1200s except for two marked "vv." We have 1220c, 1221c, 1224r, 1225r, 1242r, and four at 1243r. We would approximate the building date as between 1243 and 1245. By this time the tower would have been some 170 years old and the upper portions probably much damaged. Its abandonment in favor of a later tower on the same ridge may have occurred decades earlier.

Tree-ring records on the Rio Grande drainage in New Mexico in general indicate that 1243 was not a good year for growth, 1246 and 1248 would be worse, and half or more of the 1250s would range from quite to very difficult years for food production (Smiley, Stubbs, and Bannister 1953:54). Stallings (in Hibben 1937:57-58) gives a chart showing relative growth records for conifers, year by year, for the specific Abiquiu area from A.D. 1161 through 1335. This area is not on the Continental Divide but only 30 miles eastward. In this sequence we find as dry years 1161, 1166, 1172 (with 1173-1175 somewhat less so), 1182, 1186-1189 (with 1186 and 1187 worse than the others), 1194, 1204-1206 (with 1205 worst of the three), 1212, 1214-1218 (with 1217 the worst), 1220-1222 (with 1220 worst), 1224-1225 (with 1225 worst), 1227 dry, 1233-1236 variable but dry, 1240, 1243, 1245-1246 (with 1246 worst), 1248, 1250-1256 a seven-year drought in which 1251, 1252, 1254, and 1255 were especially bad, followed by 1258 quite bad, 1260-1261 somewhat less so, 1263-1264, 1269, 1270, 1271, 1273-1274, 1276, 1278, all bad but 1264, 1276, and 1278 the worst. The years 1280-1282 and 1284 through 1288 all were bad, 1280 and 1286 being the worst in this group; 1291, 1292, 1294-1296, all were bad, with 1292 the worst. 1303 and 1304 were not good, but after this 1311-1312, 1315-1316, 1322, 1324, 1326, 1327, 1328, 1331 and 1333-1335 were the only poor years, with 1312, 1316, 1328, 1331, 1334, and 1335 drier than the others.

Since the beginning of tree-ring studies in the early 1900s, one special interest has been the relation of amount of annual ring-width growth to seasonal and annual precipitation and temperatures. Douglass (1914) and Schulman (1956) demonstrated the strong positive relationship between ring width and precipitation of the winter immediately preceding each growing season through holdover of soil moisture into the following spring. By the 1960s biologists familiar with the details of tree growth were putting some concentrated study into dendrochronology. Multivariant statistical techniques were applied to the interactions of the many environmental variables known to influence tree growth, and the great quantity of pertinent data could be practically handled by the recently devised electronic computers. The models representing the relationship between tree growth and the climatic variables behind that growth gave rise to the new specialization known as dendroclimatology. Our present comments on weather as deduced from tree-ring records are relatively simple. For references and examples of the detailed complexities that can be derived from the new type of elaborate approach, see Rose, Dean, and Robinson (1981), a study done in connection with interpretation of the excavations made by the School of American Research at Arroyo Hondo, a short distance outside Santa Fe, New Mexico.

It is clear that from 1172 to 1296 in our Gallina area many years were bad for connifer growth and probably for crops. The most difficult period was that between 1250 and 1258 with but a single "normal" year (1257). The 1260s and 1270s had 6 and 4 poor years respectively. The 1280s had 8 bad years, and the 1290s had 7. It is not surprising that the high country which originally drew them with promise was abandoned, fairly certainly between A.D. 1270 and 1300.

But the people did not give in easily.

Construction of the unit house adjoining Tower 1, and probably renovation of the lower part of that tower for storage, took place about the same time as the widespread Gallina effort at renovating abandoned unit houses for the same purpose and adding storerooms to the outer ends and even sides of homes. Not storerooms to hold surplus food from good crops but to conserve any foods they could manage to garner and hide away rather than consume. Mackey and Green (1979:151) report one tower as having been used only for storage because it did not appear to have been very high or thick-walled. It still could have been a signal station. Our own small but thick-walled tower at GBN 5 (see Volume II for description) in the Llaves district certainly never was intended as a refuge for besieged villagers. It could have held food and at the same time been used as a link in the line of pyro-signal stations, the crew presumably living at hand in the unit house that was a part of this tower complex. The date on one of the unit house beams was A.D. 1275vv, the latest date yet obtained for any Gallina site.

It was at this time, we surmise because we do not have a specific date to lean on, that although some of the people continued to struggle with their farming, others of the family members were sent to camp on Canjilon Mountain to collect wild foods as part of what must fill the recently added home storage facilities. From artifacts and houses, we know that patterns of living were different in the camps from those of home villages. No pottery was made, but each representative household seems to have brought a cook pot, a water jar, a food bowl, and probably a canteen, the types represented duplicating those in the 13th-century Llaves home sites. From a study of the volumes of vessels in each of the four shapes, we can be fairly certain that the camp households contained from two to ten persons, with the majority in the lower and middle range.

Cooking was done outside the camp houses, but a bit of clay-covered floor provided an area large enough for a heating pit where coals could be laid whenever heat absorbed by the lava boulders and radiated later was not sufficient to dispel the chill of high-altitude nights or of storms. The arrow points, knives, and scrapers present in these houses and their vicinity are evidence that daily life in the camps largely revolved around hunting, the slicing and drying of meat for future use, and the tanning of hides. The other side of mountain-camp economy, collection and preparation of plant foods for later use, left less evidence than the hunting.

Use of mountain camps by the Gallina is a pattern of which no one had been aware before these Canjilon Mountain sites were investigated. The intentional choice of lava beds as locations for camp structures, probably because of retention and radiation of the sun's heat by the black mass and also because the vertical-sided boulders could be used as large sections of house walls, similarly is new. Nor is the concentrated use of chinking, even to the extent of its becoming paving for floors and for pathways, known for home villages.

New Evidence of Gallina Religious Activity: "Mini-sipapus," Ritual Items, and the Kiva

What part did religion play in the 13th century, whether in Gallina camp or at home?

We can be sure it would not have been left out of any Pueblo program planned to contend with increasing economic blows dealt by nature. Pueblo religion is not a matter of precepts on ethical behavior; ethics is an important but separate category. Religion, cooperation with the forces of Nature, is aimed at the basic problems of economy: orderly succession of the seasons, reproduction, and the fertility of plants and animals.

Curing, the native term for returning anything to its healthy natural state, comes into the picture secondly. In a period when the people must have been desperate for the return of normal growth conditions, increased emphasis on religion should be expectable. In camp and home sites we found a worn chunk of hematite, an occasional but rare quartz crystal, and a few chunks of what may have been pigments. They merely hint at ritual use. Then, to our complete surprise, we uncovered a "mini-sipapu" in a home site, a definite sign of religious activity.

Little has been said about religion in reports on Gallina culture, but a nagging problem to some of us has been why no structures dedicated to religious use, such as kivas, ever had been found in the area. The sipapu, best perpetuated today in the Hopi kivas, symbolizes the opening to Mother Earth's underworld where she continues to dwell, whence the Pueblo people originally emerged, to which the dead return, and where living Pueblo people prayerfully communicate with her when needed. The living Pueblos revere and make pilgrimages to caves, springs, or other openings in the earth considered to be natural and exceedingly important avenues of communication with that underworld. These, the most significant and sacred natural representations of the sipapu concept, usually are kept entirely secret from outsiders.

The large kivas of today's Rio Grande Pueblos do not have visible sipapus in their floors, though we have evidence that a hidden substitute does exist in at least some. Sipapus are known for certain of the great kivas of the prehistoric past but not for others. The floor sipapu was widely, though not invariably, built into the majority of small kivas used by religious societies from Pueblo III up to or after A.D. 1700.

For the early periods we can review existent data in the hope of seeing patterns emerge where regional differences are marked, though much remains to be discovered. If we look back at our resumé of evidences of family-oriented rituals and development of the kiva in the Four Corners country, we find the sipapu in floors of 6th-century Basket-maker III pithouses in Chaco Canyon and often but not always in the proto-kivas of Basketmaker III-Pueblo I in the La Plata, Mesa Verde, and Navajo Reservoir districts. In these areas some villages appear to have functioned as religious centers in which the people of several sites could meet for observances in a single great kiva (Eddy 1966:35). There was a sipapu in that kiva, but none in homes within the participating villages.

Floors of domiciliary pithouses of what may be called the Western Basketmaker III people (generally west of the Four Corners area) usually included a sipapu north of the fire pit, and the people are believed to have concentrated much of their ritual activities within the household. By Pueblo I an occasional great kiva appeared in that area.

In contrast, sipapus are rare, if present at all, in domiciles and proto-kivas of the Durango district (Gooding 1980:42) whence the culture and probably blood of the Gobernador and descendant Gallina groups appear to have been derived. There is a chance, however, that the Durango and the Gobernador people, instead of neglecting this feature so important to their near neighbors, simply hid it.

Thirty years ago Stubbs, briefly discussing the two floored-over sipapus he had found in Kiva B, the jar-shaped example he found floored over in Kiva F, and the open sipapu in Kiva D, all in the Pueblo III 13th- to 14th-century site of Pindi a few miles south of Santa Fe, appended a footnote at least as appropriate today as then.

> Roberts [1930] notes the absence of *sipapus* in Piedra kivas and further states that sipapus are rare in the kivas of the Chaco Canyon [he is referring to kivas of 10th-13th century Chaco peoples; those of the McElmo Phase people of Mesa Verde background in the Chaco usually contain sipapus as well as other Mesa Verdian traits] and that at present there is no satisfactory explanation for their absence. In the case of one Piedra example he states, "The floor of the room was in such good condition that traces [of the *sipapu*] would have been apparent at once." We suggest that the absence or presence of this characteristic kiva feature in the Piedra and Chaco has not been fully demonstrated. In Pueblo Pindi all the *sipapus* except one were floored over and were not apparent until the flooring was removed, which has not been a general practice in past excavation. There is no published statement regarding the examples cited by Roberts which would indicate that the structures were thoroughly examined for subfloor features. [Stubbs 1953:39 fn.]

Roberts found a sipapu in its appropriate place in the floor of each of the four small kivas and the one great kiva he excavated at the Pueblo IV Village of the Great Kivas near Zuni. He also uncovered what appears to have been a sipapu in the bottom of a footdrum in one of the small kivas there (Roberts 1932:58, 89). A similar sipapu inside a footdrum has been reported from the main kiva at today's Acoma Pueblo (Roberts 1932:59), and in 1971 we found the same feature present inside a footdrum in a religious society kiva in the Pueblo IV ancestral Tewa site of Tsama, 6 miles downstream from Abiquiu. A second hidden sipapu was discovered in another kiva of this same ruin.

(Report in preparation: Ellis.) As Earth Mother is supposed to be notified that appropriate rituals are in process when she hears the sounds via the sipapu, putting this feature into a chamber used for ceremonials or into a footdrum on which certain participants dance is a reasonable arrangement. The concept of uncovering its top on ritual occasions we admittedly have from the Hopi; others may have believed that the sounds could penetrate the covering (such as a layer of floor plaster) or that the covering should be removed for ritual periods but otherwise left to preserve a clean sanctity to the feature. Comparing the sipapu to a Christian altar stone in function is not undue.

Our intent certainly is not to make a survey of Pueblo sipapus, of which dozens if not hundreds are known. Rather it is to point out the largely unrealized fact that the concept of hidden sipapus is not new and that investigation might show wider distribution than presently supposed.

Our own first find of a Gallina "mini-sipapu" was entirely unexpected. It resulted from our decision to follow the slabs which lined a house fire pit but appeared to have their bases set somewhere below the hearth's sandstone slab "use-floor" at the bottom of the pit intended for heating and cooking. On lifting out that "use-floor" slab, we found clean and very light-colored wood ash filling a shaft which extended downward for an arm's length, still lined by the slabs we had been following. A lower bottom was marked by two slabs meticulously mortared into place with clay. The northeast corner of that lower floor to the pit had been left uncovered. There, careful work with a soft brush revealed a small jar-shaped opening, neatly lined with bright yellow ochre plaster, as we found in cleaning it out with a teaspoon. (For details see Volume II.)

This appeared to be a perfect and hidden type of tiny sipapu, the first of those several we later found with openings 3-5 cm across. None of our other mini-sipapus have been done in yellow, and some were more tubular than jar-shaped, as is true for many full-size sipapus, but the position of all was the same. The area beneath the upper "use-floor" or "fire-floor" and the bottom floor of such a fire pit never had been intended for practical use as a fire box. The slab walls were only slightly reddened as if a single fire once had been kindled and left to burn itself out, perhaps as part of the Pueblo house blessing required for domicile construction in modern times and probably in prehistoric days. The fire had been hot enough to harden the clay mortar between the stone slabs. The light-colored ash, with occasional pieces of charcoal, certainly had not accumulated but had been packed into the pit.

Gallina emphasis on Earth or Corn Mother is seen in our weighty conventionalized stone images, approximating those in historic Tewa shrines, identified by Pueblo persons, and clearly related to the modern and prehistoric tiponis discussed in several publications (see Steen 1982:48-51). They had been left behind in some of the GB houses. The Pueblos also revere Fire God and his son or younger brother, Ash Boy. The spirit of the latter is said by conservatives to live in Pueblo fireplaces or in any deposit of ashes, whence he assures the security of the householders. The fireplace poker and the ash, including that deposited with worn-out objects on a Pueblo "ash pile" (unfortunately commonly referred to by archaeologists as "the dump") are sacred because they are his symbols. In native concept, ash piles are shrines, and prayer plumes are (or were into the 1980s) placed upon them when other shrines are decorated. Here we learn one reason excavation or even setting foot onto the "ash piles" of the living Pueblos customarily is forbidden to outsiders.

In native Mexican legend, the Old Fire God was first in importance until the Sun God succeeded him in that position. In Zuni Pueblo the elaborate long sequence of public Shalako ceremonies which close with private celebration of the Winter Solstice is opened with the Little Fire God (Ash Boy) leading the Council of the Gods, representatives of other major supernatural beings, into the plaza. Meanwhile his father, representing Old Fire God, remains in retreat, keeping a fire burning in a special kiva.

At first we thought of our mini-sipapus in the bottom and otherwise unused floor of the deep ash-filled shaft beneath the upper "use-floor" of domicile fire pits as probably shrines to Earth Mother, a hidden parallel to the more standard sipapu found in the floor of many Basketmaker III – Pueblo I domiciles in the Four Corners country. Our initial hypothesis that these could have been required for the house of a religious society leader who used his dwelling for the rituals of his group, as often done today (Hawley 1950; Green 1964; Mackey and Green 1979:150), appeared unlikely when we discovered that most houses had mini-sipapus at the bottom of their deep fire pits. (See Volume II for details.)

A second possibility is that the mini-sipapus could have been shrines to the Fire God-Ash Boy complex, especially as they were carefully covered by the deep deposit of clean ash fill in the shaft between the lower floor of the fire pit and the upper or "use-floor" a short distance below floor level. We cannot settle this problem with certainty at present. Our guess is that the ash-filled shaft and the concealed mini-sipapu were shrine symbols of a relationship to Earth Mother and to Fire God-Ash Boy, whose cult still is celebrated by the Pueblo Fire Society, said to be one of the most important and oldest organized by Pueblo ancestors.

Interestingly, in Kiva B of the 14- through 17th-century Jemez site of Unshagi where one finds such Gallina traits as room bins and the great jar-shaped cist, a pit of 3.6 x 2.5 feet lined with rough stones to a depth of 3.5 feet was found 4 feet out from the curve of the east wall. The lower 2 feet of space were filled with charcoal, small amounts of ash, and several large pieces of unworked antler. Three charred bits of two-ply cotton string, such as used to tie prayer plumes, lay in this deposit. The upper 1.5 feet were filled with charcoal in which six charred poles, 1.5 feet in length and ranging up to 6 inches in diameter, were embedded. These charred pieces of wood are reminiscent of the two found in the lower section of the firebox shaft at GBN 4. The slabs which lined the walls in the Kiva B pit showed no sign of having been heated. The pit top had been covered by the plaster of the later floor (Reiter 1938:61-63). Did it indicate a special recognition of Fire God or Ash Boy? Occasional covered pits filled with ash, though not ash pits as such, also have been reported from other Anasazi sites. But we have no other definite reports of mini-sipapus in fire pits.

Have the "lower flooring" of Gallina fire pits and the mini-sipapu we so commonly find there been overlooked by other Gallina excavators who may never have removed the upper use-floor ("fire-floor") to see if anything were below? Did they accidentally dig out a clay use-floor and continue downward but miss noting an unexpected mini-sipapu in the dark corner of its second, or deepest, floor? Or might that second bottom and the sipapu belong only to a late period of Gallina occupation, perhaps not yet encountered in other excavations?

Again we cannot answer with certainty. However, some other Gallina sites have been dated in the 1260s or later. From noncutting dates, characteristics, and contents, all the houses of our GBW village appear to have been roughly contemporary with those of GBW 4, which quite definitely dates as constructed in A.D. 1261 or very shortly thereafter. No cutting dates have been obtained from the GBN settlement a quarter mile to the north. But the noncutting date of 1275vv on wood from the large room or house adjoining the tower at GBN 4 probably is not far from the actual date of cutting. It could represent either house construction or repair, but it definitely proves that this structure was occupied to at least a few years after that date. We continue to think of the Gallina people as probably having left the Continental Divide for the northern stretch of Jemez country before A.D. 1300 when, as tree-ring records indicate, the weather throughout the old northern Anasazi country so improved that abandonment no longer would have been necessary..

Our second find of religious significance was the considerable cache of ritual items carefully set away in a niche inside an otherwise empty, great jar-shaped floor cist in unit house GBN 1, where we already had uncovered a mini-sipapu in the lower floor of the fire pit. The cache contained a number of pieces of water-deposited dripstone and travertine from the cave a few miles distant out of which a branch of the Gallina River flows. There also was a large collection of worn quartz "lightning stones," such as are still energetically rubbed together to produce a flickering glow like sheet lightning during some Pueblo rites for rain. Two bird-shaped sandstone concretions would have been water fetishes. As any naturally shaped image of a living creature is believed to carry more of the spirit and hence "power" of the supernatural prototype of that creature than would be present in a man-made fetish, this figure probably found a place on an altar.[*] These, the dripstone, and the lightning stones reflect characteristic Pueblo belief in the efficacy of display and "use" of objects symbolic of moisture. They represent prayers for water but also are believed to compel precipitation by means of the cooperation of man and supernatural beings. The combination of magic and religion is typically Puebloid.

A group of "potato-shaped objects" and an old stone axe head (perhaps to cut them?) also had been tucked away in that cist. The potato-shaped objects are not altar pieces.

---

[*] Altars, as we know from the historic Pueblos, were not permanent features of a room used for rituals, but were set up on the floor on appropriate dates derived from sunwatching. In historic times altars commonly have consisted of a simple sand painting, a carved and painted reredos background, and symbolic images and materials.

Fashioned of plant fiber, clay, and human feces, as determined by the Castetter Laboratory for Ethnobotanical Studies at the University of New Mexico (for details see Volume II), these may have been made and kept to provide the ingredient which in small amount must be added to water to make a drink required for initiates and members of the most powerful of the eastern Pueblo religious societies, the Koshare, sons of the Sun. To other Pueblo individuals, excreta is as much to be avoided as by ourselves, but it is thought that the inner "power" acquired in becoming a Koshare permits and requires this drink as a feature distinctly separating these individuals from all others. Parsons (1939:415, 434-439) has suggested that the symbolic ingestion of feces may give the Koshare "power" to cure certain ailments, including those presumed to have been caused by contact with excreta. This would be in line with old Pueblo-type thought. Parsons also reminds us that urine, used by various native peoples of the world internally or externally, was a favorite remedy of our own early European ancestors.

Apart from the fact that pollen in these objects (which may be referred to as modified coprolites) provides us with some information on corn, sunflower seeds, and other foods probably used by the Gallina group, our special interest in them relates to Pueblo tradition that the important Koshare society, best known as a fertility group, is the oldest of all Pueblo sodalities. If our deduction is correct, that society would date at least from the 13th century. Today the duties of this group have more to do with encouraging conservatism and advising native governmental and religious activities than with curing, but the society is said to have been created originally to entertain the people with clowning and merriment which would minimize their ailments. Jemez tradition specifically tells of a Koshare having come into the plaza to cheer the discouraged women shortly before the hungry Gallina people abandoned the then dessicated area around Cuba, New Mexico, for the Jemez country. Our earliest definite material evidence pertaining to the Koshare hitherto has been a painting of one of these "religious clowns" on a large mid-14th-century potsherd of Abiquiu Black-on-white ware from Sapawe, a Tewa ancestral pueblo in the Chama drainage. (Ellis: Report in preparation.) A second such sherd from Pecos Pueblo, which obtained this ware from the Chama country by trade, shows a similar depiction. Among the ritual objects of painted wood found in one of the back rooms of Chetro Ketl (Chaco Canyon) was a wand carved with a head topped with two horn-like projections jutting out at an angle. Another very similar figure had been broken from its original mounting. Both are spoken of by Dodgen (in Vivian, Dodgen, Hartman 1978:89) as having a "snake-like head," We would not characterize these heads as snakelike but Koshare-like, both in contour and the horizontal black striping of faces and tapered horns or "pokes." Anyone acquainted with the sacred clown society so revered by the living Pueblos of New Mexico, and even the Hopi-Tewa of Arizona, might at once wonder if this was not strong evidence for existence of the Koshare concept and representation as early as the 10th to 12th centuries. The only foreign touch in the Chaco examples (?) is the bit of blue-green paint, not seen on today's representations. The society appears to have developed among the Tanoan-speaking Pueblos and to have been borrowed by the Keresan speakers and, eventually, others (Ellis 1964).

Our third, and most fortunate major discovery in relation to religion, was the "probable kiva," the first to have been found for Gallina culture. This subterranean ceremonial structure was the more intriguing in that it was connected by a tunnel to the surface house, GBN 1, in which we already had found a mini-sipapu and the cache of ritual items just discussed. The sealed cist in which those objects had been left was beneath the eastern side of the house floor, though its manhole opening was in a "hallway" between the long storage bin on that side and the small storeroom in the southeast corner of the house. On the western side of the big room, a soft area in the floor at first was thought to mark the manhole to a second cist, but excavation showed a shaft which dropped vertically to an enlarged base chamber. Later this chamber would be found to hold a big cist filled with still usable stone artifacts beneath a flagged paving laid to cover a portion of its floor. GBN 1 was not merely a dwelling; it was an institution!

Excavation had shown that the supposed pithouse just to the south of the surface structure had a horizontal tunnel running from the edge of its floor northward. One hardly could doubt that the shaft and tunnel would connect, and this was found to be so after laborious excavation, much of which had to be done with the worker squatting or lying at full length. That the pithouse might have been a kiva was a tentative guess after we had traced the shaft; that it *was* a kiva became fairly certain when in clearing the floor we uncovered (to our amazement!) a beautifully made full-size sipapu in its typical location directly north of the fire pit.

Sealed into place by a raised rim of clay was its cover, a neatly made disk of smooth, deep-red sandstone which contrasted with the wide band of yellow paint outlining the sipapu and extending a few centimeters outside it. And what was below the lid? Smooth soil in the center of which a small conical pit had been cut, the opening toward the underworld down which sounds should funnel. It was as fresh as if the task had been done that day rather than almost 800 years before.

Nor was that all, for a little closer to the fire pit and in a direct line to the north from it, was a second sipapu like the first in size, type, and yellow rim outlining except that it had only clay for its lid. Two sipapus are very rare in Southwestern kivas. We have no explanation except the suggestion that the one nearer the fire pit, possibly constructed first, could have been found to be so close that it picked up ashes or was an obstruction when the fire was being fed. It then may have been closed and the second one constructed for continued use. The entire kiva floor had been cleaned and, like house floors, left in perfect shape when the structure was abandoned. In this custom we obviously see the exemplification of some important precept merely guessed today. As for the two sipapus, we can call attention to the pair, close together, found in a kiva at the Pindi site, near Santa Fe, of approximately the same period.

We had known that the Gallinas-become-Jemez had kivas. At the 14th- to 17th-century site of Unshagi there were three, the smallest with no sign of a sipapu, Kiva B with a sipapu (4 inches square, 8 inches deep, lined with "small flat rocks"), located north of the fire pit, and the third with a highly polished oval slab of basalt set into the floor north of the fire pit but with nothing found beneath it. Reiter (1938:61-63, 90) suggests this may have been a sipapu substitute. For 16th-century Guisewa at Jemez Springs we have one possible sipapu in the larger of the two kivas. Our first question to ourselves when

41

we discovered the shaft and tunnel at GBN 1 was "how can one recognize a kiva with certainty?" This puzzle has been mulled over by archaeologists since the 1920s. A somewhat parallel problem would be sorting out which structures had been used as churches should some cataclysm destroy the people of the United States, even if our architecture were not flattened. Some churches are easily recognizable through their duplication of old historic architectural styles, but others are ultramodernistic or may resemble a secular fraternal hall or even a small warehouse. The complex of features most commonly associated with a "religious society type kiva" (in contrast to the large or great kiva) has included subterranean locations, circular shape, a bench running partly or entirely around the walls, a fire pit, deflector, ventilator shaft, and sipapu, all derived from early pithouses of the Four Corners area.

No single one of these features is invariably found. Yet today's generally used definition, that a kiva should be somewhat different from other structures typical of a specific culture, and probably larger than the houses in order to accommodate more people, is almost as fallible as the earlier concept. For example, we know that in the historic Pueblos, religious societies and their meeting places varied greatly in size. One of the last religious society kivas to be abandoned by the historic Jemez Pueblo had such a small floor that when the society members associated with it convened, the raised knees of the men seated on opposite sides of the floor, met.

We do not yet have a neat lineal ancestor for our Gallina kiva, but if we return to our background history for Gallina culture, we cross some useful trails. Except in the Durango district, on the eastern side of the Four Corners area we have clear evidence for the use of a sipapu. At first we find them in many of the homes, then in the proto-kiva, prototype of the later religious society or small kiva dedicated primarily to religious activities. Sipapus of varying types appear in some great kivas. With the concept of possible hidden sipapus in mind, it may be that wider distribution eventually will be known.

Secondly, we have knowledge of general adoption of north-south orientation for the pithouse and then placement of kiva features, including sipapu, on a north-south axis. This is of importance because in the Gallina pithouse, surface house, and kiva, orientation is consistently north-south.

Third, we have the hitherto unconsidered evidence for veneration of Fire God-Ash Boy appearing in the clean ash-filled vertical shaft between the upper use-floor and the ritual deep bottom floor in house fire pits. We also have the filling of all fire pits (as in some of the earlier pithouses) to the rim with ash at the time of house abandonment. Then a great mass of ash was thrown as a blanket over the aligned ventilator shaft opening, deflector, and fire pit. This custom was duplicated in treatment of the religious society kivas in the Pueblo IV Tewa sites of Sapawe and Tsama in the Chama, though their orientation was consistently east-west. Next we have the repeated evidence that our Gallina houses, at abandonment, were given a quick ritual burning possibly with dry, piled brush, after their floors had been cleaned. Our guess is that this was a purification rite: a cleansing from all materials with which the occupants had been in contact and which could be used by enemies in attempted witchcraft. Finally the roof timbers were removed, letting the roof debris of stones and sherds as well as hardened clay, interior plaster, and outer surfacing fall over the swept floors.

There also is another avenue of comparison, contemporary with or slightly earlier than the period of Gallina culture we are investigating. This is the early Pueblo III complex (originally considered to represent Pueblo II) known as "Prudden's Unit-Type Structure."

These unit-type sites,[*] concentrated from the Montezuma Valley immediately west of the Mesa Verde to Comb Wash, Utah, consist of a single or double bank of one-story dwelling rooms, sometimes with an extra room projecting forward from each end, plus a kiva out in front. Their distinctive characteristic is the underground passageway which drops as a shaft from one of those rooms and continues as a tunnel to open onto the north side of the bench in the Mesa Verde keyhole-type kiva (Kidder 1924:67; Morris 1939:33). Such kivas had a fire pit, deflector, ventilating shaft, sipapu, bench, and elevated south recess at bench height.

Prudden's unit-type structures were contemporary with our GBN 1 domicile-plus-kiva complex. The difference between the kiva-house complex in Prudden's sites and our Gallina kiva-house example lies primarily in the different type of elaboration of the latter. In the Gallina, where 13th-century pithouses and surface houses equally were fitted with a fire pit, deflector, ventilating shaft, and bins projecting from east and west walls, these features all appeared in the kiva as well as in the attached house. Pueblo conservatism is notable in this example, but other peoples of the world similarly bring religious tenets and also the type of structure in which they are celebrated out of the history of their group. The fire pit, deflector, and ventilating shaft actually were practical. We really do not know that they ever carried the religious overtones archaeologists are inclined to ascribe to them. The bench, as pointed out by someone adept in engineering, served a major function in giving support to the side walls of any pit structure. The Gallina people were at home with use of the projecting storage bins in some of which we have found nested vessels as well as corn. Conveniences for storage otherwise consisted primarily of the beamed roof from which some items could be hung or of pits dug into the floor or the bench. We have mentioned the big cyst beneath the house floor, holding ritual items, and that other beneath the bottom of the tunnel shaft, apparently to hold still usable household equipment. We also found a small cist, left empty except for a bit of trash, off the tunnel just outside the north wall of our kiva.

Would its original contents have been ritual equipment? Not necessarily. The proto-kiva, in its day, had held its share of metates, manos, and other stone implements for use of the family in charge. Women members of a Pueblo religious society today cook for the entire group in a house equipped for that express purpose or in a similar room attached to the retreat house.

---

[*] It is unfortunate that in the 1930s the Gallina surface house was given a designation so close to this earlier published name for a different architectural style in an apparently unrelated area.

43

Where outside of Gallina country does one find great jar-shaped subterranean cists? Beneath Room 23 in Building VII, Site 41 in the La Plata, Morris (1939:97-103) found a "ramified storage pit" with a short tunnel and extension opening off it. Beneath Room 29 in the same building was another jar-shaped pit, off the end of a vertical shaft about 1 meter in height. A longer vertical shaft led down from the floor of Room 30 in the same building to reach a similar pit which had been dug to reach an older kiva floor. All of these pits were empty when found; each would have looked appropriate in a Gallina Phase site. From this same Building VII came 6 "skinning knives," unquestionably of the same type as our "skinning pry-knife," although their materials differed. The period of construction and use of these La Plata rooms would have been in the 12th or fairly early 13th century.

There seems little question that the Gallina culture branched off from an original La Plata stem and remained in close enough contact with the La Plata and Mesa Verde branches to have shared some details of architectural and artifact styles.

There is, however, one other known site much closer to the Gallina area in which the single kiva was found to have been connected to the bank of rooms by a tunnel. This is Riana Ruin (Hibben 1937), located at the confluence of Cañones Creek and the Chama River, some 30 miles northeast of the south Llaves district. To judge from the pottery, of which the dominant decorated type is Wiyo Black-on-white, this was an ancestral Tewa village of the 14th century. Several parallels between details of the Gallina culture and that of this and other neighboring Tewa sites in the Chama lead one to wonder whether there was some overlap in time between the Tewa and Towa (Gallina-Jemez) occupation of adjoining territory. Tewa archaeology before the stage of Pueblo IV still is far from well known.

The small Riana pueblo consisted of a masonry wall-outlined plaza with parts of two sides made of adjoining rooms, and the third side entirely edged with rooms, two deep at one corner. Most had been of only one story. The kiva was almost entirely subterranean, with large rectangular stone-lined firebox (3 x 2 feet, and 3.5 feet deep), slab deflector at east end of fire pit, sipapu, and ventilator, all oriented to the east, as remained typical for Pueblo IV Tewa sites. The tunnel began with a shaft which dropped 7 feet from the interior of Room 13 and ran beneath its wall on the plaza side. From there, for its entire length of 22 feet, it was actually a trench passageway covered with a roof at ground surface. A ladder, of which remains were found in place, eased the initial drop into the tunnel. At about two-thirds of the distance to the kiva, large lava boulders beneath the ground level had necessitated a jog in the trench construction, and some posts had been set in for additional roof support. The opening of the tunnel into the kiva (30 x 22 inches) was outlined by fitted large sandstone slabs. An irregular pile of boulders made something of a wall curving out from the row of house rooms and part way around the kiva. The pueblo was burned a few years after A.D. 1348. The nearby Palisade Ruin (Peckham 1981) was very similar except that its single kiva (oriented slightly south of east) was without sipapu and had no tunnel. It is possible that the Gallina people borrowed the concept of kiva and tunnel from the Riana site, or vice versa, but it seems more probable that both took the concept from Prudden's unit-type house of the Four Corners country.

To judge from our one example, the floor of a Gallina kiva took on but a single feature distinctive from those of the Gallina pit and surface houses. That was the sipapu or, less conceivably, two sipapus if the pair we found saw contemporary rather than successive use. The yellow clay paint with which their rims were sometimes decorated and our first mini-sipapu beneath a house fire pit was lined is a distinctive trait to date not elsewhere reported.

We are not permitted to forget that to the Jemez this ancestral area still is known as "Yellow Mesa."

Surprises in archaeology are fun, but it is largely workaday grubbing that provides the pieces of information needed to outline the development and adjustments necessarily made by a people struggling to stay alive when ecological patterns changed. The Gallina area, without question, still warrants many years of excavation and discovery. Pollen studies, tree-ring data and other information and concepts borrowed from non-archaeologists can do much toward rounding out a picture of men and women endlessly but courageously struggling to make a life for their families when nature's cooperation with man was less than man's cooperation with nature.

Turkey Spring Site I

Area Map of Agricultural Plot and House Relationships

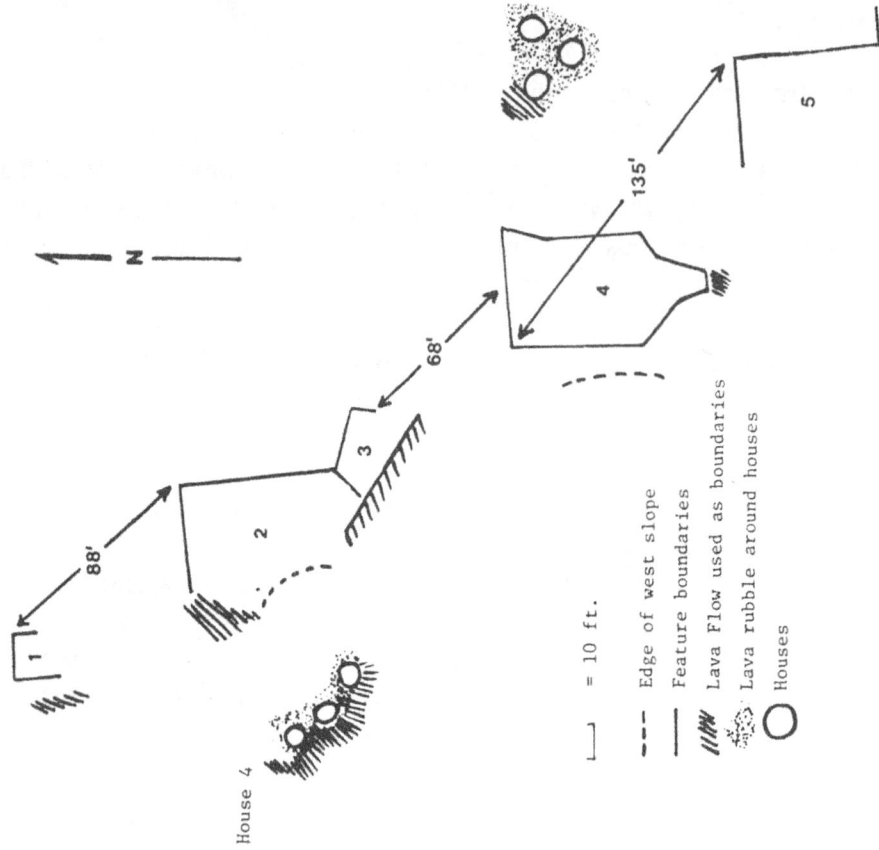

Figure 2

SITE I, HOUSE 1   LA10641

Turkey Spring Site, Carson National Forest, New Mexico

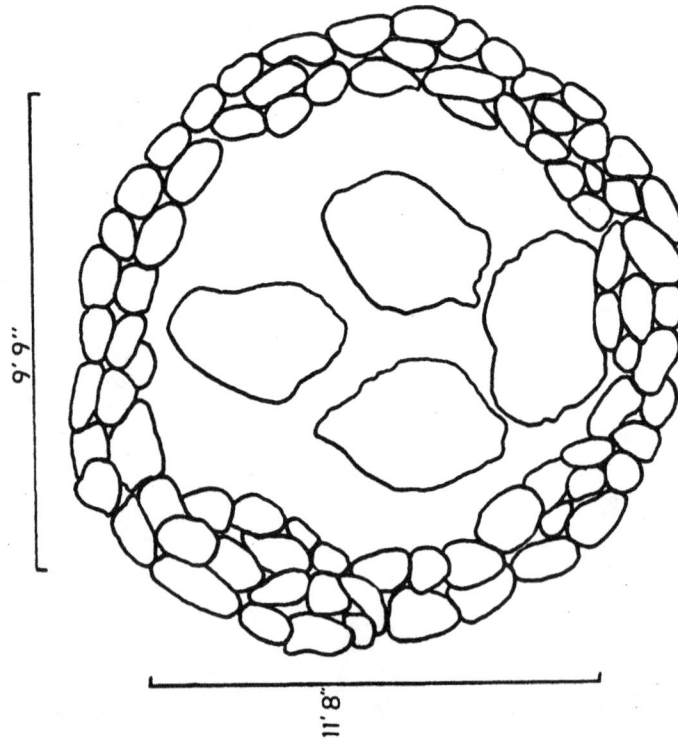

Figure 1

The Canjilon Mountain Hunting-Gathering Sites as One Expression of Gallina Culture

Little ever has been known about the hunting and gathering that comprised the second most important endeavor of the prehistoric and historic Pueblo peoples even after they had become adept in the cultivation of corn, beans, and squash. Hunting and the collection of piñon nuts still are considered important to many Southwestern families. Gathering has so far disappeared from today's acculturated economy that even in such a conservative pueblo as Santo Domingo a grant-supported class recently planned to acquaint native adults with the old survival techniques had to be cancelled. Of all the elderly women polled, none had enough knowledge of regional plants and their uses to act as teacher.

In the historic period recalled by living Pueblo men, groups of males expected to do considerable hunting in the fall and winter. At least in some villages, one duty of the hunt chief was to designate where they could go each season so that no one area would be over hunted. Men of neighboring pueblos, even if not of the same linguistic stock, might hunt together for antelope and buffalo. Buffalo hunting, requiring as much as two or three months away from home on a trip to the Plains, commonly involved representatives from more than one pueblo. The meat was sliced thin and dried on the prairie grass to be carried home in hide bags. Antelope traps of brush and perhaps some stone are remembered in various pueblos. These had a large opening at the far end into which the animals could be directed by brush beaters. The near end was more constricted and men with bows, arrows, and clubs were posted along it to do the killing. Old examples have been found from the Rio Grande to Hopi. Deer traps consisting of a covered trench or stone crevice little longer than the creature were excavated on animal trails. Deer also could be hunted by simple pursuit with bow and arrow or, like turkey, from a blind.

In general, winter was considered to be a season dedicated to hunting just as summer was dedicated to agriculture and gathering. This meant that the ceremonial activities designed for propagation of plants and animals and the acquisition of such food products tended to be seasonally concentrated, but it did not mean that no animals were killed in summer, especially if foodstuffs were short.

During years when the weather was dry or frosts lasted late in the spring or came too early in the fall to permit crop maturation, the people had no recourse but to open their emergency stores, designed to stave off starvation for one to two years if augmented with everything still obtainable from the wild. Dry weather affected not only cultivated crops but also wild plants, and a shortage of wild plants cut the number of wild animals in an area. As the countryside close around a pueblo was scoured to its limits by anxious and hungry families ordinarily primarily dependent on local agriculture, people had to go farther afield at their own altitude or higher where more moisture might have provided still unexhausted wild stores. The final recourse, of course, was abandoning their area and moving elsewhere, but this posed the problem of locating another, unoccupied area which was better economically, within walking distance for an already malnourished population. It also left the serious problem of abandoning psychologically important shrines. Pueblo people are very tightly tied to their lands and ritual sites.

In the scarcity of sites with tree-ring dates for the last quarter of the 1200s in all the northern Southwest except the Rio Grande, we have plentiful evidence that what areas had not been abandoned during the previous century now were given up, possibly because of decreasing available moisture or headward stream-cutting or both. As we cannot definitely track into the next century some of the cultural groups which had to abandon their home territory, they obviously must have lost identity in their necessary amalgamation with other peoples. Such eventualities, as well as the physically difficult move itself, would have been hard to face. We are fortunate in being able to trace the final exodus of the Gallina people to the northern portion of the Jemez area where their descendants live today. Reiter (1938), one of the first to suggest this, called attention to numerous parallels, including corner bins; Mackey (n.d.) has pursued this matter to the same conclusion especially through investigation of pottery development, architecture, and physical type.

As discussed in relation to the home villages, we now can give our own date for abandonment of the Llaves area as post A.D. 1275, when a considerable drought climaxed a long period of increasingly difficult climatic conditions. (Date obtained from wood used in construction of the tower at our House GBN 4, Llaves area.) Although we have no tree-ring dates for the hunting-gathering sites on the southern slopes of Canjilon Mountain, it seems probable that the considerable activity for which we found evidence represents the time of mounting food-provision stress shortly before the Gallina people gave up the area they had occupied for some two centuries along the Continental Divide. We would not contend that the exodus of all the Gallina groups occurred in a single concerted move, but there is no question that the second half of the 13th-century, in which tree-ring records for the area east of the Divide show many long alternating good year-bad year sequences, must have been exceedingly difficult for all the Gallina people, as for others living away from major water sources.

The Turkey Spring (LA 10641, LA 10643), Dulce Springs (LA 10642), and Red Hill (LA 10644) prehistoric sites on the slopes of Canjilon Mountain first were brought to our attention (1971) by John Hayden, at that time in charge of the United States Forest Service Ghost Ranch Living Museum, on Highway 84. He had picked up arrow points in the vicinity of what appeared to have been some sort of crude habitations and a long dry-laid wall stretching down a ridge. The area was in a very rough and broken portion of the Brazos volcanic flow and scree in the Canjilon Ranger District of Carson National Forest. The sites had not been disturbed. Fortunately, on our initial visit to Turkey Spring we found a few potsherds in the heavy ground cover of pine needles and thereby gained our first clue that the people who had camped in this area were of Gallina culture though the majority of their home villages were scattered twenty miles or more to the south.

The Canjilon Mountain sites (also known as the Turkey Spring sites) ranged in altitude from the 8,200-8,300 feet of Turkey Spring Site I to 8,300-8,400 feet for Turkey Spring Site II only a quarter mile to the north, 8,600 feet at the top of Dulce Springs site III, one mile farther up the mountain, and almost 10,000 feet for Sites IV and V near Red Hill, three miles to the northeast. These elevations place the mountain campsites from approximately 1,000 to 2,800 feet higher than our Gallina Butts (GB) home village sites (7,200 to 7,300 feet altitude) two to four miles east of the Continental Divide area in the Llaves district. Some others not far distant reach an elevation of around 8,000 feet. (Ellis Report 1982)

The significance of these mountain sites lies in their representing an economic effort primarily different from and supplemental to the basic economy of their home area, agriculture. The Canjilon Mountain area still is well supplied with berries and many other plant foods, deer, elk, and smaller animals. Construction of domiciles for summer use took advantage of the great volcanic boulders in the broken lava fields, using them as partial walls and filling gaps with apparently dry-laid unshaped lava stones. Wall bases were thick and upper portions tapered. Floor features were much simplified. Entrance was through the roof, as in most Anasazi communities. Caves of adequate size in the lava were used for dwellings or for workrooms. Structures for storage had basal walls of lava stones but, to judge from the shortage of fallen rock at their bases, must have had low roofs or upper walls of jacal (posts within a casing of clay) topped by a roof. Within the lava beds, naturally protected crevices and small caves including some of those in which we found hidden vessels, would have provided extra storage facilities. Certain flat areas in the lava beds were adapted for group workplaces or for drying meat or plant foods by edging with a low wall. Some of these were reached by pathways "paved" with slabs or filled in with chinking stones.

What appear to have been garden plots, partly outlined by low, dry-laid walls along the ridge at Turkey Spring I, point to some of the people having attempted farming here, but we can not prove this hypothesis. None of the other villages here were of low enough elevation to permit cropping, and it is possible that heat reflected from the lava bed only a few feet distant could have tipped the scale in favor of crop maturation at an altitude close to the limit for maize. No pollen from corn or other cultigens was found in our soil samples but this could result from erosion. The walls, which did not totally surround the plots, were placed to prevent fast runoff of precipitation. The five plots might be construed as the holdings of five families, but this is uncertain. The roasting pit not far above the highest plot may have been intended for roasting meat or perhaps corn before drying and shelling it to be taken home. It is quite possible that other fields, without the rock walls which called our attention to those on the ridge, may have been laid out on gentle slopes or even better, on the flats below the ridge, near what appears to have been an efficient natural reservoir. People of Turkey Spring II and of the Dulce Springs camps may have cut their stay in the mountains shorter, but it is also quite possible that they were doing some farming in the valleys below their camps. These would have been as easily reached on foot as various of the deep valleys where we know farming was done by historic Pueblo peoples living in the western foothills of the Sangre de Cristo Mountains.

We presume that the carelessly built mountain camps were not used during the winter because of the certainty of bitter cold at those altitudes. Thus far in our reconstruction we are on relatively safe ground, backed by our data. The problem of dating the years of use of the mountain camps is more difficult. Our tree-ring material, carefully collected and all sent to the Laboratory of Tree-Ring Analysis at the University of Arizona, was not datable, the major difficulty being that where water usually is plentiful for the needs of conifers, growth rings follow each other with little change in width, except in relation to age of the tree. Their record, dubbed "complacent", is not distinctive enough to permit identification of the period in which the trees lived.

Another technique now often used for prehistoric dating is that known as the archaeomagnetic method. The direction of alignment of molecules of clay from well-burned areas, such as the sides of a hearth, are checked in relation to the known, changing locations of the magnetic pole through time.

As described for each of the houses we excavated, the hearths were not well built neatly lined clay basins. Nevertheless an attempt was made to see whether archaeomagnetic dating, today not far from as accurate as tree-ring dating, might possibly be used to solve our problem. Tom Windes, trained in collection of samples for archaeomagnetic work by the Chaco Center (University of New Mexico and U. S. National Park Service), was asked to examine our best hearth, that of House I-4 excavated by Peter McKenna in Turkey Spring I. The result was disappointing. Windes found that the fire pit had not been burned enough to warrant such testing. He further noted that the presence of the surrounding basalt would have an adverse effect on the local magnetic fields, thus creating a local anomaly. His comments in explaining the lack of hard-firing of this shallow pit were that it must have:

 1. had very brief use, or

 2. held only a small "cool" fire, or

 3. held only a few coals, these having been transferred from a "parent" fire pit elsewhere (presumably in the open), or

 4. had a fire built on rocks above floor level so that only ash and coals filtered down into the pit (a concept for which no material evidence whatever exists), or

 5. it could have been an ash pit instead of a fire pit.

The latter point is most unlikely, as an ash pit presupposes a fire pit nearby, and no other pit was found in this house. We do not say that a small fire never was built in a Gallina camp house for warmth during summer storms, but bringing coals for heating into the house from an outside fire intended primarily for cooking is more probable. This method has been recognized as the typical "heating pit" system used in some of the Mogollon phases of western New Mexico and during Basketmaker II by Anasazi of the Four Corners country.

Finding much actual evidence of out-of-doors fires for cooking hardly is to be expected in the broken lava; ash and charcoal would have washed away. We do have, however, the little "cave" (Functional Structure II-17) in Turkey Spring II, thought to have served as a combination storage cist and cooking area for House II-19 only thirteen feet distant, and possibly also for nearby House II-18. (See description under Turkey Spring II.)

As all the other "fire hearths" found in our mountain sites were less structured than those of House I-4, we are left to surmise that all may have been "heating pit" areas, a device recognized as diminishing the likelihood of accidentally burning down one's domicile through sparks reaching the roof. The heating pit is another interesting feature not previously suggested for Gallina culture, though in home villages, the walled deflector in horseshoe shape, its base often filled with ash, well could have served that purpose as well as protecting the fire pit from ventilator shaft drafts.

We still are left without any concrete evidence of the time period during which the mountain campsites were in use. Gallina pottery does seem to have changed somewhat in shape through time and the pottery we have from Canjilon sites does not appear to differ from that of the home villages, for which we also have tree-ring dates in the second half of the 13th-century. It is for that period that we have evidence of increasing numbers of intermittent dry years, and the studies of Holbrook and Mackey (1976) and Mackey and Holbrook (1978) indicate that the type of mice living in or near the home villages changed because of their physiological requirements for relative dampness. Corn also was found by the same investigators to have become more irregular in kernel pattern, a sign that its growth was impeded. This was the period when the last of the Four Corners country was abandoned, supposedly because of arroyo-cutting and shortages of moisture available for crops.

Our guess is that the use of summer mountain camps to increase food supplies was considerably accelerated, if not begun, during this period, and that here we have a picture of economic adaptation within the Gallina culture.

PHYSICAL ATTRIBUTES OF THE TURKEY SPRING AREA[*]

Geography

The two Turkey Spring sites (LA 10641 and LA 10643) are located respectively in Sections 30 and 31, T27 North, Range 5 East, NMPM, within the Cebolla Quadrangle. Turkey Spring is about fifteen miles south of Tierra Amarilla but only about two miles from the village of Cebolla. According to Doney's (1968) description:

** John Hayden

51

A north-trending escarpment nearly bisects the Cebolla quadrangle; west is the Chama Basin, east, the Tusas Mountains, ... on the west side of the escarpment, there is a precipitous drop to the level of the Chama valley.

Canjilon Peak (elevation 10,913 feet) is the most prominent feature along the escarpment. Roughly one mile west of Canjilon Peak and similarly along the escarpment is a small volcanic cone known as Red Hill. The ridge on which the people established their highest sites extends west and slightly south of that cone.

Geology

Periglacial activity during Pleistocene glaciation shaped the Cebolla area, forming the characteristic landslide topography along the west side of the Canjilon escarpment, including the basic shaping of the ridge. Recent movement along the escarpment brought volcanic activity and the volcanic cone, Red Hill, the southernmost of six cinder cones along and in front of the slope (Doney 1968). Lava, which must have extruded from the base of Red Hill, covered the ridge-top along its length for approximately 4.1 miles to the west. This lava is fine-grained, medium gray in color, and of the "aa" type. It is slightly to very vesicular. The rock contains much olivine, and for this reason can be classified as an olivine basalt. The basalt flow capping the ridge ends abruptly in the center of Sections 30 and 31, forming a north-south aligned and generally west-facing front (slope), approximately one mile in length within these sections.

Along the southern portion of the flow's west edge in Section 31 and along the northernmost portion of the flow in Section 30, the fractured basalt rock forms a steep slope of jumbled boulders. Crevices, caves, and tunnels were created among the loosely "stacked" boulders. Many interspaces are extensive and interconnected; some are quite deep. It is within these two extremely rugged, broken sites that most of the prehistoric structures are found.

Slopes below the flow are covered by volcanic scree, a thin veneer of unstratified, angular rock fragments (Doney 1968; Place 1). This is rock which has broken free of the actual flow and tumbled downslope.

The basalt flow appears to overlie unconformably a deposit containing conglomeratic rock which is similar to rock from formations found on Canjilon Peak. Along the contact zone at the base of the flow (covered by scree in some places), one finds gravels composed of well-rounded cobbles and pebbles of granite, gneiss, schist, quartzite, etc. Smith (1961:28-29) describes similar "high-level terrace deposits" capping other ridges in this general area. If, prior to being covered by the lava flow, our ridge was topped by this so-called terrace gravel, the metamorphic gravel which is sparsely evident at the contact zone, especially near Turkey Spring, well may have been the source of material for many of the various artifacts of metamorphic rock found in association with the prehistoric structures excavated.

The physical makeup and environmental factors of the Turkey Spring area attracted the former occupants of the many rock house structures in offering building material, suitable exposure to the sun, partial protection from wind and oncoming weather, visual control of the surrounding lands, defensibility, and access to nearby water and food sources. On these boulder slopes the basalt rock acts like a natural heat radiator, absorbing heat from the sun during the day and releasing it during the night, an advantageous feature at this altitude. The nearby area also would have provided rich high-altitude plant and animal life.

Climate

The elevations range from 8,200 feet m.s.l. at Turkey Spring to approximately 8,400 feet m.s.l. at the top of the ridge near Site II. The climate at this elevation level is moderate. The overall climate of New Mexico is generally considered to be semiarid *(Climate and Man,* 1941:1028), but the climate at this site is neither semiarid nor moist: it probably is submoist. A good compromise term is simply "moderate." Estimation from area weather records indicates that the average annual precipitation is 16 to 18 inches. During most years, half the precipitation comes from winter snows and half from summer and early fall rain showers. The precipitation pattern and amount are known to fluctuate greatly from year to year.

The Yearbook of Agriculture, Climate and Man (1941:1014) gives the following information:

Averages for station to 1938:	Chama	Bateman Ranch	Turkey Spring (Hayden estimate)
—Temp. January ave.	21.5°F.		
—Temp. July ave.	63.0		
—Temp. maximum	99		
—Temp. minimum	-28		
—Killing frost:			
Ave. date of first	9/24	9/19	(9/21)
Ave. date of last	6/4	6/4	(6/4)
Ave. growing season length	112 days	107 day	(109 days)
Ave. annual precipitation	21.93 in.	23.98 in.	(16-18 plus in.)

Flora and Fauna

The Turkey Spring sites lie within the Transition and Canadian Life Zones. North- and east-facing exposures as well as sheltered situations are expressive of flora and fauna found in the higher, more moist Canadian Zone, whereas south and west aspects are likely to show flora and fauna of the Transition, or in some cases, the Upper Sonoran Zone.

Stream-side and spring-oriented riparian sites enrich this area with an added diversity of plant and animal species. Of note are:

- a. The main drainages north and south of the ridge which presently flow during much of the year may have been perennial during slightly wetter periods in the past.

- b. Turkey Spring, for which this archaeological area is named, is just east of Site I. Another small, unnamed spring is located south of Site II, at the contact zone between the basalt flow and underlying formations.

- c. Depressions within the basalt rock near the base of the flow form natural reservoirs. One such place is found at the bottom of the slope, west of House 4, Turkey Spring Site I, where a trail can be distinguished leading from near the ridge-top down to the depression. (This reservoir always has contained some water during the five years I have known the site, and shows high-water marks indicating a depth of more than ten feet at times.) Another similar impoundment is located at the base of the flow north of Structures 17, 18, and 19 of Site II. It was dry during 1972 but probably collects water during wetter periods.

Changes in the area's flora and fauna may not be readily determined from the paucity of evidence at hand. I have no reason to suggest that the flora and fauna have changed substantially within the past 1,000 years, except for recognizing the extinction of certain animals such as the mountain sheep, wolf, and possibly one type of elk. The presence of mature Ponderosa pine, white fir, and Douglas fir would indicate that the area has been covered with the existing forest type for 300 years at a minimum.

Until more substantial evidence is recovered and interpreted, perhaps the following brief inventory of existing plant and animal species can serve as an indication of food and cultural "raw materials" presently available:

Partial list of animals known to occur in the Turkey Spring area (by common name)

Tiger Salamander	Band-tail Pigion	Mule deer
Rocky Mt. Toad	Blue Grouse Wapiti (Elk)	
Chorus Frog	Red-shafted Flicker	White-tailed Prairie Dog
	Eagles, Hawks, Owls	Rock Squirrel
Bull Snake		Golden-mantel Squirrel
Garter Snake	Black Bear	Tassel-eared Squirrel
Prairie Rattlesnake	Raccoon	Red Squirrel
Horned Lizard	Weasel	Colorado Chipmunk
Fence Lizard	Badger	Pocket Gophers, mice
	Striped Skunk	Woodrats, Voles, etc.
Steller's Jay	Coyote	Muskrat
Clark Nutcracker	Grey Fox	Beaver
Robin	Cougar	Porcupine
Mourning Dove	Bobcat	Cottontail Rabbit
		Jackrabbit

Partial List of Important Plant Species Known to Occur in the Turkey Spring-Cebolla area (common name and scientific name)

Western Wheatgrass	Agropyron smithii
Little Blue Stem	Andropogon scorparius
Pine Dropseed	Blepharneuron spp.
Bromegrass	Bromeus spp.
Arizona Fescue	Festuca arizonica
Junegrass	Koeleria cristata
Mountain Muhly	Muhlenbergia spp.
Indian Ricegrass	Oryzopsis hymnoides
Timothy	Phleum spp.
Bluegrass	Poe spp..
Sedges	Carex spp.
Rushes	Juncus spp.
Verbina	Abronia spp.
Yarrow	Achillea lanulosa
Wild Onion	Allius spp.
Sego	Calochortus spp.
Thistle	Carcium spp.
Spring Beauty	Claytonia spp.
Hiddenflower	Cryptantha spp.
Herb. Buckwheat	Eriogonum spp.
Cow Parsnip	Heraculeum spp.

Wild Iris	Iris missouriensis
Peavine	Lathyrus spp.
Indiansfoot	Lomatium spp.
Alpine Sorrel	Oxyria digyna
Dock	Rumex spp.
Herb. Cinquefoil	Potentilla spp.
Mallow	Sphaeralcea spp.
Dandelion	Taraxacum spp.
White Fir	Abies concolor
Common Juniper	uniperus communis
One-seed Juniper	J. monosperma
Rocky Mt. Juniper	J. scopulorum
Piñon Pine	Pinus edulis
Ponderosa Pine	P. Ponderosa
Douglas-Fir	Pseudotsuga taxifolia
Rocky Mt. Maple	Acer glabrum Utah
Serviceberry	Anelanchier utahensis
Narrowleaf Cottonwood	Populus angustifolia
Aspen	Populus tremuloides
Chockcherry	Prunus virginiana
Gambel Oak	Quercus gambelii
Scouler Willow	Salix scouleriana
Kinnickinnic	Arctostaphylos uva-ursi
Sagebrush	Artemisia spp.
Oregon Grape	Berberis repens
Buckbrush	Ceanothus fendleriana
Hairy Mt. Majogany	Cercocarpus breviflorus
Rabbitbrush	Chrysothamnus spp.
Winterfat	Eurotia lanata
Snakeweed	Gutierrezia spp.
Skunkbush	Rhus trilobata
Currant	Rosa spp. (2)
Wild Rose	Rosa spp.
Raspberry	Rubrus spp.
Snowberry	Symphoricarpos spp.
Red-sier Dogwood	Cornus stolonifera

Narrowleaf Yucca	Yucca spp.
Ferns	(family: POLYPODIACEAE)
Cacti	(family: CACTACEAE)

The above lists are by no means complete; they indicate the more common species only. The lists are based on my personal knowledge and study of the plant and animal life of the general area.

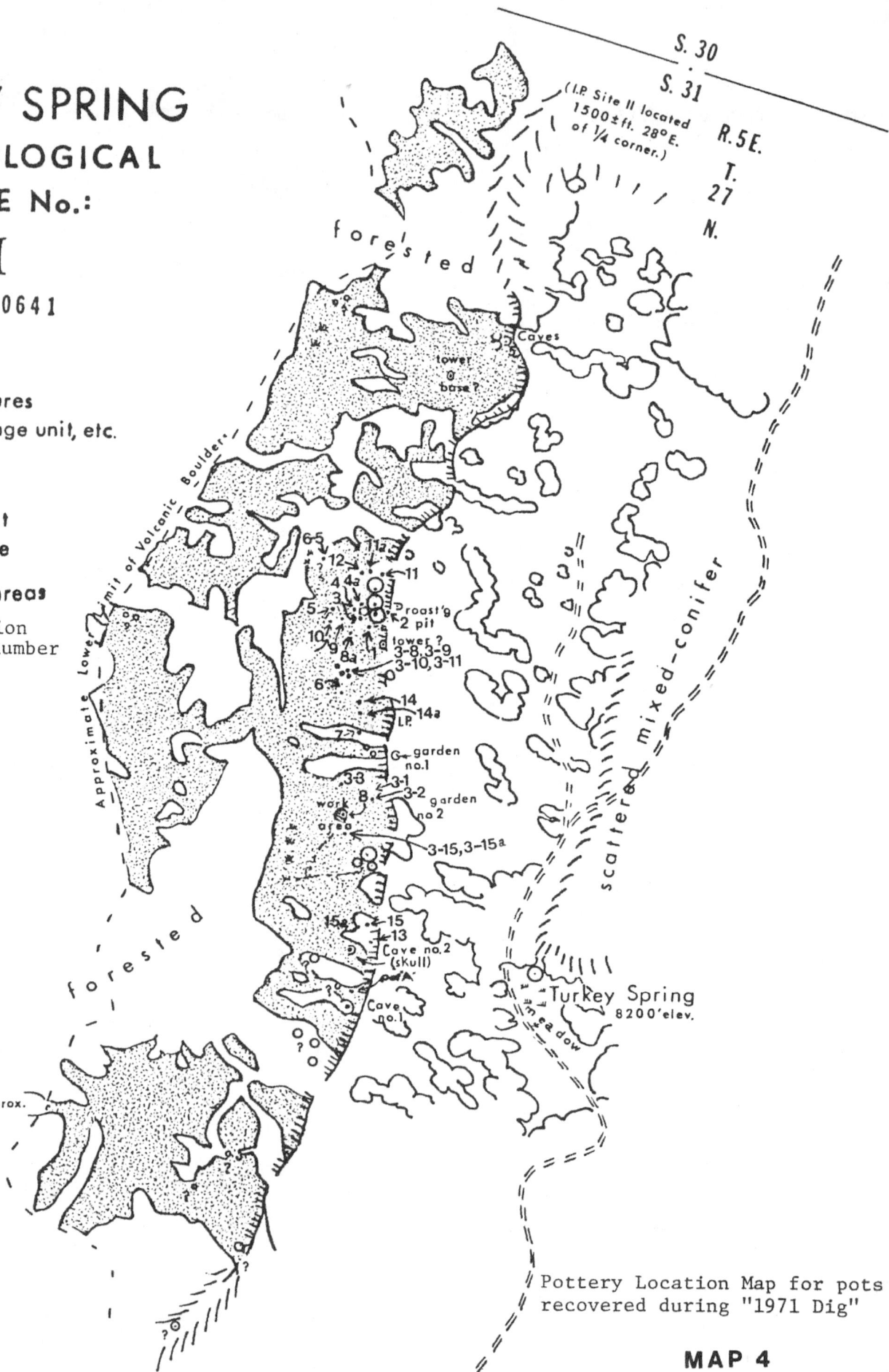

TURKEY SPRING
ARCHEOLOGICAL SITE No.:
I
LA No.: 10641

LEGEND
surface features
- ⊙ house, storage unit, etc.
- ◖ cave, lrg.
- ◣ " , small
- ⊙ ?
- ⊐ roasting pit
- basalt slope
  volcanic flow
- timbered areas

9⤵ Pot Location and field number

N

0   .5   1
390
scale
1 in = 390 ft. approx.

jsh 11/73

forested

Caves

tower @ base?

6 5   11
12
4 4a
3   11
5
10   Roast'g
9   2 pit
8a 1 tower?
6   3-8, 3-9
       3-10, 3-11
       14
       14a
I.P.
       garden no.1
3-3   3-1
8   3-2 garden no.2
work
area
       3-15, 3-15a
15a   15
       13
       Cave no.2 (skull)
pot "A"
Cave no.1

Turkey Spring
8200' elev.
meadow

S. 30
S. 31
R.5 E.
T. 27
N.

(I.P. Site II located 1500 ± ft. 28° E. of ¼ corner.)

scattered mixed-conifer

Approximate Lower Limit of Volcanic Boulder

forested

Pottery Location Map for pots recovered during "1971 Dig"

MAP 4

II

The Overall Picture of Turkey Spring Site I
(LA 10641)

The Village Layout

Turkey Spring Site I, consisting of an extended group of seasonally occupied habitations and other features, is strung out for over a mile along a north-south ridge, in and at the edge of the very rough western edge of the lava flow on the lower western slope of Canjilon Mountain. With an altitude of 8,200 feet, the climate would have been pleasant in summer, though in spring, early fall, and even on days of summer storms, the warmth captured and reflected by the black lava mass must have been a comfort. Winter would have been cold and snowy, and it is obvious that if the houses were constructed, as seems certain, with walls of unfitted and unmortared stones, they never were intended for winter use. We know from archaeological remains and the statements of living Pueblo peoples that seasonal occupation of field houses (small structures near cultivated fields) provided welcome vacations away from the main village for many Pueblo farmers in the historic and middle-to-late prehistoric periods. It also settled them near enough to their plots for efficient cultivation (Ellis 1976) and permitted the customary field protection provided by children whose summer duty was to frighten away deer, rabbits, birds, and other creatures prone to feed on what men planted.

Turkey Spring Site I was at the upper altitude limit for farming, but the people apparently laid out irregularly shaped, stone-walled plots along the ridge above their houses with the thought that more rain would fall here than in lower elevations and that such moisture plus what accumulated from winter snows would be held within those walls. Much of the local precipitation which fell here must have cascaded rapidly down the precipitous slopes, even as today. This would have been a most important consideration in the second half of the 13th century, dry throughout the northern Southwest, and on the eastern side of the Continental Divide plagued by recurrences of alternating normal and drought years. We know that low, wall-enclosed rectangular plots at elevations higher than those of home villages were an important agricultural device of the 14th through 16th centuries, especially for the ancestral Tewa along the Chama and for other pueblos, such as Zia and Jemez. To judge by the pottery types associated with Turkey Spring Site I, these Gallina "agricultural walled plots" preceded the Chama stone outlined plots by a century or more.

A far more important primary use for such summer sites as the two at Turkey Spring and the others on Canjilon Mountain would have been collection of wild plants to be dried for food and other purposes and of meat to be thinly sliced and "jerked" (dried in sun or shade for a few days). Many wild plants and animals originally would have been available in parts of their own home territory at comparable altitudes, but such natural resources undoubtedly came to be largely eliminated by overuse through two centuries of Gallina occupation, and especially the difficult 1200s.

A survey of the various features of Turkey Spring Site I resulted in a map which, compared with a similar map made to show locations of crevices in lava from which whole or partial vessels were recovered, gave us the following picture of this village.

Moving from north to south:

- 3 utilized caves at north edge of lava bed.

- 2 structural remains (use unknown) to the south a short distance.

- Circular enclosed area thought of as possible "tower" base for watchmen and signaling, possibly as workspot, or possibly as base for a storage structure.

- Crevices holding vessels L71.2.29, L71.2.2, and L71.2.30 apparently associated with nearby House I-3.

- Crevices holding vessels L71.2.22 and L71.2.25 associated with nearby House I-2. Vessels L71.2.18 and L71.2.14 may belong to same group.

- Crevice holding vessel L71.2.17 near House I-1. Vessel L71.2.9 was hidden behind and under a slab in House I-1.

- Walled structure on the ridge above, without fill and in open space, which conceivably could be the base for "tower" for watchmen and signaling, or base for storage structure.

- Crevices holding vessels L71.2.13, L71.2.12, L71.2.1, L71.2.28, and L71.2.6, all more or less opposite Garden Plot 1, but not near enough any known house to indicate definite association.

- Gardens 1 through 5 on the ridge above tumbled lava. 3 houses to the east.

- "Work-area flat" out in the lava, floor partly paved by chinking, and with trail intersecting another trail running from House I-4 down to spring at base of lava on the plain. 2 small unidentifiable structures near the work area.

- Crevice holding vessel L71.2.8, found at edge of work area. Other vessels found near work area and Garden 2 were L71.2.5, L71.2.36, and L71.2.37.

- Crevices holding vessels L71.2.20 and L71.2.34.

- Shallow Cave 5, on the floor surface of which the skull cap of a human being was found. Vessels L71.2.33 and L71.2.31 were not distant.

- Bain's Cave (Cave 1), near which L72.2.2 was found.

- 6 more possible habitations were found south of Bain's Cave, 3 in the most northern group, then 2, and finally 1.

- Below these, near the southern end of the village, was a stone circle with an adjoining circle only 5 feet across. This could have been a signal "tower" or watch place, or house and storehouse, or 2 storehouses.

- The most southern evidence of structures here was a short distance below the southern "tower" or watch place. Some areas which appear to have been "chipping stations" where men sat and flaked implements also are found toward the south end of this village.

This gives us, perhaps, a dozen domiciles, but excavation might increase this number.[*]

Our guess as to the purpose of the three structures marked as possible towers has nothing to do with their architectural shape but rather with their use. When we were working on the land claims of Zia, Santa Ana, and Jemez, the elders told us of their old system in which watchmen or guards stationed at a distance lighted one, two, or three fires (the number depending on the degree of danger) on high spots if the home pueblo or another needed warning. Because of hills, Jemez could not signal directly to Zia but employed a relay near the present location of San Ysidro. From Zia, the message could be picked up by Santa Ana guards, for whose use a low-walled, open, signal station was situated on Santa Ana Mesa above the pueblo itself. From there Santa Ana could signal to a signal station maintained on the mesa above San Felipe which then signaled down to San Felipe (Ellis and Ellis Dodge, report in preparation) and Sandia Pueblo. Sandia, in turn, down the Rio Grande valley to Isleta or up the river to San Felipe. San Felipe easily could contact Santo Domingo and the latter Cochiti, one of whose villages on the east side of the Rio Grande is claimed to have had a tower consisting of a two-story house at the southern end of the village, which since has been torn down (Ellis 1956; Ellis Dodge, Report in preparation). We find mention of fire and smoke signals in various Spanish and early Anglo reports dealing with Pueblos and the Navajo.

The second type of information comes from recent Chaco studies in which a signal system was found to have existed over a distance of a 150 miles north-south, and for lesser distances east-west. As checked with modern flares, the Chaco Pueblos and their outliers were connected by actual towers and low-walled, high, bare spots where fires could be lighted (Hayes and Windes 1974; Lister and Lister 1981:164-168). Such signals may have been relayed into, and throughout, Gallina territory by means of fires or smoke from the tops of large and small towers and the many high ridges. The only requirements would have been the posting of watch guards and visibility from a single spot to at least one other such spot.

[**] We have used the terms: a structure is a constructed unit such as a room, path, or roasting pit. A "structure by function" is not man made but shows evidence of having been used as a domicile or storage room. A feature is a form added to a structure such as a ventilator shaft, fire pit or bins, and a garden plot is an area with stones or a low wall outline presumably used for farming such as any of several shapes of grid gardens.

As the Chaco culture extended eastward to a few miles west of the Continental Divide near Cuba and Gallina culture extended in a strip from south of Cuba to (in some spots such as our mountain sites) a short distance north of the Chama River, knowledge of signaling certainly could have moved from the Chaco to the contemporary Gallina culture. That the two did have contacts is proven by presence of more sherds of Chaco pottery than of any others in the scanty Gallina trade collections.

No fill was found in the exposed north and south ridge circular walled-remains at Turkey Spring Site I or in that other similar rock circle toward the center of the village, but no certain means of functional identification has been devised. The open line of sight from the high, barren ridge overlooking Rattlesnake Point village, with its towers, to Turkey Spring Site I is apparent on a contour map (Ellis 1976). Ireland (1982), following our suggestion of combined use of towers and elevated open spots for signal stations, has used a contour map covering most of the Gallina and Jicarilla Reservation areas (into which Rosa and Gallina sites extend) to show the possibility of an interlocked communications system of 270 links connecting 57 possible stations in the Llaves area, from which 11 Gallina sites (and probably numerous other Gallina villages and towers not yet checked) in this district are visible. It could have been easily tied into a similar system which we both hypothesize might have relayed messages to a mass of other Gallina and non-Gallina sites in the upper San Juan Basin. A message traveling from the most southern to the most northern areas on Ireland's preliminary map would have covered 60 miles.

After our site survey, testing of some features and excavation of others were carried on by our 1972 group. Ten or fewer persons were assigned to work on each structure under the immediate supervision of a crew chief with previous experience in archaeological fieldwork. Work was to proceed in 4- or 6-inch levels, depending on the general depth of fill. Overall direction and later studies of pottery and stone work were handled by Florence Ellis. Tree-ring specimens were sent to the Laboratory of Tree-Ring Analysis at the University of Arizona. From a total of 20 structures, plus the walled cultivated plots, we trenched or excavated 6 structures and 3 of the gardens at Turkey Spring I. Pottery, artifacts, and sherds at present are exhibited or stored in the Florence Hawley Ellis Museum of Anthropology (opened 1980) at Ghost Ranch Conference Center, Abiquiu, New Mexico. The new data, including that on hidden vessels, provided our first glimpse of Gallina summer-occupied, hunting-gathering sites.

The "Structures"[*]

Structure I-1[**]

This approximately circular domicile (11.6 feet north-south by 9.75 feet east-west) stood on a south-facing slope below a rough and precipitous drop from the ridge crest. The many roots from trees presently growing immediately outside the walls made excavation exceedingly difficult. (Frontispiece and Figure 1)

In Level 1 the top 4 inches of fill consisted of moist humus which included a few clumps of burned and unburned clay, probably from the roof. Under this was dry soil containing an occasional small chunk of unburned clay and bits of decayed wood. A few small bones and scraps were scattered in the humus layer and below, suggesting possible accidental deposition after abandonment of the structure. The small charcoal fragments, burned clay, and ash which continued through the fill could have resulted from ritual burning of the original roof at the time of abandonment, as surmised after finding similar items in other of the mountain structures and home sites in the Llaves area. An alternate possibility is that it was debris from post-occupational forest fires, an early suggestion made by Hayden. No evidence of a floor could be distinguished.

One broken obsidian bifurcated point was found in Level 2 between 6 and 8 inches below the surface, close to the north wall of this house. Near it lay an approximately circular obsidian flake knife 2.8 cm in width. There also was a small obsidian blade with retouched edges, an obsidian flake knife dulled by use, 2 small blades each of which carried a projecting burin, 5 unshaped small flakes used as blades, 2 broken unclassifiable points and 1 large Type 3 obsidian point, 1 heavy white chert and 1 gray gneiss scraper, 1 snubnosed scraper and a chunky gray chert scraper. One small end-scraper of red chalcedony was found on the surface, near the house. The only ground stone artifact was a piece showing a small area that had been used for crushing or smoothing.

It is apparent that the Gallina people of the mountain campsites greatly favored obsidian for flaked tools but either were not consistent in point types or may have collected and brought home points made by other peoples. Also, hunters of different cultural backgrounds and periods may have come here earlier, or later, and lost points, a few of which

---

[*]   Measurements on features were taken in feet and inches because long metric tapes were unavailable in Santa Fe at that time. Measurements on artifacts are given in the metric system.

1 inch = 2.54 cm, 1 cm = .3937 U.S. inches
1 foot = 3.048 cm,   1 m = 39.37 U.S. inches

[**]   Supervised and reported by Mary Lu Moore.

conceivably could have washed into house remains, though more might be expected in the open. (See chapter on stone implements for discussion.)

One sherd of Gallina Plain Gray Utility ware was found in Level 1 of House 1, indicating it washed or fell in from the collapsing roof. No evidence of a clay floor was discovered.

Structure I-2 [*]

After most of the loose rocks had been removed from the surface, the outline of this could be seen as roughly circular. (Dimensions were 12 feet northwest-southeast and 14 feet on the opposite axis.) The south wall, approximately 2 feet high, obviously was incomplete, but there were no rocks nearby which would appear to have fallen from it. The southwest wall, which stood 9 feet from floor to top, was made up of large lava boulders. The north and northwest portions of the wall still were piled to 5.5 feet high. As the wall extended at a decreasing height around the southwest side, it reached what might have been an entrance on the south side of the house. That gap could have been a ventilator opening if entrance was through the roof, but we found no actual evidence of a ventilator in any of the mountain structures. And the opening may have been only where rocks had been "robbed" by someone building a later structure, a possibility which might explain the low height of remaining walls.

This house was trenched, northeast to southwest, halfway across its floor in 4-inch levels on a line drawn to avoid boulders, too heavy to move manually, which had rolled onto the old floor surface. No fire pit or fire place was encountered, but either could have been to one side of the trench. On the red clay floor, which test holes indicated went entirely across the house, some chunks of fire-hardened adobe and a few sooted sherds were found. The house may have been burned by accident or with the ritual "light firing" upon abandonment, as we later were to find typical of the home village Gallina structures in the Llaves area.

Level 1 consisted of loose rocks, humus, and windblown sand. Mixed in the fill were a triangular obsidian Type 4 point 2 cm long, 1.8 cm across the base, well flaked, and with serrated edges. There also was a complete, very small, obsidian end-scraper made from a flake, concave on the backside with the lower edge worked from both sides. Such a tool would have been useful on the skins of small animals. The lower half of a large flat knife of coarse, gray-black obsidian, 2.6 cm wide and 3 cm long, appeared on the same level. One unusual small obsidian flake, one glittering unused quartz chip, and one sharp piece of red chert which showed no use made up the remainder of the lithics.

From Level 2 (4-8 inches below surface) came one broken triangular Type 4 point 3 cm long and 2 cm across the original base, made from a delicate flake of obsidian. The base was thinned and straight; there never had been a stem. In type this duplicated the point from Level 1. Also in this level was a rim sherd of Gallina Gray Plain Utility ware,

---

[*]   Excavation supervised and reported by Frank Saffarans and Mary Lu Moore.

oxidized to orange. Chunks of fire-hardened adobe and a few sooted sherds from the floor level indicated the house had been burned, either by accident or by the ritual "light firing" already mentioned. A blackened area in this level may have been caused by a fallen burning roof beam.

Level 3 reached the hard-packed clay floor which covered the base of lava boulders *in situ*, with other lava rocks set between them to provide a fairly level foundation. At the northwest side, clay was found packed to a depth of 18 inches. By removing some of this and some of the floor chinking, we could look down into a cave more than 6 feet below. Two men slid into the cave and found three natural rooms, but there was no outside entry nor sign of use. One piece of deer bone was the only "find".

Structure I-3[*]

This house appeared to be more or less pear-shaped, a modification presumably resulting from dislocation of some of the natural, rough boulders. Northeast-southwest it measured 11.1 feet, north-south 11.75 feet, and east-west about 10.8 feet. Irregularity in the rock outline prevents one from considering any measurement exact. The volcanic boulder walls showed no evidence of chinking, mud mortar, or plaster. The surface was covered with 2 to 5 inches of overburden, largely soft pine needles.

Beneath the overburden were several chunks of hard yellow clay about 1 inch thick, presumably from the original rooftopping. A charred beam, 6 inches in diameter, lay on the north side under the clay. A second charred beam, also 6 inches in diameter, lay parallel to the first, on top of roofing material of reeds and small branches that had overlaid the beams. One clay chunk showed what appeared to be fine impressions, probably from grasses comprising part of the roof covering. A layer of charcoal and speckled white-to-gray ash, 4 inches thick, was found directly above the floor on the south. In the northwest quadrant, beneath 5 inches of charcoal-free humus, was a 4-inch layer of charcoal and ash, with another layer of ash alone, 2.5 inches thick, covering the floor of packed yellowish clay. A test pit, sunk in the southeast quadrant, showed clay 2 inches thick. There was no evidence of any entryway, a fire area, or postholes.

Masses of roots from two large trees growing in the center of this house complicated excavation, but the fact that the fill was only 6 inches deep eased the problem of observation. The only artifacts found were a single small sherd of Gallina Grey Utility ware and an obsidian flake (2.5 x 1.25 cm with one worked edge) from the northeast quadrant.

The amount of charcoal, ash, and burned clay left little question that the structure had been burned at abandonment. But, again unfortunately, the records of the tree-ring specimens collected here, as elsewhere in the mountain sites, all were too short or too complacent in growth (the result of adequate moisture) for dating.

---

[*]   Excavation supervised and reported by Mary Lu Moore.

Agricultural Plot Dimensions

Plot 1. Length – 18 ft.   Width – 18 ft.

Wall Lengths	Wall Height	Wall (rubble) Thickness
N 18 ft.	N 1 ft. 6 in.	N 3 ft. 4 in.
S 10 ft.	S ----------	S ----------
E 10 ft.	E 1 ft.	E 4 ft. 3 in.
W 18 ft.	W 2 ft.	W 4 ft. 2 in.

Plot 2.* Length – 50 ft.   Width – 51 ft.

Wall Lengths	Wall Height	Wall (rubble) Thickness
N 43 ft.	N 10–12 in.	N 6 ft.
S 12 ft. 7 in.	S 10–12 in.	S 4 ft.
E 50 ft.	E 10–12 in.	E 5 ft.
W ----------	W ----------	W -------

Plot 3.* Length – 30 ft.   Width – 16 ft.

Wall Lengths	Wall Height	Wall (rubble) Thickness
N 27 ft.	N 1 ft.	N 4 ft.
S 34 ft.	S ----	S ----
E 10 ft.	E -- 10 in.	E 4 ft. 3 in.
W 12 ft. 7 in.	W 2 ft. 2 in.	W f ft. 4 in.

Plot 4. Length – 72 ft.   Width – 44 ft.

Wall Lengths	Wall Height	Wall (rubble) Thickness
N 46 ft.	N 2 ft. 6 in.	N 6 ft. 6 in.
S 8 ft. 6 in.	S 12–15 in	S ----------
E 88 ft.	E 1 ft. 6 in.	E 4 ft. 4 in.
W 86 ft.	W 1 ft. 8 in.	W 4–5 ft.

Plot 5.** Lenght –   Width –

Wall Lengths	Wall Height	Wall (rubble) Thickness
N 45 ft.	N 10–12 in.	N 3 ft.
S 14 ft.	S 10–12 in.	S 3 ft.
E] 56 ft.	E 10–12 in.	E] 3 ft. 6 in.
W]	W 10–12 in.	W]

Rough Distances and Directions Between Plots

<u>Plot 5 to Plot 4.</u> N.E. corner Plot 5, 135 ft. to N.W. corner Plot 4. Direction N.W.
<u>Plot 4 to Plot 3.</u> Center North wall 68 ft. to center of East Wall Plot 3. Direction N.W.
<u>Plot 3 to Plot 2.</u> West wall of Plot 3 is S.E. wall of Plot 2. Contiguous structures.
<u>Plot 2 to Plot 1.</u> N.E. corner Plot 2, 88 ft. to N.E. corner Plot 1. Direction N.W.

* Plot 2 and 3 contiguous structures
** Plot 5 was more a terrace than an enclosed plot. See diagrams.

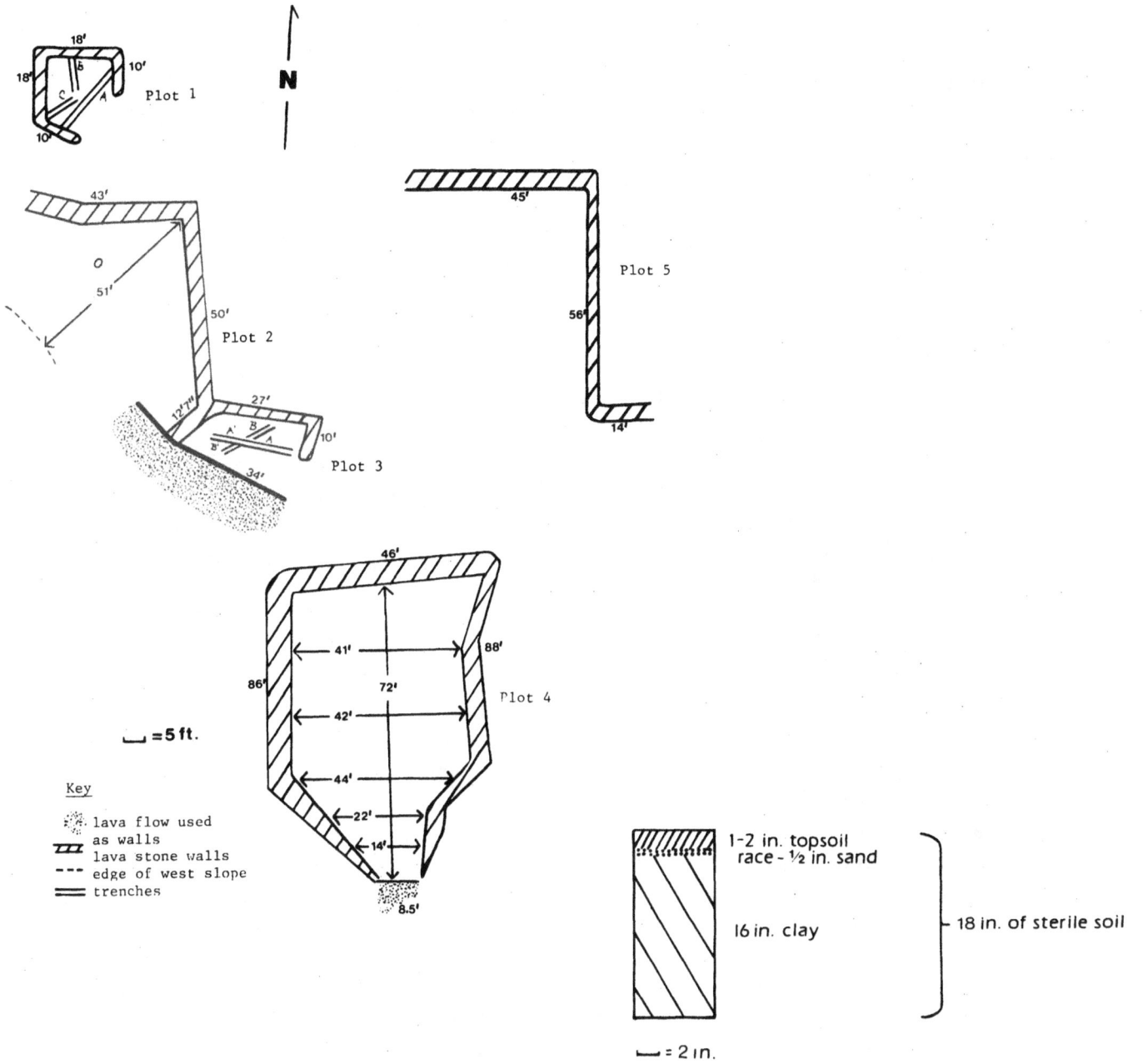

Figure 3

Structure 4 and the Agricultural Plots[*]

Houses 4 and 5, and two other probably similar structures, were located so closely together as to form a unit only a few feet to the west of Garden Plot 2 and below the crest of the ridge. The "draw" in which they had stood below the crest of the ridge was lined with lava blocks and boulders which provided raw material for building. Farther (to the south) down the ridge on the eastern side of Garden Plot 4 and 60 feet north of Plot 5 was another set of three closely associated structures which we did not examine except from the surface (Figure 3, Map of Agricultural Plot and House Relationships). In both of these groups the structures appeared to have been circular with what must be called "common walls," for lava rubble was built up around them (at least as high as the house walls presently stand) or had fallen from the original upper wall to fill entirely the space which otherwise would have separated them.

For a time we wondered whether these structures should be referred to as pithouses. Like the others we have discussed, they appear to have been, instead, surface houses which utilized and by intention were nestled into chance open spots in the tumbled landscape. Gallina pithouses and basic surface houses so resemble each other that the *only* real distinguishing trait separating the two consists of the thick above-ground roughly laid walls of the latter. We know, also, that although pithouses may have been predominant during the earlier stages of Gallina culture and the surface houses predominant later, the two definitely overlapped in time.

The low walls enclosing the northern four of the five plots of what appeared to have been gardens at Turkey Spring Site I were measured and mapped. The most prominent characteristic of the low walls was common use of large unworked lava rocks varying greatly in size and irregularity of shape. As in the walls of houses 1, 2, and 3, previously described, there was no evidence of bonding material or plaster having been used. The garden wall heights ranged from about 6 feet (single rock height) to 3 feet. However the plentiful rubble associated with the walls varied from 2 to 4 feet in thickness, so these walls originally were higher. Large natural lava formations were utilized as parts of the walls when conveniently located.

Our main concern was to determine whether the walled plots surely were intended for agriculture or contained any cultural evidence of dwellings or other special use. Accordingly, Plots 1 and 3 were trenched to see whether any features or use-strata could be identified.

The trenches in Plot 1 were excavated to a depth of 18 inches. The soil profile showed 1-2 inches of top-soil (depending on slope) overlying sand which ranged from a trace to .5 inches thick. The sand layer was thicker under the Gambel oaks than elsewhere. Below the sand was hard-packed, tan-colored clay. There were scattered bits of charcoal in the top layer.

---

[*] Surveyed, excavated and reported by Peter McKenna.

In Plot 3 the trenches were halted at depths of 8 and 12 inches when the strata were seen to duplicate those of Plot 1. Except for an obsidian chip found 2 inches below the surface in Trench B of Plot 3, all trenches were sterile.

On the western slopes just below the plots, small rich alluvial fans have penetrated the otherwise-sterile basaltic bed, good evidence that considerable water flows rapidly through the area where the plots were wall-outlined. The only cultural item found in close examination of the surface of the plots was one sherd of Gallina Grey Utility ware. (For details see tables on plot dimensions, size of trenches, and diagrammatic soil profile, Figure 3.)

Following the test-trenching of the two plots, attention was turned to the houses, with excavation concentrated on House 4, located at the base of the alluvial deposits downslope (west) from Garden Plot 2. This structure was selected because it appeared to be in good repair and lacked the heavy overgrowth of the other dwellings.

The walls to House I-4 were composed of a combination of standing basalt formations and piled basalt stones. The west wall rose 6.25 feet above the floor but on the east it was no more than 3 feet high. There was, however, a large accumulation of rubble around the lower walls on the north, east, and south. No trace of mortar or of plaster could be seen.

The fill in House I-4 consisted of 6-10 inches of heavy dark loam containing much ash and charcoal as well as small bits of volcanic scoria, probably washed down from wall chinking. The upper 2 inches were heavy with grass and its roots. Adobe chunks in the fill showed evidence of burning. On the surface lay a heavy, rough, shallow-basin metate of volcanic scoria which must have been on the flat roof of the house when it burned. It was of the one-open-end type common during the stage of Pueblo I in the Four Corners area but practical for camp use at any time. The overall measurement of the block was 50.2 x 29.2 cm, but the pecked grinding surface covered only 40 x 20.3 cm and one corner was broken off. (See Figure 26 in chapter on stone implements. Compare Woodbury 1954, Figure 16, a and c.) According to early Spanish reports, household tasks commonly were performed by Pueblo peoples on the flat roofs of houses, and this is clearly indicated for the Gallina by our finds in the Llaves area.

The floor of House I-4 (8.75 feet east-west; 9.9 feet north-south) was of fine-grained, orange-brown puddled adobe. As shown by a small test pit, this adobe had been packed to a depth of 1.5-2 inches over 1.25 inches of debris, charcoal, and ash. Beneath this were 11-12 inches of sterile soil. The underlying material proved that one earlier house, at least, had existed in this near vicinity before House 4 was constructed.

The edges of House 4's saucer-shaped floor curved upward into the wall. The western side of the room had been more eroded than the eastern. There were no signs of a surface-level entryway, postholes, or floor cists. Neither was there definite indication of materials used in roof construction, though a heavily burned chunk of clay showed the partial impression of a beam which may have been as large as 6 inches in diameter. This suggests that vigas had been laid across the top of the walls, covered with smaller poles or branches and finally with clay, much as in the home villages, though the whole would not have been as heavy.

In the center of this house was a fire pit 8 inches deep. It measured, though irregularly, 2 feet in diameter. The pit had been constructed with two large stones set on top of each other to form the bottom. A third basalt rock stood upright as lining for the north side of the pit. White ash which contained tiny rodent bones, 2 obsidian arrow points (one warped by heat but both of the same type though differing somewhat in size), and 7 lithic flakes filled the pit and had been heaped to a height of 4 inches above the floor. Several large stones apparently had been set on top of the ash. Although this fire pit certainly lacked the depth and precision of construction of those for Llaves home sites, the superabundance of ash filling and the attempt at stone lining was in accord with those home fire pits, some of which also contained points and bone fragments. (For house measurement details, fire pit construction, and use interpretation, see Figures 4, 5, 6, and the summary to this chapter.) From the 6 inches of fill above the floor came 5 obsidian points, of which only 3 (Types 1, 2, 3) were whole enough for classification. (See chapter on stone implements for shape and dimensions.) One of the latter appeared to be the lower section of a heavy point possibly intended for elk. There also were 13 "lithics," 7 being tiny obsidian chips and one similar but larger, all apparently debitage left from fashioning implements in this dwelling. One pink chert flake with a sharp worked tip could have served as a graver for incising and cutting. Two unshaped chert flakes appear to have been used as scrapers, and there was one good triangular obsidian scraper and a fine snubnose scraper.

The most unusual artifact left in the fill was a polisher (see Figure 27), possibly for a floor, though unusually small and fine if that was its intended function. The implement was 19.1 cm long, with a maximum diameter of 8.1 cm. The top surface was curved and would have fitted the hand. The flat and highly smoothed opposite side evidently had been used in polishing something. The gleaming surfaces are reminiscent of the implement widely employed by Pueblo women into this century in solidifying their clay house-floors, relaid or repaired annually, but this Gallina specimen is smaller than any we have seen. This may well have been used as a tanning stone held in the hand to protect the base of the thumb when stretching and softening hides as is still used in some of the pueblos today. This interpretation would also fit with the environment in which it was found.

Sherds, more plentiful in the fill of this house than elsewhere, consisted of two thin pieces of Gallina Plain Gray Utility ware and three somewhat heavier samples of the same type.

On the floor were 1 chert and 11 small obsidian flakes and a heavy crude scraper, 2.5 cm long and 3 cm across, of obsidian. Both edges show some sharpening by chip removal and the scars of tiny flakes such as pop off during use. There also was 1 obsidian point and a single, unusually thick (1 cm) sherd of Gallina Plain Gray Utility ware. The most interesting object was a quartz crystal. From its presence, we may sur-

Turkey Spring Site I
House 4 Floor Profiles

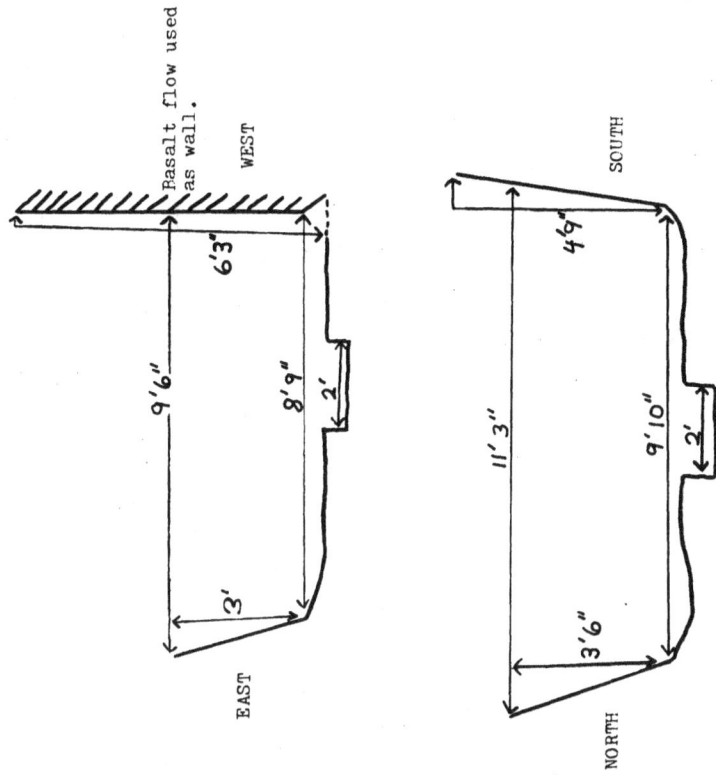

EAST

3'

9'6"

6'3"

8'9"

2'

Basalt flow used as wall.

WEST

NORTH

3'6"

11'3"

4'9"

9'10"

2'

SOUTH

└ = 6 in.

Figure 5

Measurements: House I-4

Wall Height - floor to top of rocks

N 3 ft. 6 in.
S 4 ft. 9 in.
E 3 ft.
W 6 ft. 3 in.

House 4 Surface Measurements
excludes rubble.

NE-SW 11 ft. 3 in.
NW-SE   9 ft. 6 in.

Basal Floor Measurements

N-S 9 ft. 10 in.
E-W 8 ft. 9 in.

Wall Rubble Width Around House

NE 3 ft. 9 in.
SW 3 ft. 9 in.
NW 5 ft. 8 in.
SE 5 ft. 8 in.

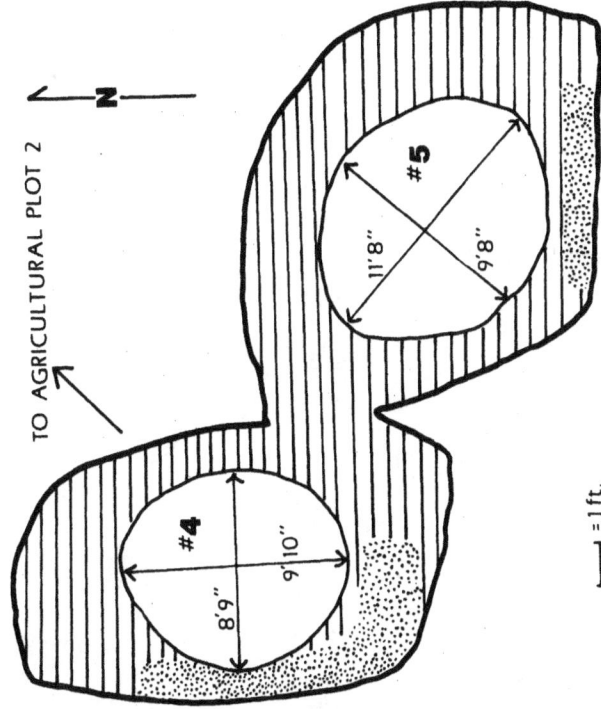

N

TO AGRICULTURAL PLOT 2

#4
9'10"
8'9"

#5
11'8"
9'8"

└ = 1 ft.

HOUSES I-4 and I-5   Surface

▤ Wall rubble around pithouse.
░ Basaltic flow used as wall.

Figure 4

71

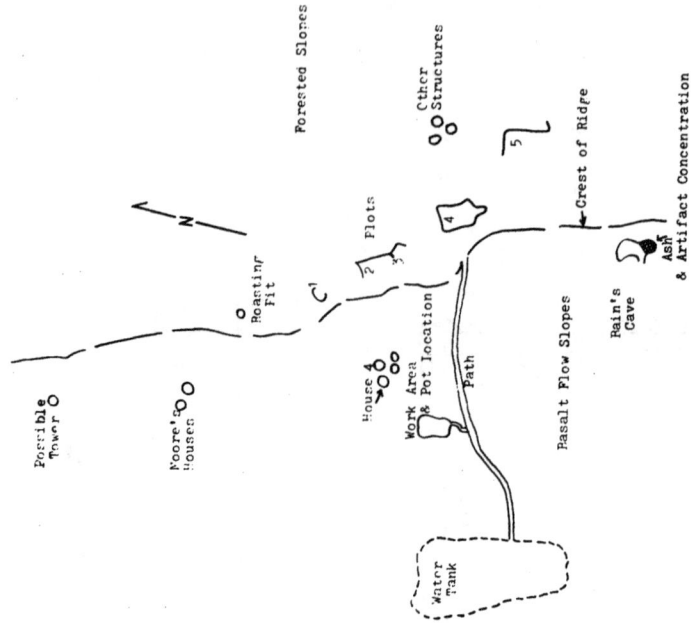

SKETCH MAP OF TURKEY SPRING SITE I
(no scale)

Forested Slopes

Other Structures

N

Possible Tower

Plots

Moore's Houses

Planting Pit

Crest of Ridge

House
Work Area & Pot Location

Path

Rain's Cave

Ash & Artifact Concentration

Basalt Flow Slopes

Water Tank

Location of Trail in relation to work area

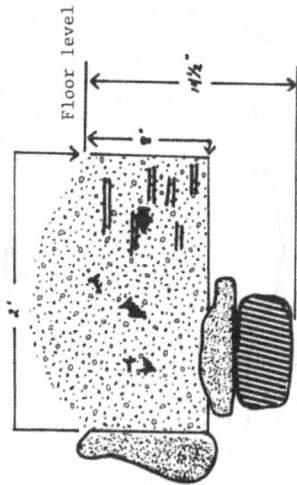

TURKEY SPRING SITE I

Key
Basalt
Fine grained rocks
Ash
Bone fragments
Points
Soil
2 in.

Firepit Measurements
Diameter N-S and E-W   2 ft.
Depth   8 in.

Floor level

14½"

Stone #2 above

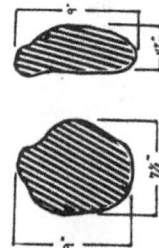

Stone #1 above

Stone #3 above

House I-4 Heating pit

Figure 6 and 7

mise that the people of this site were using magico-religious rituals in the diagnosis and treatment of illnesses in much the same way quartz crystals have been used by their descendants in historic times.

From near Garden Plot 4, westward and downslope to a large natural reservoir (depression) at the bottom of the basalt flow runs a footpath. In 1976 when Turkey Spring Site I was revisited (but no work done), the "tank" was found filled with water, though this had not been so in 1972. The manner of construction of the pathway and amount of wear was equivalent to that which had been found for Structure 20, the pathway at Turkey Spring Site II in 1973. Observed from downslope and with the sun at a pre-noon angle, the trail to the "tank" reflected light as a silvery ribbon among the boulders of vesicular basalt. Approximately midway along the trail, a short (about 15 feet) lateral and northerly trending path breaks off the main trail to reach the large open work area (about 20 feet N-S, 10 feet E-W). This work area has a basalt floor with "paving" achieved by chinking spaces with small pieces of basalt and covering some larger, irregular areas with flat slabs of basalt.

The work area is much larger than any of the house floors and may have served as a location somewhat comparable to a Pueblo plaza where men or women could sit comfortably while at their tasks and, also, where open-air drying could be done with benefit of additional heat reflected from the lava. One half of a jar of Gallina Plain Utility ware was found cached in a small overhang-niche at the northeast end of this area.

As the main pathway goes on to the ridge crest where we found the garden plots, it is possible that water may have been carried from the tank to the gardens on occasion, but its main use probably was for persons bringing water to the houses for domestic use and possibly to the work area for processing activities. Figure 7 shows the approximate position, size, and orientation of these various related features.

Movement through the village area probably was highly patterned, with north-south travel largely along the crest of the ridge just to the east of the bed of rough tumbled lava, and east-west traffic to the spring and "tank" over the described pathway.

Natural Features Utilized as Structures

Bain's Cave and Skull Cave*

Bain's Cave, irregularly shaped, approximately 12 feet north-south and 5 feet east-west, with two large oval slabs laid to overlap as roof protection above its 1.5-foot western entryway, was found in the rough lava between the sixth and seventh "draws" south of the roasting pit. A natural southern opening 2 feet wide had been blocked with stones. After the floor plan had been drawn (Figure 8) and the surface soil level marked, removal of the loose surface dust and debris and the old fill beneath was carried on with trowel and brush. All soil was screened.

*1   Excavated and reported by James Bain.

Turkey Spring Site I

Bain's Cave: floor plan

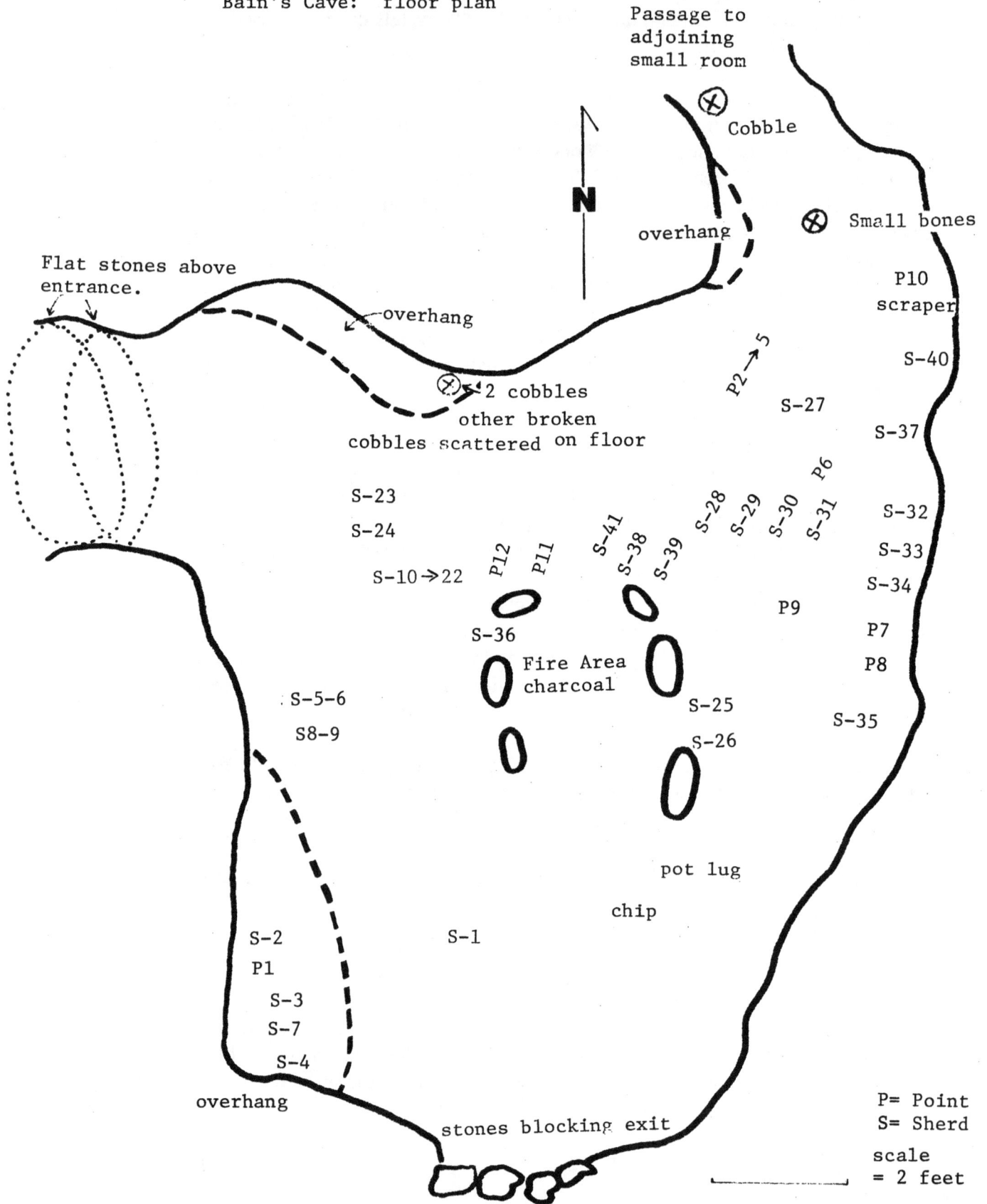

Passage to
adjoining
small room

⊗ Cobble

N

overhang

⊗ Small bones

P10
scraper

S-40

Flat stones above
entrance.

overhang

⊗ 2 cobbles
other broken
cobbles scattered on floor

P2→5

S-27

S-37

S-23

S-24

S-10→22

P12 P11

S-41
S-38
S-39

S-28
S-29
S-30
S-31

P6

S-32

S-33

S-34

P9

P7

S-36

Fire Area
charcoal

S-25

S-26

S-35

S-5-6

S8-9

pot lug

chip

S-2

P1

S-3

S-7

S-4

S-1

overhang

stones blocking exit

P= Point
S= Sherd

scale
_____ = 2 feet

Figure 8

74

The fill proved to be only 6-8 inches deep, but because this room had been well protected by the cave roof and sides, a surprising amount of cultural material remained in it. (See drawings of points and other artifacts in chapter on stone implements.) A fire area containing charcoal was outlined with six stones (not set close together) near the center of the original clay floor but not dug into it. North and east of the fire area, the floor was redder and the clay more granular.

Three overhangs cut into the wall space of this room, but sherds showed that the floor had been used to its outer edges. Six sherds and 1 point were found beneath the overhang in the southwest corner, but one cannot think of this as merely a trash area because sherds and chipped stone artifacts were widely scattered. Near the eastern wall were 6 sherds, 4 points, and 1 triangular knife to be hafted. Six more sherds, 1 chip, and 2 points came from close around the fire area, and 1 sherd from outside it. Five sherds and 5 points were found between 1 and 1.5 feet north of the fire area, 15 more sherds were near the doorway, and 3 whole and some broken cobbles were scattered on the floor.

On the northeast corner a passage only 1 foot wide led to a small adjoining room, which because of time shortage was left unexcavated.

The contents of Bain's Cave room totaled 11 points (3 of Type 1, 1 each of Types 2, 3, 4, 5, 6, 7, and 2 too broken to classify), 1 scraper, more than 40 sherds, the cobbles, a number of small animal and bird bones (mostly from near the opening to the small room), 1 larger bone (probably deer), and numerous chips. Because of the fire area, sherds, and points, we can be sure that this cave room was not primarily a place for storage.

The number of points helps to substantiate our impression that hunting was a major activity of the people of this village. The number of sherds suggests that the inhabitants of this cave were not overly meticulous about housekeeping, but the cave must have been used over several seasons for that much breakage to have occurred. Certainly the occupants had not cleaned out their domicile before they left, and this cave floor was not subjected to the amount of drainage water which washed through the de-roofed houses after abandonment.

A Gallina Black-on-white bowl was found in a crevice in the rough lava a short distance to the north of Bain's Cave and may be guessed to have been hidden by Bain's Cave inhabitants, as no other dwellings were nearby.

On the next ridge to the north from Bain's Cave, in a shallow cave through which water obviously rushed with every large storm or melt, the upper portion of a human skull was found in 1971. A careful search was made in the nearby area but no other bones or skull portions were seen. It seems likely that the skull was moved by water or by animals from a burial not far distant. This skull cap is our single example of human remains found in the mountain sites to date.

Structure 6: Roasting Pit[*]

The most northern of the structures excavated at Turkey Spring Site I in 1972 was a large roasting pit located about 120 feet from House 1 and near the edge of the ridge overlooking the main occupation area. On the surface of the depression lay the central section of a knife of well-flaked, gray obsidian but with both ends missing (4.3 cm wide; 3 cm long), which had been dropped or washed into its current position after the pit had been abandoned and filled.

When the surface was stripped, a thin layer of white to gray-beige colored ash was found to extend considerably outside the depression as well as inside it. Beneath this ash was a layer of topsoil and beneath that a thin layer of scattered small rocks.

Trenching revealed a rock-lined roasting pit. Ash continued below the small rocks to the bottom of the pit itself, where it was less hardened into pellets than higher in the deposit (see Figure 9). When all the fill had been removed, some of the lining stones were taken up. Sterile soil lay below. No charcoal, wood, or cultural material such as sherds or lithic debris was found. The general shape of the pit was a sloping and some-what squared oval. Inside dimensions of the two sides at the top were 95 and 96 inches; at the bottom they were 25 and 26 inches. Depth ranged from 20 to 27 inches.

The rocks lining this pit were of sandstone, quartzite, and other minerals of local origin. Most were about 8 inches long but smaller pieces had been wedged between them. Some of the rocks were fire-reddened, hardened, and smoke-blackened. None of the rocks were fire-cracked. The absence of charcoal suggests that the pit had been cleaned out and then filled with ash when the people left, as was consistently the case with fire pits in the home sites we excavated in the south Llaves area and as seems to have been true for the fire pits or fire areas in these mountain sites.

A roasting pit with its hot ash and coals was used by the historic Jemez for brief roast-ing of wild potatoes, only an inch and a half across but a great favorite because of their fresh flavor. Other wild vegetables and roots also were roasted for food, one root being valued only for its yellow bark which was eaten. The center of the root was discarded.

Corn to be made into *chicos,* the dried kernels so commonly used in native stews, is tossed, still in its shucks, into a roasting pit which has been heated for several hours. When the pit is filled with the ears, water is poured on top of the corn to produce steam and the pit then is covered over. Today the cover may be a piece of tin, but in the past it could have been a heavy layer of dampened small branches and leaves topped with mud. The corn is left overnight or through a day and then pulled out to be tied by its turned-back husks in long lines over a frame or branches to dry. Shelling finally prepares the kernels for storage.

---

[*]   Excavation supervised and reported by Gordon Bronitsky.

If corn was grown in the walled gardens of Turkey Spring I, the people must have arrived by mid-May, the earliest date for planting, and they would have had to remain in camp until mid-October, or even November, for it to ripen.

The Pollen Tests for this Site

We had hoped that samples from the so-called garden plots, the floors of houses, and the hearths would provide us with data suggesting something of the eating habits of the campers and certify their agricultural efforts. But fortune was not with us. Writes Anne Cully, Castetter Laboratory for Ethnobotanical Studies, University of New Mexico:

> ... we did not find any definitely identified pollen from cultivars. ... there was no positively identified corn pollen in the samples. Most of the samples were either low in pollen counts, or did not contain pollen at all. Hearth samples are often low in pollen, probably due to the high alkalinity associated with wood ashes. This may provide conditions which encourage the growth of fungus and bacteria which destroy the walls of the pollen grains. At Turkey Spring I, samples from close to the surface are low in pollen counts. This level may be subject to rapid leaching of pollen grains down to a less permeable layer. The floors of the caves yielded somewhat better results. The pollen sample from the small wall feature in Cave 2, 15 cm below the surface, was productive, although there were no indications of introduction of pollen plants used in subsistence.

The small amounts of pollens found in our mountain sites simply reflect the biome still surrounding Turkey Spring I today.

Summary for Turkey Spring Site I

This site, which introduced the concept of hunting-gathering, seasonally occupied mountain camps being used by the Gallina people, had us understandably puzzled at first. Before excavation, the structural remains appeared almost formless. Had it not been for the projectile points, many but not all of which resembled those with which archaeologists had become familiar in the Gallina home villages, and for the Gallina-type pottery found hidden in crevices near the houses, we would have been at a loss to know who the occupants of these crude structures had been.

Eventually, with the evidence examined and their connotations thought through, these sites were appreciated as more sophisticated than crude. The ridge above Site I had been walled on the lower side to prevent fast runoff and erosion. Other walls divided plots, either to show family ownership or to further minimize erosion. Some structures with only low stone-wall outlines also stood on that ridge, perhaps as relics of storehouses, perhaps as watch stations from which guards could scan the lower country and also watch for fire or smoke signals from towers in the north Llaves area, probably including Rattlesnake Ridge. The domiciles were set into pockets in the lava with one or more great boulders to serve as part of the wall structure. Connecting spaces were filled in

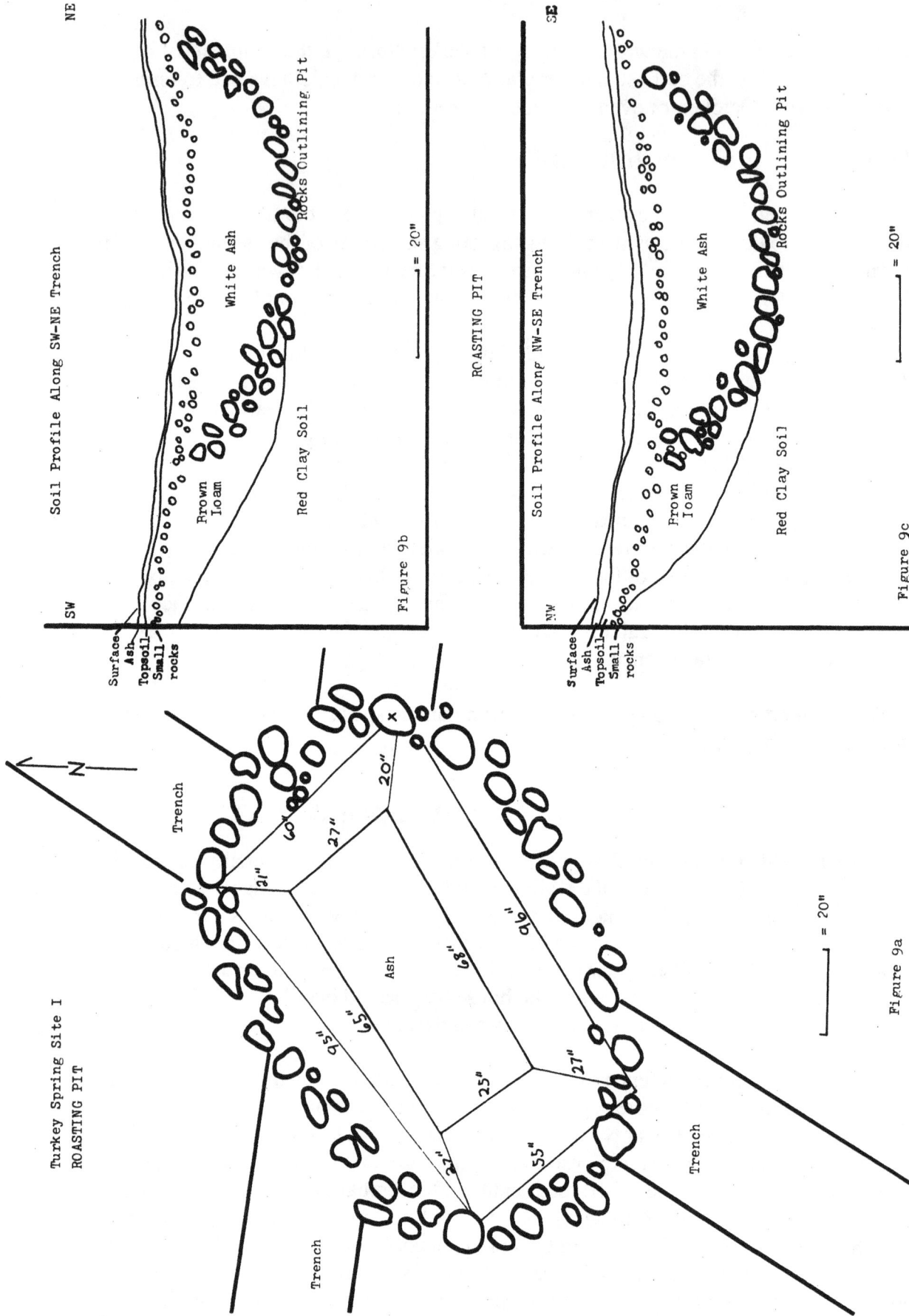

Turkey Spring Site I
ROASTING PIT

Soil Profile Along SW-NE Trench

Soil Profile Along NW-SE Trench

ROASTING PIT

White Ash

Red Clay Soil

Brown loam

Rocks Outlining Pit

Surface
Ash
Topsoil
Small
rocks

= 20"

Figure 9b

Figure 9c

Figure 9a

Ash

Trench

= 20"

Figure 9

78

with dry-laid masonry of lava "cobbles," much like the masonry which composed entire walls for houses of the home villages, even to the point of using a very thick base but tapering that thickness as the wall rose. There was no need for indoor posts to support a roof and little chance to dig holes for such posts in a lava floor. The roof of log supports covered with branches or brush for a cover could rest directly on the walls of boulders and stones.

As nature had provided "tuck-away spots" for storage in crevices and little caves in the lava, there was no need for indoor bins, above or below the floor, or for cists. That these camps were not used year-round minimized the household storage needs.

There was little opportunity for householders to excavate anything but the most shallow of fire pits, even when clay was brought in to cover all or part of the lava floor, and it seems that a fire "area" or "place," actually a "heating pit," sometimes surrounded with spaced rocks, was the usual household heating device. As it probably held only coals brought from an outside cooking fire, no appreciable depth or lining was required.

And here we call attention once more to the secret little sophistication of these Gallina folk: the black boulders and black cobbles of the walls and the mass of black lava into which the houses were set absorbed heat from the sun during the day and gently offered it back to those on the lava bed at night. The people obviously had learned, as all peoples learn, by observation. Their preference for the lava bed itself as the location for domiciles and work areas is obvious, in spite of the problem of exceeding roughness which would wear away sandals, cut into bare feet, and make every visit to a neighbor and even to the spring at the bottom edge of the flow something of a gymnastic feat. Those who lived here must have carried their own weight and that of their burdens with agility. The "paved" trail through the lava bed was an important public facility.

One cannot expect a total interpretation of the details of such sites from Pueblo Indians born in this century, for by that time the profits to be gained by hunting and gathering as an important economic aid were disappearing into the limbo of forgetfulness. The people had been closed in, possible foraging areas were limited, and the canned goods of grocery stores (could one but find a little money) were tempting. The most illuminating parallels so far have come from the account of piñon-gathering and hunting camps as recalled by Jemez Pueblo for the first quarter of the 20th century.

Pueblo people long have considered piñon crops one of their most important resources because the delicious and nutritious nuts could be stored for several years in containers, bins, or even in hollow spots cut into house walls and later plastered over. Contrary to popular opinion, piñons do not appear in bumper crops every seven years, but irregularly. Production depends primarily on the amount of moisture of the preceding year. As precipitation is known to be spotty in New Mexico, good piñon areas vary within any single year. In the past anyone out in the open for hunting or spring wood-gathering made it his duty to check the prospects of that area and relay the news to the home village.

During the late fall the Jemez made some one-day trips to good piñon areas, but after the Jemez fiesta in mid-November, many families (but commonly not all members of an extended family) would leave for one or the other of the two Black Mesas of their area. They walked for some seven miles to the highest reaches, food and water and their bedding of skins and blankets tied onto pack horses and burros. Frost brings an opening of the piñon cones with the "popping" that frees the nuts to fall beneath the tree or be blown away by heavy winds. Ordinarily, the families expected to remain in the piñon camp until December, sometimes staying even past Christmas day, but in years of unusually heavy crops they might return later for a second short period of piñon-gathering. This was considered one of the high spots of the year.

When the families arrived at the site to be exploited that season, their first duty was to clear the ground. A primary precautionwas to rid themselves of, or at least remain away from, pine or piñon trees which had died and might possibly fall if winds were high. All the camp site, which might spread a quarter mile or more in each direction, was raked- with a cast-off deer antler if one chanced to be at hand, or well swept with short brooms made from brush. Next, each family reestablished its shelter, which had seen many earlier years of use. To construct a shelter, the people tried to find a great boulder, usually in their area, of volcanic tuff, especially if the top were overhanging and the lower portion somewhat cavaeate. This would make one side of the room. A second boulder if well- positioned might make a second wall. Otherwise, a pair of forked-top tree trunks were set into the ground in front to hold a lintel beam. Roofing logs then could be laid between that beam and the top of the boulder and covered with branches. Side walls consisted of slimmer logs or branches, sometimes further insulated by tied bundles of long broomgrass laid horizontally. This provided enough strength to support some soil if that were added.

An even simpler arrangement was to make a lean-to by slanting logs between the top of the boulder and a line on the ground at what was to become the outer edge of the shelter.

Cooking was done outside the shelter most of the time, but inside if the weather were too bad. Brush always was used as a base for bedding, but when the weather was coldest the entire area of floor where persons would sleep was covered with fire until well heated The charcoal and ash then were swept off and the brush spread in place as a mat.

The men understood their first day in camp as for hunting. Grandmothers and children scurried to gather juniper and cedar berries on which everyone could munch as they worked. (In modern Jemez parlance, the "cedar" is a juniper which grows many wide-spreading trunks; the "juniper" as such has a single main stem and fibrous, gray shaggy bark over red inner wood.) The berries of both, different in size and flavor, are appreciated as a treat. The families also carried dried beans and peas to boil, and corn kernels to parch on the coals.

A special duty of the children was to hunt out packrat nests which might hold large stores of piñons. These were robbed, but if the animals themselves were not caught some food carried by the Pueblo people was put in its place so the creatures would not starve. Packrats usually are fat by that season and the youngsters strove to grab them by the tail (which frequently broke off, like that of a lizard) because when steamed, fur and all, in hot ashes, or dressed and then boiled, packrats were considered a most flavorful food.

Children also looked for signs of turkey, and, if the families returned in the spring, their happy tasks included searching for birds' eggs. But with the real danger of becoming lost in the wooded area, they always were warned not to go beyond shouting distance from camp.

The piñons collected were taken back to the Pueblo periodically, to make sure that nothing happened to them. At camp they might be stored in rawhide boxes or even in small slab-lined pits. Transportation was managed by putting the piñons into tanned buckskins thrown over the shoulder of a young man who on his return from the pueblo would bring the village news. Runners also were used to carry messages and news between Pueblo and camp.

The piñons, once the families returned to the pueblo, were shared among members of the extended family who had not been able to join in the camping expedition. Sharing also was expected for the roots, plants, and branches collected, dried, and made into bundles by men or women while in the mountains. Jemez still depends on many mountain herbs for medication. Although the majority of remedies remain secret, we can appreciate the relaxing pleasure of "smoke baths" prescribed for one with low metabolism or similar malaise. A well-heated cedar branch was wrapped in a damp cloth and placed under the arm of a patient, or between his legs. He might even sit on it as if it were a hot water bottle. The aroma and the damp heat were relaxing and soothing.

For the historic Jemez people, the group of shelters composed a "settling area" within which each specific shelter and the area about it was inherited by family members down through the generations. (The same system is found among the Jicarilla Apache in their camp settlements at Stone Lake.) Ownership of each plot was known to everyone, and thus one could find every other family if snowbound, running short of food, or merely looking for company. A family usually owned a shelter in each of the "settling areas" established where the piñon crops were known to be best, one year or another. At each, the families left implements and equipment stashed away so they need not bring them up the mountain at every visit.

Thus the early 20th century Jemez and thus the late 13th-century Gallinas. The parallels are too obvious to require comment. We cannot dismiss the Canjilon Mountain sites as piñon camps because the biome is not the same; even the lowest camp is toward the top of the piñon range. It is the type of camping pattern which carries through. The supplies for which the people came to Turkey Spring and the higher sites would have been some of the plants listed by Hayden in his introductory discussion of physical attributes of the area, plus the large animals so important as the main protein supplement to a failing, largely carbohydrate, vegetable diet.

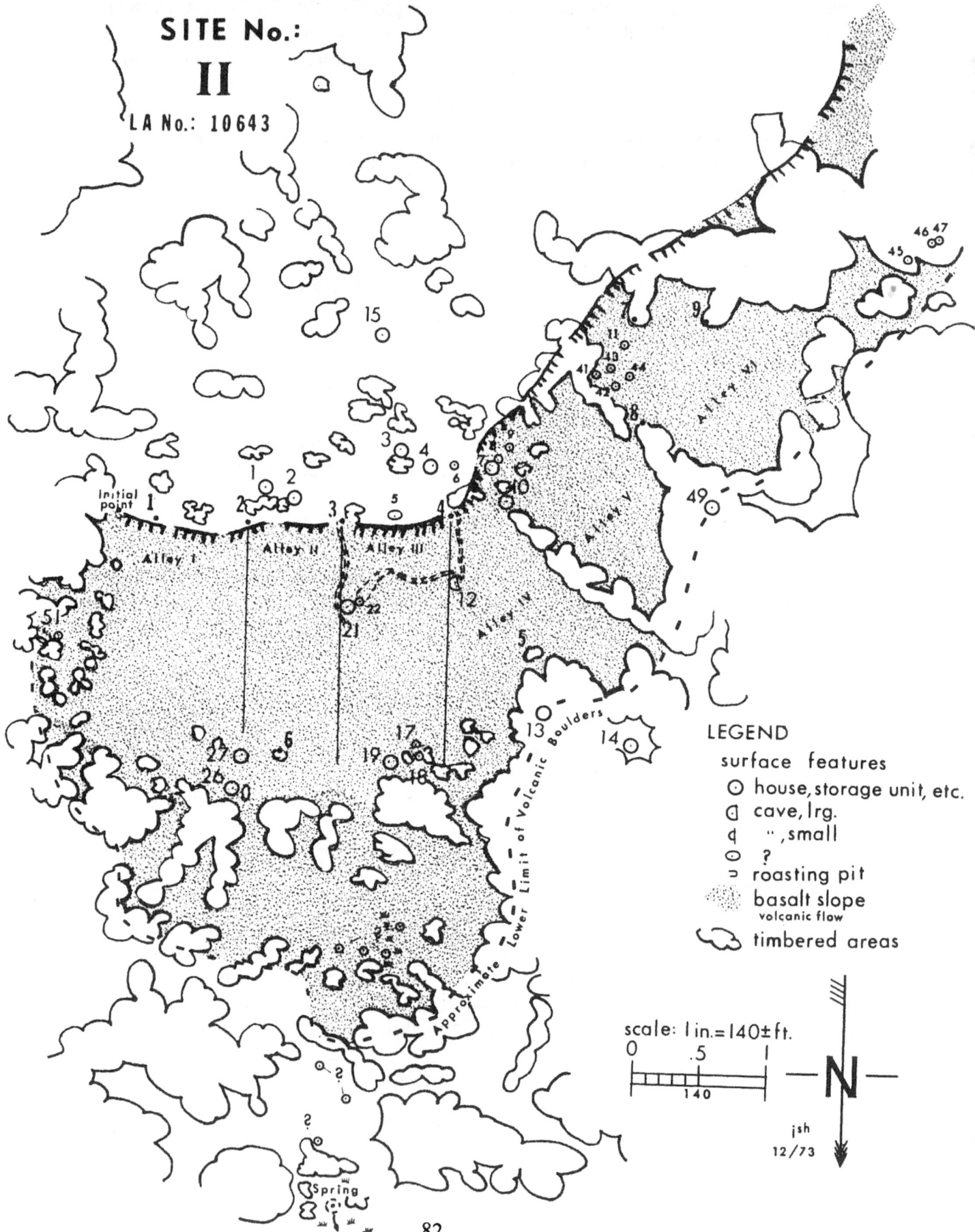

MAP 5

TURKEY SPRING
ARCHEOLOGICAL
SITE No.:
II
LA No.: 10643

Initial point

Alley I

Alley II

Alley III

Alley IV

Alley V

Alley VI

Approximate Lower Limit of Volcanic Boulders

Spring

LEGEND

surface features

⊙ house, storage unit, etc.

◖ cave, lrg.

◖ " , small

⊙ ?

⊃ roasting pit

basalt slope
volcanic flow

timbered areas

scale: 1 in. = 140 ± ft.

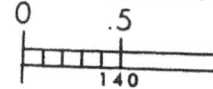

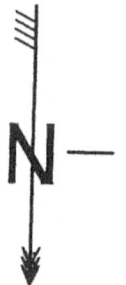

0 .5 1

140

— N —

jsh
12/73

III

Turkey Spring Site II (LA 10643)

In the summer of 1973 we concentrated our single week (the second being lost to rains) of intensive archaeological work about a quarter mile to the north of Site I for survey, exploration, identification of use areas or other evidences of occupation, and salvage of artifacts on the surface or hidden in the caves and crevices of Site II. Excavation of a limited number of structures would serve our purpose of sampling. The primary object of our program was enlarging on the data and materials obtained in 1972 from Site I. The two sites appeared to be the southern and the northern manifestations of a single complex and perhaps actually were only two parts of a single village. Recognition of Site II as a once-inhabited zone had resulted from John Hayden's previous observation of some depressed areas in the broken lava reminiscent of the stone structures of Site I, as well as his finding projectile points and chipped stone along the mesa edge. There also had been some checking of this site in 1972 immediately after the fieldwork on Site I, and a few vessels hidden in crevices were found at that time.

Site II, at an altitude of 8,400 feet, was strung through the lava on an irregularly outlined curve measuring about 400 feet along the upper edge and 500-600 feet* along the lower edge which approximated the lower limit of the volcanic flow and boulders (see Map 5). The people had chosen the lava bed for some of their domiciles, but a number of other structures lay either above or below the broken lava in the lightly forested periphery. On the gently rolling mesa above the scree, the soil was so heavily mingled with volcanic pebbles that the soles of one's shoes soon were markedly shredded. To us the mesa still would seem to have been more convenient as the setting for a house than the sharply broken desert of black rock below. On the other hand, the lava boulders reflected the sun's heat and thus provided warmth for houses. Some of the artificially paved areas we found in the scree would have served well as drying platforms with an outline of boulders and walls to cut the wind. Historic Pueblo peoples customarily have dried vegetal foods on the flat roofs of their houses, the tops of *ramadas* (shades) built nearby, and even along the edges of plazas.

Turkey Spring Sites I and II share the same ecological zone. The eastern edge of the open rockfall at Site II lies within 2 degrees of magnetic north. The steep vesicular basalt is perhaps less broken than in Site I, but deep fissures, several small caves, and massive rockfalls apparently have resulted, as in the neighboring site, from the flow being undermined when fluvial gravel and cobbles beneath its southerly edge were eroded. The lava is bordered by forest on all sides, and the wood line at the base of the open volcanic rock lies approximately 80 inches below the rim elevation. A few feet beyond the outer limit

---

*   Measurements were taken with steel tapes but because of the very broken and irregular terrain and surfaces, none should be considered exact.

of boulders is a spring, convenient for families spending the summer in dwellings below the lava. The pond which collected runoff a short distance south of the sites at the top of the lava was a second, though intermittent, water source.

As the most practical approach to our work, Site II initially was divided into three rectangular sloping alleys 100 feet wide, to which four others of irregular shapes were added. The first three were marked by flagged lines bearing toward magnetic north. Alleys I through V were numbered from east to west, and a sixth, triangular in shape, which included the remainder of the western section of the main lava rock, was identified as Alley VI. Some work east of Alley I led to designation of that area as Alley 0. Exploration and what excavation was done in Alleys 0, I, and VI were immediately supervised by William R. Perret. Similar work in Alley II was supervised by James G. Bain, in Alleys III and V by Peter R. McKenna, in Alley IV by Mary Lu Moore, and on the mesa above by Florence Ellis. Each turned in a field report, herein abbreviated and interpreted. Transit bearings, mapping, and recording finds were in the hands of John Hayden.

As at Site I, a number of the structures noted in the overall survey of Site II were given surface examination and placed on the map. Our time, briefed by the onset of heavy rains, prevented further investigation. This was felt to be advantageous rather than otherwise because no such mountain hunting-gathering Gallina sites hitherto have been known. Further thought after the initial sampling and study, including examination of apparent functional relationships with the home villages of these people, could result in the formulation of hypotheses and specialized planning of techniques to be emphasized in investigation of the remaining domiciles, storage structures, and drying or other use-areas on the mountain.

As we shall organize our present discussion of individual "features" on the basis of location in a specific alley, their numbers may not be found in sequence.

Alley 0[*]

Structure II-51

About midway down the slope in Alley 0 and only 20 feet east of the Alley 0-I boundary was a circular pit, Structure II-51, rimmed with laid-up rocks of cobble size. The diameter at the rim was 9.6 feet east-west and 9.1 feet north-south. At the level of the bottom, 6.9 feet below the top of the wall, the diameter was only 3.5 feet east-west and 4 feet north-south. This funnel shape probably was caused by rocks rolling down from the walls. Removal of rocks and some accompanying forest debris from the bottom offered no evidence of an earthen floor, but much of the uncovered basalt showed bright hematite coloration both on the surface and similarly on freshly broken surfaces an inch or two deep. This suggested an original roofing of the structure with logs, possibly topped with brush or pine branches with needles, and strong oxidation of that material

---

[*]   Supervised and reported by William Perret.

84

by intentional firing at the time of abandonment, even as appeared probable for the structures studied at Site I. Neither floor features, sherds, nor artifacts were found here. Its small size may be a clue to this structure having been used for storage rather than as a domicile. Close similarity to Structure II-41 in Alley IV is apparent.

Alley I[*]

Structures

In Alley I two evidences of use were found. One was Structure II-53, a small paved area about 120 feet north of the lava flow rim and 5 feet east of the Alley I-II boundary. This appeared to have been a "work area," conceivably for drying foods, which measured 6 feet east-west and from 2 to 3 feet, tapering, north-south. The idea that this "paving" could have been intended as chinked roofing to a rock passage below was investigated but access and, hence, use of such an opening does not seem feasible.

The second, Structure II-54, was a small shelter-room and paved area near the center of Alley I. It was made up of two large blocks of basalt which supported a 6 x 8 foot cap block about 2 feet thick, probably weighing in the vicinity of 7 tons. The interior of this shelter measured approximately 4 x 5 feet; it opened to the northwest. The floor had been chinked with small rocks until it was approximately level. Several openings between the wall blocks also had been chinked.

No artifacts were found in either structure.

Adjacent to this shelter on its north and northeast sides was a roughly level "paved" area about 6 feet on a side. In the center an erratic boulder about 1.5 feet high either had fallen or been placed.

Alley II^{**}

The architectural finds in this alley consisted of five apparent domiciles and some work areas quite possibly intended for laying out plant foods to be dried. One of these areas also may have served as a lookout.

Structures II-26, II-27, and II-28

Structures II-26 and II-27, located just at the tree line edging the north side of the boulder field (bottom of slope), and Structure II-28 which lay 67 feet farther to the north seem to have been domiciles of much the type already described for Turkey Spring Site I. The first two were approximately 18 feet east of the west boundary of Alley II.

---

*   Supervised and reported by William Perret.

**   Supervised and reported by James Bain.

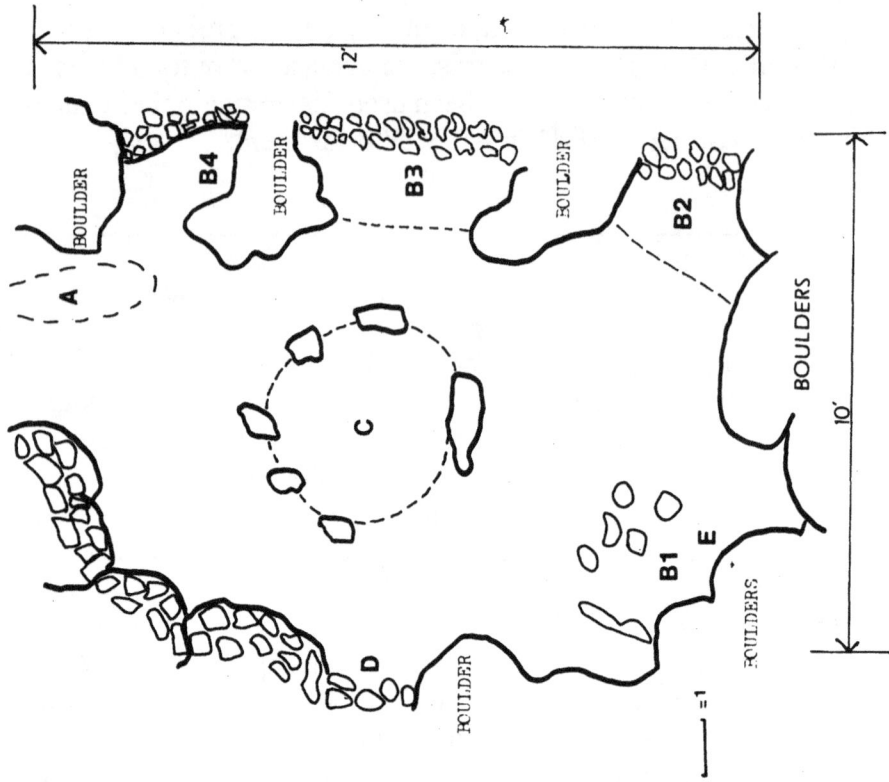

Turkey Spring   Site II, Alley 2   House II-27

12'

10'

= 1

A - Hole where large root was removed. Bones, potsherds and most points found here.
B1,B2,B3,B4 - Raised areas. Small obsidian point found at B3.
C - Possible heating pit, heavier concentration of charcoal.
D - Obsidian and chert chips.
E - Charcoal and chips.

Figure 11

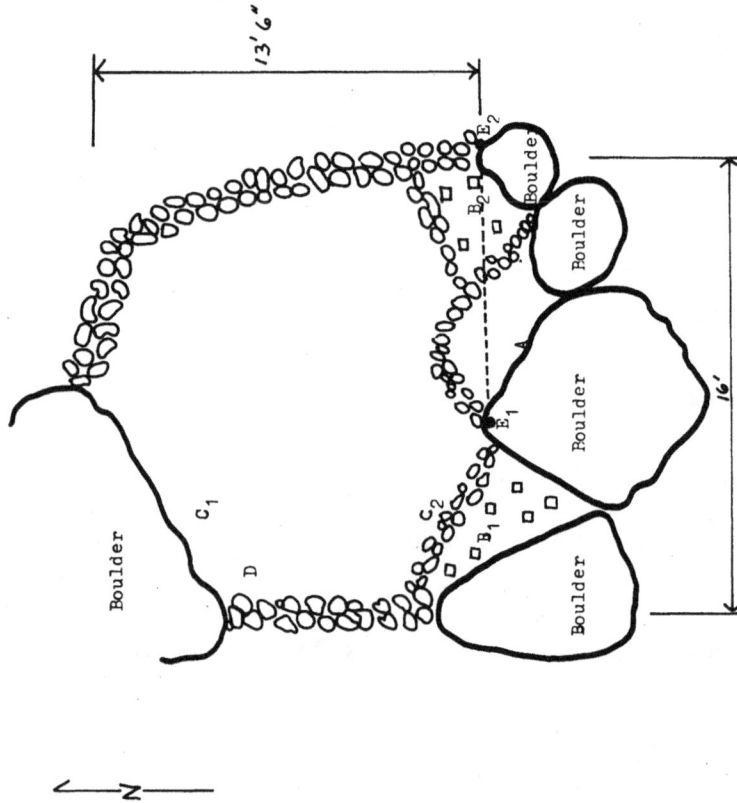

Turkey Spring Site II, Alley 2
House II-26,

13'6"

16'

= 1 ft.

A - Charcoal concentration (probably heating pit) found under overhang of boulder.
B - Raised areas perhaps for storage. Hammer stones and choppers found in B2.
C - Potsherds found in these locations. Scrapers and chips found at C1.
D - Bird point found here.
E1 - E2 Position of possible roof beam. Charcoal scattered evenly over floor except for concentration at A, and lesser concentration at C1. No fire pit in center.

Figure 10

Figure 10 and 11

Largest of the three structures, Structure II-26 measured 13.5 feet north-south and 16 feet east-west. Large lava boulders formed the walls at the southern and northwest edges of the house. Rough walls, approximately 3 feet high, laid up of stones, met the edges of the boulders. As there was no break in these walls to indicate a doorway, entrance presumably was through a roof hatchway. Beneath a foot or more of humus and pine needles lay a stratum of fairly hard gray soil about 3 inches thick. This appears to have been the floor. Below it was a layer of softer yellowish clay. Curving walls about 18 inches high outlined what appeared to have been storage areas across the south end of the room. That is the orientation for storage compartments in Gallina home sites, but the shapes are entirely different. Two of these "storage areas" in Structure II-26, marked B1 and B2, seem to have been raised and at least partially paved with small stones (see Figure 10). There was no fire pit, but two concentrations of charcoal were found. One lay beneath the overhang of the large boulder at A. In the raised area at B2 three cobbles showing some fire-cracking probably had edged a fire area or served as firedogs. A fourth stone may have served the same purpose or may have been a chopper. The smaller concentration of charcoal was at C1. Small bits of charcoal, possibly from roof-burning, were rather evenly distributed over the floor, and one log which may have been a fallen roof beam lay at the level of the raised storage areas. Like the other logs garnered from the mountain sites, it was not datable.

Forty-five sherds, including many of fair size, were found toward the two ends of the west side of the room. All were of sooted Gallina Plain Utility ware cook pots. The clay was slightly micaceous, as in Llaves area vessels.

A tiny (1.8 x 1.2 cm) white quartz, side-notched "bird point" (Type 2, discussed in Chapter VII on stone implements), the smallest of all we found and perfectly shaped, was lying on this floor. One triangular, obsidian side-scraper and an obsidian lunate burin-blade which we have come to interpret as a tool for working on arrowshafts, together with 3 small chert and 2 small quartzite scrapers and some unworked flakes, were lying near the boulder at C1 (see Figure 10). Fragments of animal bones also appeared here and there on the floor.

Structure II-27

Structure II-27 (Figure 11) was a domicile measuring approximately 13 x 10 feet which stood some 40 feet east of Structure 26. The natural lava boulders incorporated into its walls were smaller but more numerous than those in Structure II-26. The adjoining built-up stone walls averaged about 2 feet high. The large root of a tree had broken through one wall, but there was no opening for an entranceway. Removal of 4-5 inches of fill uncovered a fairly hard yellowish clay floor. Several stones which could have been part of a fire hearth were found near the floor center. The stones showed no evidence of fire but a shallow concentration of charcoal and ash lay within the space they bounded. This would have been the "heating pit" area where coals brought from an outside cooking fire were laid to warm the dwelling when needed. A second concentration of charcoal was found in the raised area at B1.

Figure 12

Turkey Spring Site II Alley 2

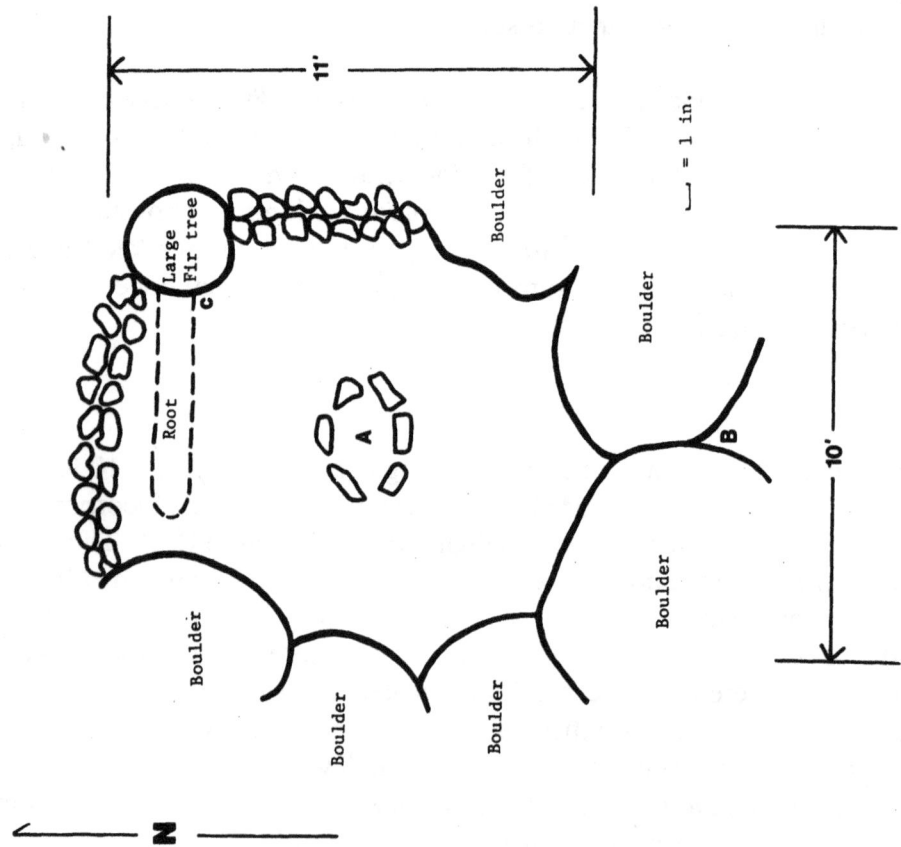

Feature II - 34 House

A - Probable Fire pit - 16 in. diameter - Charcoal encountered 3 in. below surface and still concentrated at 6 in.
B - Mouth of small cave between two boulders just south of house. No apparent signs of habitation, but one potsherd found in it.
C - Obsidian chips found beneath root at this point.

⊢ = 1 in.

Figure 13

Turkey Spring Site II Alley 2

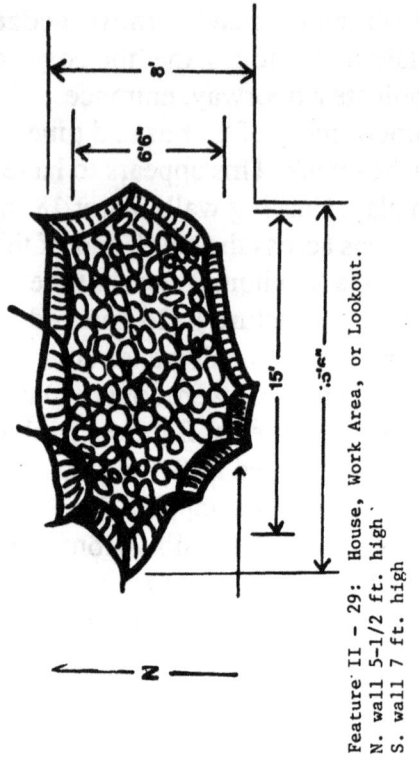

Feature II - 29: House, Work Area, or Lookout.
N. wall 5-1/2 ft. high
S. wall 7 ft. high

Figure 14

Turkey Spring Site II Alley 2

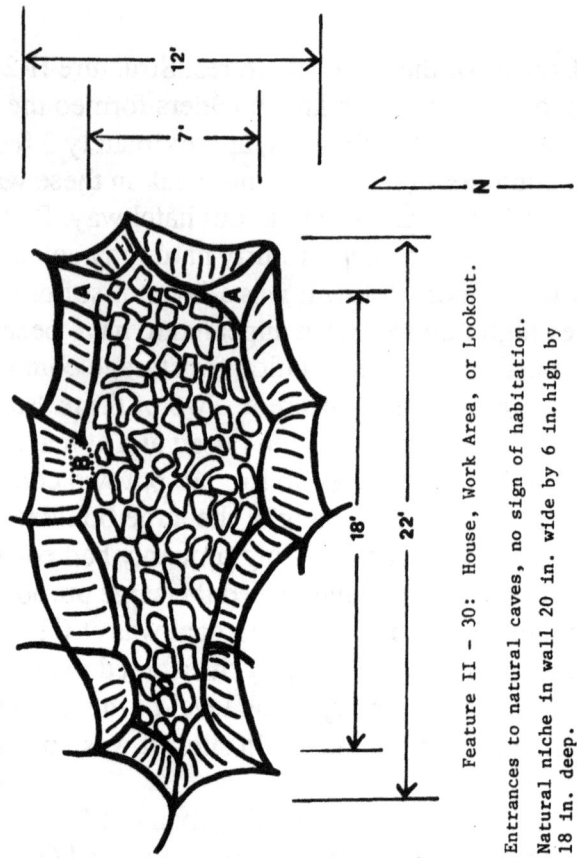

Feature II - 30: House, Work Area, or Lookout.

A. Entrances to natural caves, no sign of habitation.
B. Natural niche in wall 20 in. wide by 6 in. high by 18 in. deep.
Both north and south walls were 4 ft. high.

Probable lookout (Top of steps in crevice in North wall gives excellent view of valley.)

Fifty-seven small sherds of Gallina Plain Utility ware were found, almost all from the area where the large root was removed. A number of animal bone fragments came from the same hole. One complete, side-notched, obsidian point(Type 1) and 2 fragments of chert points were found. There also was half of a long, slender, white chert knife, well flaked and much like an arrow point except for lack of notches. The other lithics consisted of 1 slender obsidian flake with pointed end and 1 approximately rectangular small flake. There also were 1 larger, thin, white chert scraper (3.3 x 2.5 cm), 1 very rough chert end-scraper (4.5 x 3.5 cm), and 5 chert and 2 obsidian unshaped scraper-knives. An especially interesting piece was a white chert blade with the typical lunate curve for cutting hide, small branches, or reeds. It had been used enough times to have become dulled. Others were a black obsidian flake with a sharp little burin peak at the top, and a white chert flake which was leaf-shaped except for the birdshead-shaped burin extending out from one end, making the whole implement (3.4 x 1.6 cm) resemble a bird in shape. The 32 chert and 7 obsidian unused flakes, all debitage cast aside as a man sat and worked with his implements, proved that this domicile had housed a knapper whose shop was at home.

Structures II-33 and II-34

Structure 33 was a small cave near Structure 34. The only possible artifact found inside was a piece of antler which showed evidence of either having been whittled or, more probably, gnawed by an animal.

Structure 34 (Figure 12) had been a small domicile located 67 feet north of Structures II-26 and 27. Two-thirds of the wall of this house consisted of large, natural volcanic boulders *in situ*. A very large Douglas fir tree at the northeast corner of the structure had sent a root 15 inches in diameter entirely across the northern sector. When 4 inches of fill were removed, the floor, a layer of yellow clay, could be seen. In the center was a stone-outlined circle about 16 inches in diameter, a fire "place" marked by charcoal. Excavation showed a cone-shaped depression with heavy concentration of charcoal extending to a depth of 6 inches. This was clearly a "heating pit," of the type described for some Mogollon sites not far from Zuni, where coals were brought into the house and laid in a cone-shaped pit from which the heat would radiate through the night. We did not reach the bottom of this heating pit; bad weather was closing in rapidly and the rough forest road, then not even graveled, was thoroughly difficult if wet.

Even though the heating pit was not cleaned to the bottom its presence strongly suggested that Structure II-34, though small, had been occupied.

Three flakes of obsidian, 1 of chert, and 1 of quartz had been found at point C, beneath the large root. Two Gallina Utility ware sherds were in the fill, and 1 single sherd of Gallina Plain Utility ware lay in a small cave outside the boulders of the south wall.

Turkey Spring Site II Alley 2

Turkey Spring Site II Alley 3

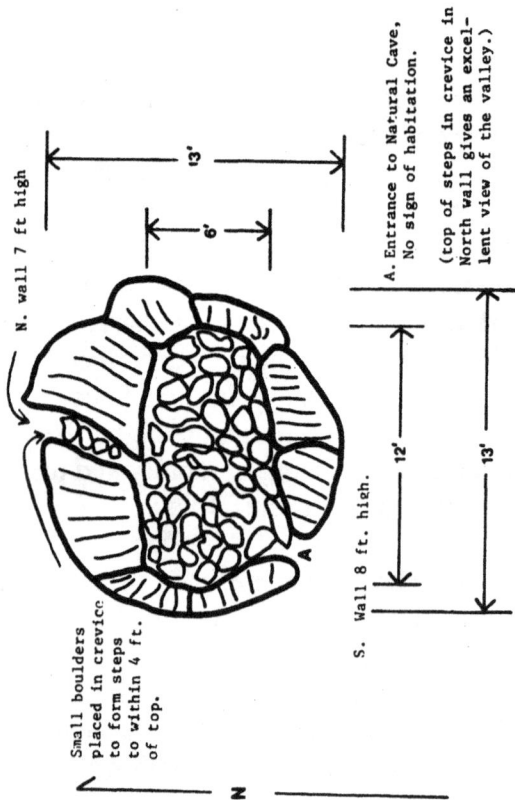

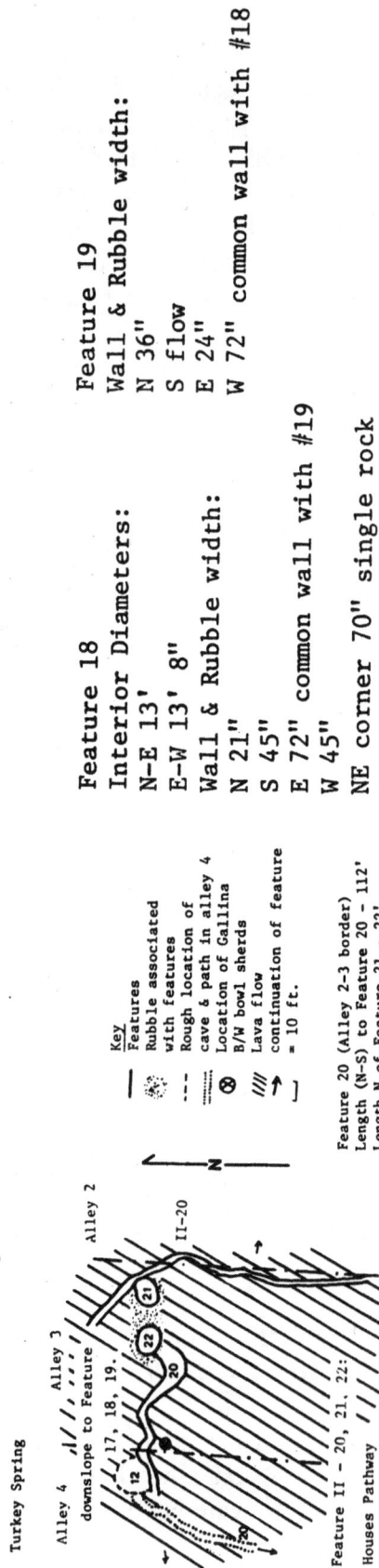

Alley 3

Alley 4

N

Upslope to Features 20, 21, 22

18

19

N. wall 7 ft high

Small boulders
placed in crevice
to form steps
to within 4 ft.
of top.

N

13'

6'

12'

13'

A. Entrance to Natural Cave,
No sign of habitation.

(top of steps in crevice in
North wall gives an excellent view of the valley.)

S. Wall 8 ft. high.

Feature II-31: House or look-out and work area.

Figure 15

Feature 18
Interior Diameters:
N-E 13'
E-W 13' 8"
Wall & Rubble width:
N 21"
S 45"
E 72" common wall with #19
W 45"
NE corner 70" single rock

Feature 19
Wall & Rubble width:
N 36"
S flow
E 24"
W 72" common wall with #18

Figure 17

Turkey Spring

Alley 4   Alley 3

17, 18, 19.
downslope to Feature

12

Alley 2

II-20

21

22

20

N

Key
Features
Rubble associated
with features
Rough location of
cave & path in alley 4
Location of Gallina
B/W bowl sherds
Lava flow
continuation of feature
= 10 ft.

Feature 20 (Alley 2-3 border)
Length (N-S) to Feature 20 – 112'
Length N of Feature 21 – 22'
Length from Feature 22 to
cave in Alley 4 – 82'
Feature 20 width 18' – 1'
average 2' – 3'

Feature II – 20, 21, 22,:
Houses Pathway

Figure 16

Figure 15, 16 and 17

90

Structures II-1 and II-2

The remains of Structures II-1 and II-2, domiciles, lie just beyond the top of the lava flow. Both were briefly tested but neither was cleaned to the floor.

On the first day of survey work in Alley I, a member of Perret's crew sighted an intact pot hidden beneath several rocks in a small passage between large boulders at the bottom of a larger passage 8 feet below the surface, 50 feet below (north of) the crest, and 10 feet east of the Alley I-II boundary. This placed it in Alley II and much nearer Houses II-1 and II-2 than to any other structure. The vessel proved to be a fine Gallina Black-on-white canteen (L73.3.1) with four vertically pierced lugs for suspension cords (see Plate 9). It was encircled by two bands, one about the neck and one just above the lugs, each interrupted by a typical Gallina "ceremonial break" in the painted encircling lines.

Structures II-20, II-28, II-29, II-30, and II-31

Three work areas designated Structures II-29, II-30, and II-31 were found in the middle of the boulder field.

Structure II-29 was a large depression sheltered by basalt boulders which, along the north edge, stood an average of 5.5 feet high. On the south or upper edge they averaged 7 feet high. The floor of this area had been filled in (paved) with smaller stones to make it more or less level (Figure 13). It measured 6.5 x 15 feet and would have made an excellent space for drying plant foods but also could have been the remains of a domicile with everything but walls and floor gone.

Structure II-30, 4 feet below the tops of surrounding boulders, was similar to II-29 but slightly larger, with a floor of 7 x 18 feet (Figure 14). Two small caves were located at the east end of this area, but neither they nor a small natural niche in the north wall offered any data as to use.

Structure II-31 was similar to II-29 and 30 but slightly smaller than either. The tops of the surrounding boulders averaged 8 feet above the floor on the south side and 7 feet on the north, which overlooked the valley. This structure differed from the two just described in that at about the center of the north side a near-vertical space between two boulders had been packed with smaller stones to form rough steps up to a point 4 feet below the crest of the boulder wall. A flat stone at the top of these steps made a convenient platform from which one could observe the valley below (Figure 15). This structure, 13 x 13 feet, well could have served as a lookout, even while it provided a work or drying space. We cannot, however, rule out the possibility of its having been a domicile. A small cave opens off the southwest corner of this floor but today retains no evidence of use.

The other structures in Alley II differed in type. Structure II-28 was a narrow crevice extending 6 to 8 feet under some large boulders. On a shelf 5 feet from the entrance, an incomplete vessel (L73.2.3) of Gallina Plain Utility ware was found with one sherd, dust, and rodent dung inside it, and other sherds close by. A large bulbous Gallina Plain ware canteen (L72.2.5), with four lugs for suspension (see pottery illustrations), and a flat-bottomed Gallina Utility widemouthed cook pot (L72.2.1) had been found near each other in a nearby crevice during brief explorations in Alley II in 1972.

Structure II-20 was a pathway made by laying smaller stones among the large boulders at the upper end of the broken lava field to form a narrow, paved trail. After about 30 feet, this trail veered to the west into Alley III where it led to walled structure II-21 (see Figure 16).

Alley III[*]

Structures II-17, II-18, II-19, II-21, and II-22

In the initial survey of Alley III four definite "birdnest" houses were found, two within the flow itself and two at the north forest-flow contact. The upper set, Structures II-21 and 22, had a clearly distinguishable path (Structure II-20) running from the top of the ridge down through the scree to the northeastern side of Structure II-21. On the western edge of that domicile was a second house, Structure II-22. The pathway continued to the southwest and then twisted westward into the Alley IV boundary (Figure 16). From the mouth of the cave the path swung southward (upslope) to end on the tree line at the lava crest.

A use-association among these three Structures must be inferred because of the inter-connecting path. The pathway itself is incomplete in spots but can be readily discerned winding over the larger basaltic boulders. It was made by placing smaller flatter pieces of vesicular basalt over the rough irregular large boulders. In places, pecking and flattening from reshaping or usage also can be discerned. The technique used in paving this path duplicated that of paved floors in the work or drying areas.

Structures II-21 and 22, the houses, were distinguishable as rounded depressions in the basalt flow, each with smaller and flatter rocks forming a circular floor, probably covered over with soil and clay when the structures were in use. Through the centuries, soil and any decomposing vegetal matter present filtered between the boulders and stones, leaving only bare rock. Because of our time limitations, Structure II-22 was left untouched, but II-21, taken as our sample for the two, was cleared. As much of the basalt inside Structure 21 was denser and more laminar than that of the lava flow into which the structures had been set, it must have been carried from at least a little distance. The fire-cracked quartzite and sandstone cobbles in the center of the room, where the fire pit or fire place originally should have been located, similarly had been brought in from elsewhere.

---

[*]   Supervised and reported by Peter McKenna.

Turkey Spring Site II, Alley 3
    Feature II - 19: house

Interior Diameters:
N-S 10' 7"
E-W 9' 5"

Wall or Rubble Thickness:
N 36"
S Flow
E 24" & Flow
W 72" common wall with 18

Wall heights:
N 31"
S 60+" (SE & SW also)
E 46"
W 33"

Firebox:
triangulation
E 36"
S 44"
N 68"
Depth 24"

Dimensions:
N 18"
S 16"
E 25"
W 19"
N-S 17"
E-W 13"
NW-SE 20-1/2"
NE-SW 17"

Test Pit:
Located 3" from SW corner
of firebox
Length NW-SE 18"
Width NE - SW 13"
Depth   33"
Crossection of firebox reflects
same evidence as does test trench

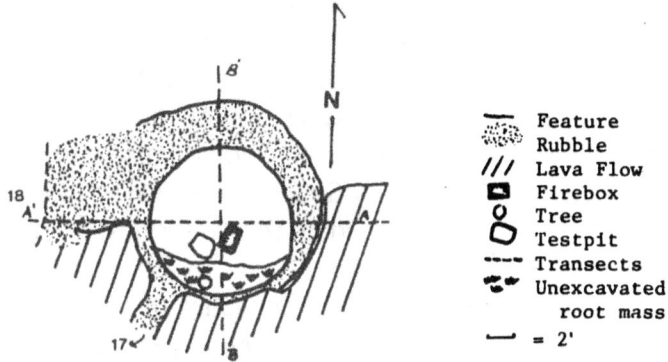

Legend (plan view):
- Feature
- Rubble
- /// Lava Flow
- Firebox
- Tree
- Testpit
- Transects
- Unexcavated root mass
- ⊢ = 2'

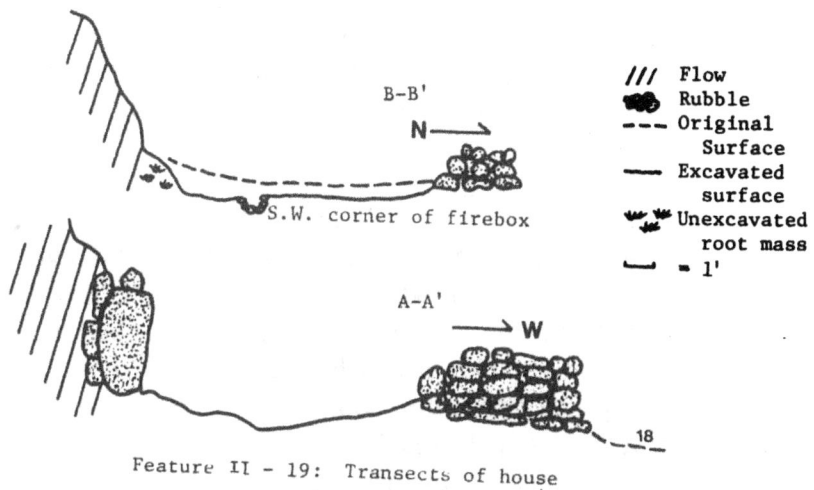

Feature II - 19: Transects of house

Legend (transects):
- /// Flow
- Rubble
- Original Surface
- Excavated surface
- Unexcavated root mass
- ⊢ = 1'

B-B'
S.W. corner of firebox

A-A'

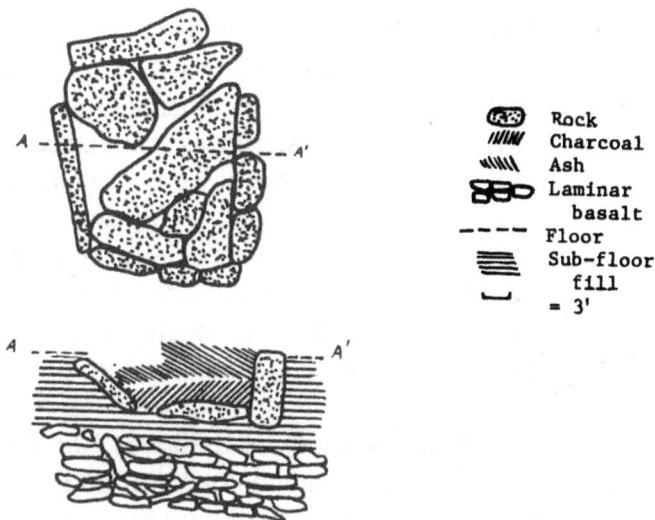

Firebox of House II-19

Legend (firebox):
- Rock
- Charcoal
- Ash
- Laminar basalt
- Floor
- Sub-floor fill
- ⊢ = 3'

Figure 18, 19, 20

The vesicular basalt boulders, which provided most of the outer wall of Structure 21, rose to a height of 6 feet. Gaps between boulders had been filled, and on the east a stretch of 45 inches was bridged by a wall approximately 16 inches wide and 4 feet high. No mortar was found between the stones. Although they were of irregular shapes and sizes, they were tightly packed together and the wall still was quite stable. The northwestern segment, however, had collapsed into a typical rubble heap such as those associated with the Turkey Spring I house sites. The floor of Structure 21 measured 13 feet northeast-southwest and 10 feet northwest-southeast. That of adjoining Structure II-22 measured 14 feet north-south and 13 feet east-west. The combined length of the two, between which there was only 34 inches of rubble, came to 115 inches. Structure 22 was not excavated, but the floor had been largely uncovered by nature. As neither in it nor in the floor of Structure 21 was there any evidence of sockets for roof supports, the roof beams presumably had rested on top of the walls.

The only artifacts remaining consisted of 1 small rose and white chert flake scraper, 1 smaller obsidian flake used as a scraper, 1 partial obsidian point, and 2 cobbles, 1 broken and 1 whole, which apparently had seen considerable use as manos or related grinding stones.

The two houses, Structures II-18 and II-19 (Figures 16 and 17), found 150 feet downslope and directly north of Structures 21 and 22 at the very margin of the forest-basaltic flow contact, had no pathway but, like the pair just described, were associated with a small cave. Structure II-18 was the larger and looked more inviting than II-19 for excavation, but the presence of three white fir trees, scrub oak, Utah serviceberry, and chokecherry growing in the room would have made uncovering it too arduous and time-consuming to justify the results. Moreover, anything found within it probably would have been considerably disturbed by roots. Consequently, Structure II-19 was selected as the sample for detailed investigation. This proved to be the best preserved and to contain the most material of all the houses dug during the 1973 season.

Structure 19 (Figures 18 and 19) had a dead white fir tree at its south wall and chokecherry, Utah serviceberry, and strawberries growing in the main area of the room. Aspen, scrub oak, Ponderosa pine, raspberries, and other vegitation flourish in the immediate vicinity. A quadrant system was established at magnetic compass points and what locations could be made were noted in the tables of measurements. Despite our efforts at maintaining intrasite control, digging and recovery were most difficult because roots had disrupted house features, especially the floor. Consequently, most of the materials here were located during the screening process and not *in situ*. The only generality we can make in relation to location and concentrations of implements recovered is to say that they came from the floor or the shallow fill.

The interior diameter of Structure II-19 was 10.6 feet north-south and 9.4 feet east-west. Wall and rubble width on the north was 36 inches, east 24 inches, and west 72 inches, where it shared a common wall with Structure II-18 (Figure 17). Its south side consisted of boulders of the lava flow. Structure II-18, the larger of the two, measured 13 feet north-south and 13.7 feet east-west. Wall and rubble width was 21 inches on the

Turkey Spring Site II, Alley 3

Feature II-17. Cooking-storage annex
for Houses II 18, 19.

Dimensions:
  Entrance:
Width Top 8"
     Center 29"
       Base 75"
Height S 19"
     Center 35"
      1/2 N 16"
          N 25"

  Interior:
Width W 44"
     Center 34"
          E 36"
Height N   6"
      1/2 N 12"
     Center 65"
      1/2 S 40"
          S 17-1/2"

Key
Exterior rocks
Interior rocks
Laminar basalt
chinking

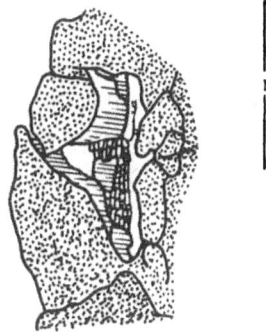

⌣ = 10"

Figure 21

Feature II-17: Cooking- storage
               annex for House II-18
               and 19. Floorplan.

"Pocket" in SW corner
Length   29"
Height   16"
Width
  Basal   18"
  Top   12"

Feature 17 Basal Dimensions
N-S
          E 44"
   Center 75"
          W 35"
E-W
          S 14"
   Center 34"
          N 16"

Key
Charcoal
Lava flow
Feature base
Small laminar
  basalt chinking

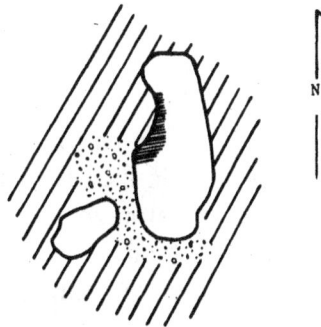

⌣ = 10"

Figure 22

Turkey Spring, Site II, Alley 4
   Cave II-12; used as a domicile.

/// Tamped Earth
     Ash
     Boulder
     Alley
  ∘ Neck banded sherd
     Scraper
     log

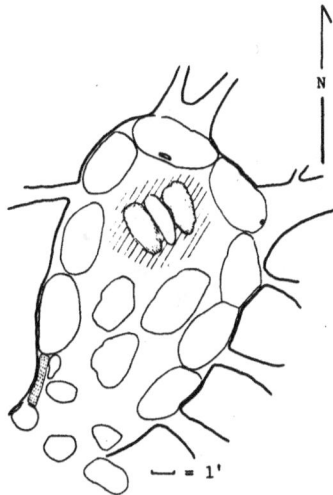

⌣ = 1'

Figure 23

95

north, 45 inches on the south, 45 inches on the east, and 72 inches on the west where it shared a common wall with Structure II-19. On its northeast corner a single boulder provided 70 inches of wall. No postholes or evidence of roofing or doorway were found.

The floor of Structure II-19, as far as could be determined, originally had been saucer-shaped, curving up somewhat at the edges to meet the walls as in Structure I-4 at Turkey Spring Site I. A centrally located deep firebox (13 x 18 inches; 33 inches deep) had been constructed of vertically placed stones and paved with flat slabs (Figure 20). The box contained a 4.5-inch layer of charcoal chunks which were covered with a lens of fine gray ash. In the charcoal was found a white quartzite projectile point, such as in structure 4 at Turkey Spring Site I and similarly in the house designated as GB2 in our south Llaves area home village, the Butts Site.

In the total excavation of Structure II-19, 12 projectile points or their fragments were found. All were of obsidian except 1 of white quartzite from the firebox, 1 of black schist or gneiss, 1 of rose and white Pedernal chert, and 1 of chalcedony. The only sherds where 3 from Gallina Plain Utility jars, 1 being from a cook pot with pointed base.

The small "cave," Structure II-17 (Figures 21 and 22), was unique (height: 19 inches south, 35 inches center, 25 inches north. Width: top 8 inches, middle 29 inches, base 75 inches. Interior height: 17.5 inches south, 65 inches center, 6 inches north. Width: 44 inches west, 34 inches center, 36 inches east). Located 13 feet southeast of Structure II-19, it apparently had served as a storage cist and/or cook area for both Structures II-18 and II-19. Two large boulders which were located in a natural pocket had outlined the original space, and smaller more laminar basalt stones were placed to form what seems to have been a continuous semicircular wall on the south, southwest, and west (Figure 22). The fill was 13 inches deep. Charcoal and other signs of fire were heaviest at the north end of the pocket, primarily under a small ledge that once may have served as a shelf. A well-flaked knife of obsidian and a broken, quartzite drill lay in the fill. Pottery was represented by 2 sherds of Gallina Utility ware (1 from the neck of a water jar with a horizontal loop handle at the rim) and 1 sherd from a Gallina Black-on-white bowl.

A large pink quartzite chopper and an obsidian graver or drill were picked up a few feet from Structure II-19, and sherds from a Gallina Black-on-white bowl were found just south of the pathway (Structure II-20) near the cave over the boundary in Alley IV. In 1972, a bulbous canteen (L72.2.8), a rotund canteen with four lugs (L72.2.4), and a widemouthed culinary jar (L72.2.3), all of Gallina Plain Utility ware, were found hidden near Structures II-17, II-18, and II-19. These would have been sufficient for the kitchen needs of this complex. One might have expected to find a water jar as well, but either the two big canteens took its place, or the jar was hidden so efficiently that we did not find it.

Structure II-10, II-12, II-13, II-14

In Alley IV, but close to the division line with Alley III, we have the already mentioned western section of paved trail, Structure II-20, where it runs from Structure II-12, the cave habitation, up onto the edge of the mesa. At the top of Alley IV is Structure II-10, a small structure possibly for storage. At the bottom of this wedge-shaped alley, but a short distance out beyond the lower edge of the volcanic boulders, were three or more other houses of which two, Structures II-13 and 14, were excavated.

Six passages led off the main room of Structure II-12, a cave, the largest being 8 feet in width and all spacious enough for a small person to crawl into. In 1973 each was carefully explored. No artifacts were found, but it seems probable that these openings would have been used for storage. A large sherd of a Gallina Black-on-white food bowl, approximately 18 cm in diameter, was picked up in 1972 on the surface nearby.

Structure II-10 was constructed at the upper edge of the lava spill with pine trees nearby. Tree stumps and roots made methodical excavation most difficult. The structure was roughly oval in shape, 5 feet north-south, 9 feet east-west. Depth from tops of walls to fill was 2-3 feet, increasing north to south. Those walls consisted primarily of large volcanic boulders 2-4 feet thick, but some chinking with small rocks could be seen.

In Level 1 the area within the boulder confine was covered with scrub oak, small lava boulders, and moist humus 6 inches deep. In Level 2 clayey soil and small-to-large chunks of charcoal which disintegrated on contact with air appeared. At a 12-inch depth, heavier clay, lava rocks oxidized to an orange color from intense heat, charcoal pieces 1.5 inches in diameter, and small chunks of burned clay indicated a floor. The charcoal was scattered everywhere, and a section of burned beam, 3.1 feet long and 9.5 inches in diameter, pieces of two smaller beams, and more burned clay lay on the floor. No evidence of a fire pit or of postholes for roof supports could be found. There were 84 sherds of sooted Gallina Plain Utility ware from two or more thin-walled cook pots, one with a short outcurving rim and one with a direct rim. Corn cob or grass brush texturizing on the surface of the former is clear. Stone work consisted of one flake.

We can sum up the data only as pointing toward Structure 10 having been a storage structure, well cleaned out and with its roof burned upon final abandonment. Other structures apparently of the same use were numerous in the general area near the upper edge of the lava flow. (See discussion in "The Mesa Top Ridge at Edge of Flow.")

Structure II-12, a cave used as a domicile (Figure 23), was roughly oval (10 feet north-south; 15 feet east-west) in shape. It was easily entered through a natural gap 2.5 feet wide and 4 feet long, facing approximately west. Several large spaces around the slabs

---

[*]   Supervised and reported by Mary Lu Moore.

which formed the roof at the top of the cave provided light and air. The distance between the roof of the cave and floor measured 7.6 feet.

The walls of this cave consisted entirely of lava boulders. At one time there may have been some chinking, but we had no evidence of plastering. Some of the small niches in the stones could have served for tucking things away, a thought encouraged by finding a sherd from a Gallina Plain Utility cook pot with a rim fillet in an opening midway up one 5-foot boulder. Halfway up a 6-foot boulder of the back wall, a small hole held soft loose soil and a chert scraper. An 8-inch-diameter pine beam 6 feet long was wedged horizontally into boulders which comprised walls and roof just south of the cave entrance. (The beam was taken for study, but was not datable.) This could have been part of a supplement to the slab roof covering, or it might have been used as a rod on which to hang clothing, skins, or even the water jar-canteens.

The fill above the floor consisted of dry sandy soil with which ash, charcoal, burned and unburned lumps of clay, heat-fractured stones, sherds, flakes of obsidian both worked and unworked, and two broken points were associated.

Beneath its soil and debris, a floor base for this cave had been secured by fitting small rocks among the boulders *in situ*. Strewn on that floor were 5 blackened pine beams about 3.5 inches in diameter and 1.5 feet long. In the rear center, tamped-down earth provided a better flooring surface and a little depth for 2 heating pits. Heavy concentrations of charcoal and ash containing burned and unburned turkey and rodent bones covered much of this area.

One unlined heating pit was vaguely rectangular, 13 inches north-south and 16 inches east-west. Close to its east edge was a boulder with, on its farther side, what appeared to be a second heating pit the same size as the first.

Near the heating area were 2 broken points. One had been a large Type 3 point of obsidian; much of the blade and one barb are missing. The base of the stem was thinned near its center with longitudinal flaking which left a dip in its outline. The other, a small Type 2 point of obsidian, had lost its tip.

One chert flake had been utilized as a blade. There also was a circular chert blade which showed where a lunate flake had been removed to provide a sharp curved edge. It may have had a burin, now dulled. The use of circular and semicircular blades by the people of these mountain camps catches one's attention, but even more surprising is the number of cutting blades with burins. One rose chert lunate burin-blade of the arrow-shaft-working-tool type, a lunate burin-blade of quartzite, and a long obsidian blade with a burin at one end also were found in the Structure 12 fill. The number of implements with similar function suggests concentrated interest and experimentation by the knapper of this household.

Three unshaped flakes had been utilized as blades. In the category of scrapers and scraper-knives we have one basalt side-scraper, a large, gray quartzite side-scraper, and a quartzite snubnosed scraper. This household evidently worked the skins as well as using the meat of animals killed.

In the fill we found 2 Gallina Gray (probably Gallina Plain Utility) sherds from a narrow-necked water jar with rim fillet as well as 7 other sherds of Gallina Plain Utility ware. One was from a cook pot with a nipple-like protuberance close to the lip to make handling the vessel easier. Only 3 Gallina Black-on-white sherds were present, the decorated ware always being more scarce than the undecorated Utility ware types.

Structure 13 was a relatively circular domicile constructed on a terrace at the lower limit of the volcanic boulders and approximately 50 feet southeast of Structure 14, which stood on a lower terrace. Structure 13 measured 14.5 feet in diameter and 2.5 feet from the tops of the walls to the surface of the fill. The roots of a pine tree growing within the area encompassed by the walls had disturbed the heating pit and ash. Walls plus fallen rubble measured 3 to 6 feet across. Redish oxidation was obvious on the lava boulders. Small stones from outside the lava area had been brought in for chinking, but there was no evidence of mortar or plaster.

The uppermost 6 inches of fill consisted of loose lava rocks, moist humus, and a few roots. Loose sandy soil appeared in the second 6-inch level. Small bits of charcoal were found in both levels, especially in the northwest and southwest quadrants. Level 2 also held a considerable amount of whitish-grey ash. Burned clay and charred pine beams 3 to 4 inches in diameter were present.

Hard-packed clay at a depth of 12 to 15 inches below present fill surface indicated that the floor had been reached. A test pit showed that this clay, considerably eroded on its surface, was 18 inches thick. The question of whether an original floor had been laid and later had received new toppings of clay, though in the test pit no actual differentiation of layers could be seen, remained unanswered.

At the center of this house, in the midst of large amounts of charcoal and ash, was a fire area. Above it lay a flat sandstone slab, only 7 inches below the surface of the fill. Could it have fallen from the hatchway, presumably directly over the fire area? That area was irregular in shape and seemed to stretch 3 to 4 feet in each direction, quite possibly now larger than originally because of root disturbance.

Beneath the slab in the mass of ash were a number of heat-fractured and blackened rocks, together with 17 chert and obsidian flakes, 10 of which proved to be artifacts. The others were mere debitage. The most ingenious of these implements (5 x 3.3 cm) was made from a thin flake of pinkish chalcedony which had been carefully worked on both sides and sharpened by delicate pressure work on all edges. On one side a lunate concave depression had been struck. The sharp ends of this curve provided 2 burin points for cutting or scoring. The other sharp edges of the implement could have been used for splitting one end of a reed to hold a wooden foreshaft, and then using the burin to split the end of that foreshaft to take the projectile point. The bow-maker also could have clipped his string, presumably of sinew, or cut a piece of buckskin or mountain lion hide into the pattern for a quiver. This arrowshaft-working tool almost might be called an "all purpose implement", as any of the sharpened sides of the thin blade could have served as a knife or, when it dulled and the owner was less concerned about risking its edges, as a scraper. Burins alone, burins flaked onto blades of various shapes (of which an obsidian example was found in the fill of Structure 13, a house), and burins associated with a lunate curve were far from uncommon in these mountain sites. The "arrowshaft-working tool", varying in shape and material used, was the most developed of these several related implements. (See discussion in chapter on stone implements.)

A large unworked flake of grey quartzite (8.7 x 5.7 cm) had seen much use on its long edge as a blade. There also was a small blade of brown flint (3.2 x 1.6 cm) with one keeled and one somewhat concave face. It was rather reminiscent of a point but without notches and probably was held in the fingers when used. A pink chert scraper together with 3 chert and 3 obsidian nonshaped flakes which had been put to use as scrapers or blades, 1 Type 7 small obsidian projectile point, 1 point fragment, and 6 flakes of chert, quartz, and obsidian completed the collection from this house. Here again is proof that the flint-worker of this family sometimes worked at home.

The complex of artifacts from Structure 13 can be thought of as quite typical for one of the mountain domiciles which had not suffered from extreme run-off erosion of the floors.

Structure II-14, had stood in an area of huge scattered boulders, tall pine trees, scrub oaks, and mountain flowers. In shape it was oval: 12 feet east-west, 16 feet north-south. From the tops of the walls to the surface of fill was 4.8 feet. As in a number of other structures, some of the boulders forming the wall showed clear signs of oxidation resulting from the intense heat of a fire against the lava. There was no surface-level opening to the house.

In preparation for excavation, loose rocks, rotting tree trunks, and brush were removed from the surface. Numerous roots in the humus impeded excavation, and attempts to remove those roots may have damaged part of the flooring.

The first 6 inches of soil beneath the humus of Level 1 was light colored, fine, and sandy over most of the area. Slight discoloration resulted from ash mixture and variations in dampness. Small pieces of charcoal were found throughout this level. Fractured blackened rocks also were present. As work progressed through the center of this house, one serrated obsidian point fragment, flakes of obsidian and chert, concentrations of charcoal, lumps of burned clay, sherds, and bone fragments (burned and unburned) appeared. Near the center of the room were numerous rocks.

The floor of hard-packed clay was exposed 5 to 6 inches below the surface. A test pit proved the clay to be 12 inches deep. Near the center of the house, beneath a group of apparently unrelated rocks, was a roughly square fire pit lined with several broken sandstone slabs and some imported cobbles. Within the pit were ash, charcoal, heat-fractured and blackened cobbles, flakes, and several sherds with blackened areas. (From secondary firing?)

The total of sherds found in this house was 27, all of Gallina Plain Utility ware on which the original gray color had been oxidized to brown during the fire which had burned the house. There were 15 lithics, including 2 obsidian point fragments, 1 worked obsidian side-blade knife (4.5 x 1.7 cm), 4 small chert flake scrapers, 1 small quartzite flake scraper, and 1 heavier brown stone flake scraper, all with edges worked or serrated by flakes. Six others appeared to be debitage.

Northwest of Structures 18 and 19 (houses) in Alley IV is a depression which now is filled with lush overgrowth. In times of heavier precipitation this depression may have provided an additional source of water for local inhabitants, like the similar structure in Site I which even today collects water in rather substantial amounts.

Alley V[*]

Structure II-49

The only excavation southwest of 10 was on Structure II-49, a small shallow structure from 21 to 58 inches across (Figure 24) in the forested area at the immediate base of the lava flow on the Alleys V and VI line. The small amount of rubble left above the present surface is not enough material to represent stone construction of a unit of adequate dwelling height. The upper walls, then, must have been of perishable materials, as in most of the Jemez piñon camps of historic times. The east-northeast portion of this structure was directly against the lava flow.

The fill of forest vegetation and rich brown humus was only 7 to 10 inches deep. Beneath this the floor was hard and contained so much ash that it gave a gray-white appearance. A test trench against the south wall showed that the clay floor was 7 inches deep, but it had been laid on similarly colored soil containing unburned brownish inclusions. The depth of the two layers totaled 15 inches above the basalt rocks. On each side of the floor, southwest and northeast, was a single, fairly large rock, one 26 x 17 x 19 inches, the other 11 x 10 x 7 inches (see Figure 22). Ten small chunky flakes of quartzite varying from 2 to 3.7 cm in length and 1.3 to 3 cm in width looked as if they might have been used as unworked scrapers. One tiny used obsidian flake (1.7 x 1.5 cm) possibly had been a burin. The almost complete dearth of artifacts, the presence of the two rocks that appear to have been left in the room during use, and the minimal lithic materials would have combined to make the structure questionable as a dwelling had it not had a heating pit. The pit (14.2 x 10 inches and 5 inches deep) was located off-center to the south. It was not similar to the partially slab-lined heating pits found in Structure 19 of Site II and Structure 4 of Site I but had a curved adobe lip on three sides, the south, east, and north. On the west and southwest sides the lip had eroded away; the pit was not

---

*   Supervised and reported by Peter McKenna. Structure II-49

lined, and no charcoal was present. A layer of fine gray ash about 2.5 inches deep covered the bottom of the pit.

A 2-inch layer of ash extending over the floor to a distance of 70 inches out from the walls indicates the structure had been burned on abandonment. The curved adobe lip of the fire pit is duplicated in many fire pits of the home villages, although there the great majority, but not all, are lined with sandstone slabs. Such slabs were not available in the near vicinity of the Turkey Spring sites, and the lava pieces used in some heating pits here were a poor substitute.

The Mesa Top Ridge at Edge of Flow[*]

Structures II-1, II-2, II-3, II-4, II-7, II-55, and II-15

A number of structures were found along the top of the ridge, either just above or a very short distance below the break between mesa and lava (see Map 5). Our original surmise that the smaller examples might have been storerooms and the larger examples summer homes seems to have been borne out by excavations.

Structure II-1, Alley II, which appeared to have the surface outline of a house, was dug, but if there had ever been a floor it had entirely weathered away from what once had been the stones of the old surface. Nothing was left.

Structure II-2, very near Structure II-1, was located only 15 feet from the lava edge in Alley II. The walls were difficult to define. They consisted of irregular large lava stones rolled into place, but the amount of stone present would have been sufficient for a wall only up to 2.5 feet in height. The outline was approximately circular. A large pine tree growing directly at the outer edge of the ring of boulders had sent masses of roots through the structure. Inner measurements were 6 feet east-west and 8 feet north-south.

The uppermost level consisted largely of humus. In the lower part of this layer a little charcoal was found. At 10 to 14 inches under the present surface was the floor, a hard clay layer from 6 to 8 inches thick. A single large rock which protruded through the floor proved to extend under the house wall and hence had been a part of the original landscape. Some charcoal bits were embedded in the clay surface of the floor, but no fire pit or fire area was seen. One fire-reddened stone and some burned clay chunks which probably had come from the roof rather than the walls were noted. A single obsidian chip was found 1 inch below the floor surface. No other artifacts were found, and no evidence of holes to hold roof supports or of a ground-surface entryway was seen.

Our conclusion was that Structure II-2 had been a storehouse, either with low walls or with some sort of jacal (slender poles plastered over with clay) upper wall, and that its roof had been burned at the time of abandonment.

---

[*]   Supervised and reported by Florence Ellis.

Structure II-3 had stood approximately 140 feet back from the lava breakdown edge of Alley II. It was oval in shape, 9.25 feet north-south by 7 feet east-west. It had been outlined by moderate-size lava chunks, now fallen, which would have made a wall 2.5 or 3 feet high at most. The house foundation now stands only 1 stone (12-15 inches) high above the present surface of the ground.

An irregular floor of yellow clay was found 11 inches below the surface. Some rocks from the walls had rolled onto it before the protective covering of humus had accumulated. There was no evidence of a fire pit, but on the west side some ash and charcoal were present. Charcoal, 2 culinary sherds, and our largest obsidian point (Type 2, measuring 2.5 x 4 cm) were found 2 inches above the floor on the north side of this room. More charcoal was scattered throughout that level, and a few sherds lay directly on the floor at a depth of 14 inches.

The presence of charcoal on the floor indicates roof-burning at the time of abandonment of this structure. That it was a domicile rather than a storehouse seems probable because of the sherds and point. No evidence of a ground-level entrance or of interior postholes for roof support was found.

Structure II-4, only a few feet distant from II-3, similarly seems to have been a domicile. It was oval, 10 feet northwest-southeast and 5.8 feet on the opposite axis. Stones sufficient to make a wall up to 2 feet high outlined the structure. It is possible, of course , that the upper walls were made of jacal with supporting posts set into the lower lava boulder wall-base. The floor of this house was found 8-10 inches below the present surface.

One peculiar find in this structure was a deep cone-shaped heating pit (27 x 10.5 inches) against the west wall. A large whitish volcanic stone had been used as lining at its front side. Three stones lined the remainder, and the clay making the back wall immediately above those stones was well burned. Considerable charcoal lay in this pit 12 inches below floor level. A mass of very heavy and now solid brown clay had washed into the north side of the pit after it was no longer used. Our experiments showed that the clay was suitable for pottery, but we have no trace of evidence that ceramics were made in any of our four mountain sites. The clay may have been used on the house roof or inside walls (if they were of jacal above the stone foundation) and had washed down into the pit after abandonment of the house. Without charcoal scattered throughout this structure, as in the others, our supposition must be that for whatever reason, its roof was not burned. Neither sherds nor flakes were found in this house, but there was a portion (12 x 7.5 cm) of what had been a sandstone grinding implement reminiscent of a mano, with roughly worked edges. One face showed an exceedingly smooth abrading surface and the other about the degree of smoothness expected for a mano back.

Structure II-7, just at the sloping edge of the lava area at the top of Alley V, seems to have been a roughly circular storage pit measuring 4 x 5 feet, without an obvious floor. Some charcoal flakes were found 6-8 inches below the present surface and others under the south wall. Next to the southwest was Structure II-8, a similar storage house though more oval, 5.1 x 4.6 feet, with a definite clay floor 43 inches below top of the south wall and 25 inches below top of the north wall. Structure II-9 appeared to have been another storage structure of approximately the same size. These three small cells showed no evidence of habitation use and, closely adjoining each other, may have made up the storage complex for a single family.

Structure II-55, near Structure 4 in Alley III, was an oval storage house, located only 10 feet from the mesa rim and with fairly curved walls and many large rocks somewhat more closely fitted together than in most structures. The top of the saucer-shaped floor was encountered 2 inches below ground surface, but it dipped to 8 inches below at its center. Some scattered charcoal was found at and slightly above floor level.

Structure II-15, a small circular structure measuring 7 x 7 feet and set 300 feet back from the lava edge in Alley III, had stone enough for a rock wall which originally would have stood 2 feet above the surface. Depth ranged from 11 to 17 inches. Bottom and walls were irregular and rough. Charcoal flakes occurred throughout the fill. Two possible scrapers were found at 11 inches and 2 flakes at 12 inches below surface. One large triangular scraper lay on the surface 3 feet from the structure.

Summary for Turkey Spring Site II

We learned appreciably more about the Gallina hunting-gathering living complex at Site II during our second short season and later study of data and materials from that area. Much of this information solidified our Site I findings, but a number of discoveries were new. Site II was larger than Site I, with something over 50 structures and the paved pathway. Only 22 of the structures were excavated. Very little was left of some which originally had been storehouses or were so exposed that erosion had washed almost everything away except for wall remnants. Many fewer pottery vessels were found hidden in the crevices of Site II than of Site I. Some may have been found by Indians or Whites coming into the area in the past, though it seems probable that if a few vessels had been plucked from the lava, the search would have been augmented and the others retrieved.

The structures found in Site II clearly were of three types: (1) definite domiciles which varied in size but contained identifiable heating pits, (2) similar structures, though sometimes appreciably smaller, which did not show identifiable fire areas of any type and probably were intended for storage, and (3) a cave habitation with two heating areas separated by a small boulder.

The structures of Site II provided appreciably clearer data on construction than those of Site I, though in both areas the excavators were plagued with the problem of damage done by roots and the difficulty of removing or working around them. We now are certain that except for the cave, domiciles had no entry openings in the walls at ground level. Entrance must have been gained through the roof, as in the pithouses and the surface or "unit type" structures of Gallina home sites.

The mountain structures were set down into spots where the lava boulders around them could provide a considerable amount of wall with known heights up to 6 feet. Their being "set down" at first gave the impression that these had been pithouses, but that was not so. The only major difference between Gallina pithouses and surface houses is the fact that the former actually are pits dug into the ground, which engulfs them except for roofs. Home village surface houses were built with thick but tapered walls of what may have been dry laid masonry of largely unshaped stones. They were roofed with beams and *latillas* (small poles) and heavily covered with clay. The roofs met the walls but were supported in part by four posts seated in sockets in the floor. Interior walls were plastered and floors were covered with several inches of well-laid clay-mix, into which flagstones sometimes were set, especially in the fire pit area.

In contrast, houses and most storerooms in the hunting-gathering camps had walls which consisted, as far as possible, of lava boulders *in situ*, with the gaps filled in by thick dry-laid areas of smaller volcanic stones. Crevices were chinked with small pieces of scree. The roof apparently rested on the walls themselves. Some structures, especially on the mesa top, may have had jacal upper walls and floors a few inches below ground level, but evidence is scanty.

The type of chinking found in house walls was used to fill space between boulders which chanced to form the basis of a floor. Some hard working family or families also cleverly adapted the same chinking to their desire for a relatively smooth pathway across the exceedingly rough terrain. If the lava cut into our shoes, it would have rapidly torn their sandals into pieces and lacerated even heavily calloused feet.

As noted for Turkey Spring Site I, the problem of digging a fire pit into a floor with a lava base would have limited some structures to a fire area rather than a pit. Laying a floor would have been heavy work under any circumstances, not the least of which was bringing water and in this case the clay, as well, from a distance. Some houses were given a partial packed-clay floor to allow for digging a fire pit, but of only shallow depth. As sandstone slabs suitable for lining fire pits were not available in this mountain region, a few such pits were roughly lined with pieces of lava. The most common heating device was the unlined heating pit into which coals from out-of-doors cook fires were placed. Spaced stones often outlined heating areas. The rounded fire pit lip customarily found in home sites would have required a fairly hard clay, which may not have been easily available. Attrition from winter erosion where snow was heavy would have cut into roofs and floors alike, and rivulets of clay would have trickled through the multiple crevices. Repairs must have required considerable time every spring.

In general, it seems that most structures intended for storage were located toward the edge of the lava breakdown, though some probably were built in the flow itself. Certainly there was usage of caves and crevices in the flow. Domiciles in part were below the lava, but others were in its midst. A few were on the mesa above. Some of the storehouses may never have had walls more than 2-3 feet high, with roof openings as has been generally surmised for the freestanding storerooms constructed in some Gallina home settlements. As a number of the latter were built with jacal walls, it is possible that

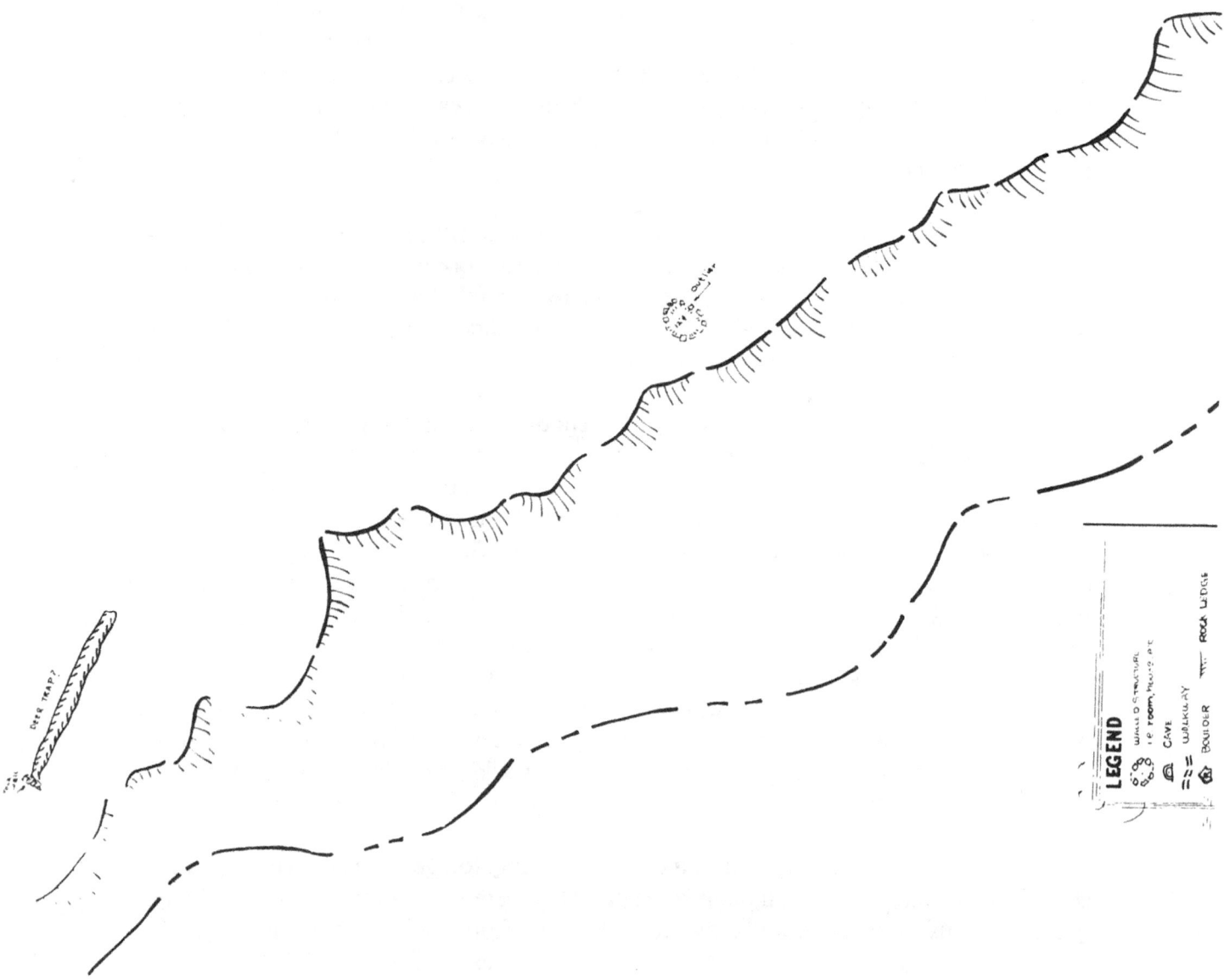

MAP 6

LEGEND

WALLED STRUCTURE

1-2 ROOM, FIELD HOUSE

CAVE

WALKWAY

BOULDER

ROCK LEDGE

DEER TRAP?

106

Note:

Archeological features mapped using compass and steel tape. Locations of some features may be slightly off due to strong local magnetic attraction.

Initial survey party:
John Hayden
Bill Pavit
Jim Bain
7-3-74

TURKEY SPRING ARCHEOLOGICAL AREA
SITE No. III   LA-10642)   Dulce Springs

NE4 SW4 SE4 Sec. 29
T27N R5E N.M.P.M.
Rio Arriba Co.

	SCALE	1 in.=20 ft
DRAWN BY J. S. HAYDEN	REVISED	

Composite map showing archeological, geological topographical and vegetative features.

| DATE 8/74 | APPROVED BY | DRAWING NUMBER |

Approx. Elevation at reom No.1 = 8520±10'

RIDGE   Direction of slope

SPRING   Drainage

BOULDER FIELDS:
Broken vesicular lava

Broken slab or tabular type lava

TREES   SHRUBS

DULCE SPRINGS

107

the mountain structures with enough stone for only low walls may have had upper parts of wood or jacal.

We do not have evidence of any pottery having been produced here (no pottery-scraping or polishing tools were found), and the number of vessels hidden away in Site I and Site II assures us that the kitchen equipment of these families was scant. The people brought from home only the necessities required, cooking pots, water vessels, and bowls, almost all of undecorated ware. One would think they might have had a few vessels for storage, but no large jars were found. Those would have been very difficult to carry over a distance. (See discussion in chapter on pottery.) Baskets, which we know the Gallina people had, would have been much lighter than pottery and may have been of considerable importance, though lack of bone awls suggests that little if any basketry was made in the mountains. From the stone implements found, as we have shown, it is clear that the preparation of dried meat and hides for future use was of major concern.

The possibility of a forest fire having been responsible for the burning of which we have evidence in all the structures investigated in Sites I and II was raised again by the charred semirooted tree trunks on the surface of Structure II-14.

Our answer is that there must have been various forest fires in this area since the time of use by Gallina people. But the fact that there is evidence of burning in habitations located in the midst of the lava bed, where no trees would have been growing nearby, seems to substantiate the hypothesis of intentional ritual firing of houses or here in the forest the burning of roofs (though in the home area most beams were saved for re-use), when the camp finally was abandoned, as is explained by today's Pueblo peoples. Heavy ash, charcoal, and charred beams found in contact with house floors also point to structures being burned at the time of abandonment rather than later. Otherwise, there should have been a layer of soil deposited by wind, accidental washing, and roof decomposition found on top of the floor but beneath the charcoal, ash, and charred beams attributable to roof-burning by forest fire. We found no such sterile layer anywhere. There were no artifacts of any importance, such as pottery vessels and stone work other than flakes, points, and an occasional scraper or blade, left in the mountain houses. The people had totally moved out before the roofs were burned. Preparation for leaving included hiding in the nearby crevices and niches what vessels they could not conveniently carry. Stone tools such as axes were needed and taken with them. Metates and manos probably never were brought into this area in numbers. Some corn flour could have been among goods carried from home, as by the Jemez families who went to piñon camps in the historic period. But it seems likely that most of the foods eaten in the mountain camps were locally obtained, and, if we may guess from historic Jemez data, greatly relished.

IV

Dulce Springs Site III (LA 10642)

Our Site III at Dulce Springs is approximately wedge-shaped. The top consists of the front of a broken, vesicular basalt slope at the south edge of which is a much smaller but wider slope of broken tabular basalt. The parent vesicular lava had come angling in from the northwest, spreading as it flowed. The bed of broken tabular basalt curves around its south end like a ruffle. (See map 6.)

The entire archaeological site slopes downward and southward, the tabular basalt being rough but broken into smaller units and with far fewer great boulders and much smaller crevices than in Turkey Spring Sites I and II. At Dulce Springs everything but the man-made structures is on a smaller scale and less overwhelming than at Turkey Spring. The altitude of Structure III-1 (house: domicile) just below the front (lower edge) of the tabular basalt slope is 8520± 20 feet. On the northwest, the entire area is flanked by mixed conifer-aspen forest among which four structures were located, with two others nearby between the edge of the forest and the approximate edge of the ex-posed tabular basalt. A house and three caves, one of which held two vessels of Gallina Plain Utility ware, a canteen (L74.2.3), and a water jar (L74.2.2) with two rows of 3 lugs apiece, lay toward the southern end of the broken vesicular basalt slope. Most of the "houses" and caves in the mountain sites seem to have served as domiciles.

The survey in the area of broken tabular basalt where several clumps of scrub oak, chokecherry, and mountain mahogany shrubs now grow, located 7 circular structures, 5 semicircular structures built against cliffs, and 2 small caves. Just to the north of the eastern portion of that area in a patch of oak and rock spirea were 3 more circular structures. A few feet beyond the southern edge of the tabular basalt were 2 adjoining circular structures, and to the west of the basalt flow in mixed conifer-aspen forest were 4 more of similar shape. Two others lay between that forest edge and the edge of the tabular basalt.

The Dulce Springs, which supplied water for the village, lie in riparian vegetation directly opposite the most southern tongue of the lava.

The most intriguing feature of the site is the walkway (Structure III-4) of chinked and in some cases smoothed lava rock, easily traced and similar to, but more extensive than that of Turkey Spring Site II. Beginning at Structure III-14, a house toward the southern end of the vesicular basalt, the walkway quickly sprouted an extension to Structure III-13 (house) and then wound down to Structure III-8 (house) built against the lava cliff. (See Map 6 of Site III.) From Structure III-8, the pathway today leads through a con-siderable patch of shrub in its winding to Structures III-1 and 2 (houses) just within the southeastern limits of the exposed tabular basalt slope. Before reaching those houses, it passes, on its immediate edges, four stone platforms (Structures III-5 and 6) of single or several large stones with evenly smoothed tops. They looked to us as if they would have been most useful as drying platforms where plant foods, such as berries pressed into the little cakes Pueblo women stored away in the historic period, could have been laid out in the sun. Whatever their purpose, those smooth surfaces certainly give the impression of having seen appreciable use.

From Structures III-1 and III-2, the walkway leads up toward the northeast on a graded trail to Structure III-22, one of the houses built directly against the cliff forming the edge of the exposed vesicular basalt. The trail ends at the upper edge of the slope of tabular basalt which meets peripheral forest area where Structures III-24, 25, and 26 (all houses) had stood.

We found ourselves using the old pathway daily because it provided, by far, the easiest route through the broken lava. It obviously tied the eastern structures of this site — and presumably their occupants — into a unit. The six western structures, all outside the basalt area, and the two to the south of the basalt could be reached easily without a prepared pathway. One would simply skirt the flow. It seems probable that a short branch of the pathway once may have broken off in the region of the platform-like features to permit eastern-area water carriers to reach the Dulce Springs more easily. Were those "platforms" merely seats on which carriers could set down their vessels and rest? Perhaps. The problem of carrying heavy jars of water over rough and steep territory certainly was one good reason for construction of a walkway. We might add, incidentally, that as no habitations have existed within many miles of any of these sites in the historic period, the pathways cannot be attributed to historic man.

The second intriguing feature at Site III is a deer trap, approximately 480 feet northwest of the northern houses in this prehistoric village. The fissure basic to its construction must have been located on a recognized deer trail.

The entire Dulce Springs area and its archaeological features were mapped by Hayden, Perret, and Bain using a compass and steel tape. Hayden, who prepared the map showing 30 structures and functional structures including 4 small caves, warns that some locations may be slightly off as a result of local magnetic deviation. Our group's 1974 work, the excavation of 11 structures at Dulce Springs and 3 structures at Site IV near Red Hill, as well as the surveys, was intended to be a sampling, but it was further limited by the excessively stormy July weather of that year. Toward the end, access roads, ungraded and poor at best, were made slow to impassable by heavy mud. Rain and hail also cut into work time, and excavation of two structures at Site III was not quite completed because of water covering some floors on our last day.

The Eastern Half of Site III[*]

Structure III-1)

This feature at the eastern base of the tabular basalt flow at Dulce Springs proved to be the best example found of Gallina summer camp house construction where great lava boulders *in situ* were not available to serve as part of a wall. The walls of this house consisted entirely of dry-laid lava slabs carefully piled on top of each other with smaller wedges as chinking. Except for the structure being circular in overall exterior appearance, it would have been very much like those constructed by Gallina people living in the Llaves district. The walls measured 6 feet through at the base, as commonly found in the Llaves area, and one could guess that it must have been tapered as it rose. On the north side it still measured 49 inches above ground level, on the east side 34 inches, on the west 31 inches, and on the south 21 inches. The interior diameter of the room was 8.8 feet north-south and 9.2 feet east-west.

Level 1, the upper 6 inches of fill inside the house, consisted preponderantly of moist humus which held a few lava slabs fallen from the walls. There also were small bits of charcoal, 1 obsidian chip, 1 chert scraper blade, and 2 sherds, 1 of Gallina Plain Utility ware toward the east wall, and the other of Gallina Black-on-white toward the north.

In Level 2, we found many larger rocks, considerable charcoal, some chunks of red and ochre-colored burned adobe, probably from the roof, and a great many troublesome tree roots. A total of 34 sherds of Gallina Plain Utility and 12 of Gallina Black-on-white ware (10 from 1 or more bowls and 2 from 1 or more jars) came from near the north wall. In the southwest quadrant a fire area 18 inches across, with copious amounts of ash, was uncovered at the bottom of Level 2. There had been no pit, probably because of lava rock directly beneath the floor. A few stones and 1 quartzite flake came from the ash; 2 scrapers were uncovered nearby.

Level 3 reached a somewhat irregular floor at the fire area level. On the floor were found 12 obsidian flakes, a Gallina Plain Utility sherd, and 4 fragments of a burned bone awl.

The total of stone tools from this house runs high: 1 point-shaped asymmetrical obsidian knife, 1 obsidian flake used as a blade, 2 semicircular obsidian flakes and 1 semicircular chert flake used as knives, 1 thin oval flake retouched around the entire periphery, 2 obsidian lunate-burin blades, 1 obsidian knife (not lunate) with burin, 4 unshaped small flakes used as blades, and 4 obsidian Type 1 projectile points, 1 Type 2 obsidian point, 2 Type 3 obsidian points (1 possibly reworked), 1 Type 4 obsidian point (or knife), 1 Type 5 point, and 1 Type 7 obsidian point. There also were 3 obsidian endscrapers, 1 large chert scraper blade, and 12 flakes of debitage. The most unusual floor

---

[*]   Supervised and reported by Mary Lu Moore.

find was a well-polished piece of hard dark hematite approximately 1 inch long and over 1/2 inch across, possibly an item for ritual use.

Final clearing was prevented because the rainwater which rushed down the slope toward the end of our work accumulated over the floor and disappeared very slowly. However, no postholes, evidence for bins, or opening into the structure at ground level had been found before the rain.

Structure III-2

Structure III-2 was adjacent to the east side of the house just described. Excavation began with removal of a shrub and a fallen tree trunk. North-south the room measured 10 feet; east-west it measured 8 feet; from top of wall to fill surface was 16 inches.

Level 1 consisted of 6 inches of soft moist humus containing traces of charcoal and burned wood.

Level 2 held some decayed wood as well as intrusive fist-sized rocks fallen from the disintegrating dry-laid outer wall. A number of large roots slowed methodical digging. Remnants of what apparently was the heating area, with a quantity of ash but no pit, was uncovered in the northwest quadrant, together with fire-blackened and reddened rocks and more charcoal. Beneath it was a thin and narrow lens of clay, not large enough to be considered a floor. Near the fire area was 1 burned bone and a tiny obsidian flake. A little farther away but on the same level were a small obsidian knife possibly reworked from a broken projectile point, a gray obsidian knife, 3 lunate-burin blades of obsidian, 2 obsidian small flakes used as blades, 1 quartzite scraper, and the fragment of a large obsidian point.

Again rains interfered with completion of excavation, but we had reached floor level. As in Structure III-1, there was no evidence of a ground-level entrance or of postholes for roof supports, and well-spread charcoal at floor level suggested roof-burning at time of abandonment. Presence of a fire area and of projectile points would seem to indicate use of this structure, like that of its close neighbors, for living rather than for storage.

Structure III-3

At a distance of about 8 feet to the north-northwest of Structure III-1 was a small roughly oval room against a cliff. To provide floor space, lava boulders had been removed to leave an approximately level lava base. Earth then was brought in and tamped for the floor. From the top of the dry-laid lava-chunk wall to the fill surface was 6 feet. Width of the wall was 3.7 feet. From north to south the room measured 7 feet; from east to west 10 feet.

In the 6-inch layer of humus above the floor were small pieces of charcoal and traces of clay which probably had come from the roof. Screening produced 5 flakes of quartzite and obsidian, 1 of which had been used as a blade. A very fine obsidian knife designed to be hafted (7.5 x 3 cm), 2 obsidian projectile points of Type 1 (so similar one felt sure they had been made by the same worker), and 1 chopper made from a white quartzite cobble were found on the floor. There was no sign of a fire area, ash, a ground-level entrance, or roof support pits.

Whether one should think of this structure as a storeroom or as an extra sleeping or workroom for persons associated with the family occupying Structure III-1 is a question.

Structure III-22

This structure (Figure 25), located against the cliff at the top of the flow of tabular basalt, would have commanded a clear view over the entire village except for those houses among forest trees west of the lava, and it is possible that all nearby trees at time of occupation had been cut for roof material. The structure first attracted attention because of large amounts of black ash visible through the present ground cover of leaves and needles.

The walls consisted of big lava boulders at three points between which lava slab walls were piled. This produced a polygon-shaped room of 8.8 feet north-south and 7.2 feet east-west. Three sherds of Gallina Plain Utility ware and 2 small obsidian flakes lay on the surface. A small cave extended beneath a layer of flat rocks at the north end, but it contained only several small chunks of red ochre (or burned clay?) and a piece of slightly charred wood.

Rain and hail cut one day's work short and with heavy rain on the following day no one could reach the site. When excavation began, a great deal of black ash, much charcoal, and bits of red ochre (?) were found throughout Levels 1 and 2 (each 6 inches deep), especially near and even between the wall slabs. Flat rocks covered the floor area. One large triangular obsidian blade (4.5x3 cm with a vaguely defined lunate area and a sharp little burin beak on one end), 2 obsidian large non-shaped flake blades, 1 Type 2 point, 2 Type 7 points, 2 obsidian point fragments, 5 obsidian and 1 quartzite non-shaped small flakes used as blades, 57 flakes of obsidian debitage, and 5 more sherds like those from the surface were retrieved. There was no evidence of a fire place or heating pit as such, or of postholes or entryway at ground level.

One may wonder whether this enclosure could have been a spot where watchmen were posted and large fires or smokes produced on a soil-covered roof for signaling. Could such procedures have anything to do with the large amounts of black ash and charcoal found at and near the surface, which might represent the top of the fallen flat roof? As an observation post, its location was perfect, but we had no chance to check whether a signal from here would have been visible in the other villages. The lithics could have pertained to watchmen on duty who lived or at least spent long hours here but not in boring nonactivity.

A Gallina Black-on-white bowl (L74.2.4) of the size for serving a meal to a relatively small group was found hidden in Structure 23, a small cave only a few feet south of

Turkey Spring II, Alley 5
Feature II-49: House

FEATURE II-49 TABLES AND DIAGRAMS

FEATURE 49 MEASUREMENTS

Materials Recovered

Diameters:
Length N-S 144"
Width E-W 131"
Long axis 30°E 210°W

2 Obsidian lithics
10 Quartzite specimens unworked

Wall Heights:
N 12"
S 14"
E 24"
W 19"

Wall or Rubble Thickness:
N 21"
S 28"
W 37"
SW 58"
E & NE Basalt flow

Fill and Test Trench Profiles:

] = 6"

▤ forest debris 1-4"
⋯ brownsoil 6"
▥ floor 7"
▦ sub-floor soil 8"
//// basalt rock

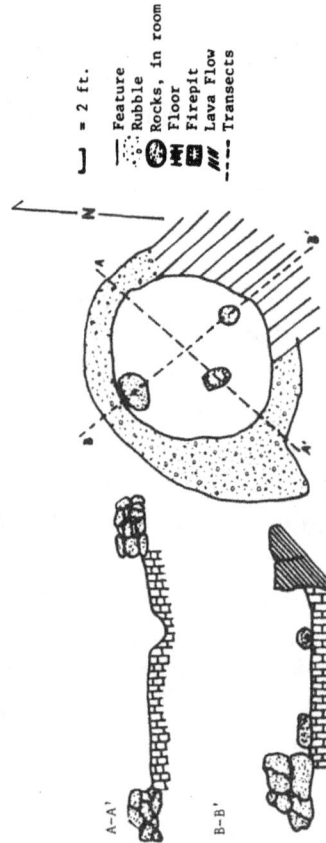

Firepit Measurements:
Length (E-W axis) 14-1/2"
Width   10"
Depth   5"

Basalt Rocks in Feature 49:
West Rock (next to wall)
Length (N-S) 26"
Width   17"
Height above floor 9"

East Rock (20" from E wall)
Length 11"
Width 11"
Height above floor 7"

Dulce Springs

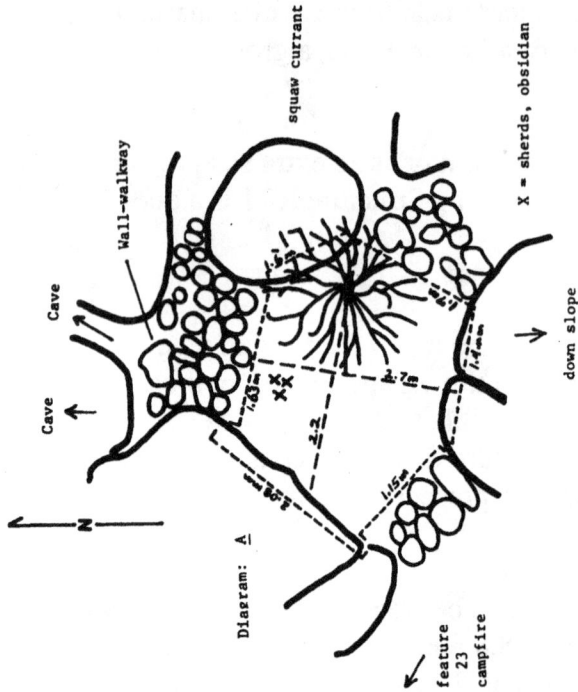

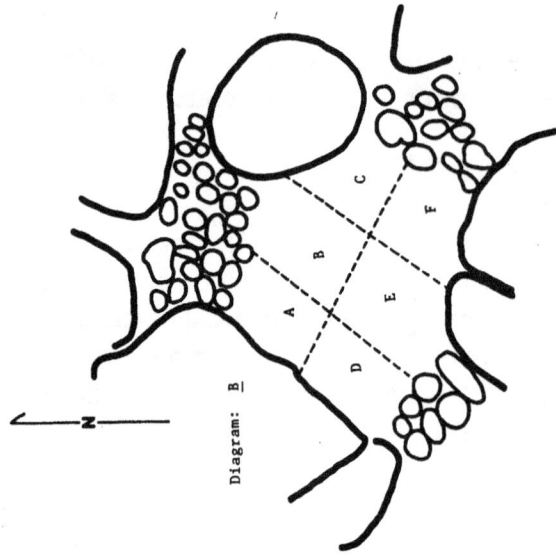

Diagram: A

Wall-walkway

Cave
Cave
Cave

squaw currant

X = sherds, obsidian

down slope

feature 23 campfire

Diagram: B

A B C
D E F

Feature III-22: polygon house of boulders and rock walls

Figure 25

] = 2 ft.

⋯ Feature
◉ Rubble
● Rocks, in room
▦ Floor
▣ Firepit
/// Lava Flow
--- Transects

A-A'

B-B'

Figure 24

114

Structure 22. From another small cave, a short distance west of Structure 22 and north of Structure 23, came an unusual implement which may have served either as a big scraper or as a saw. This began as a natural spall of basalt, 14 cm long and 7 cm across, with a flat triangular cross section. The long edges had been serrated with rather large irregular notches.

Such finds neither add to nor subtract from the hypothesis that Structure 22 could have been a watch and signal station, for the original floors of big towers known for the home Gallina sites in the general Llaves area show the interior built-in furnishings (fire pit, deflector, ventilator shaft, bins protruding from walls) expectable in a domicile. Unless we erase this data from consideration, we must suppose that two to three men lived in the base of such a tower to which they were assigned (according to our hypothesis) as watchmen-signalmen. The remodeling of such towers into storage facilities would have come after the original floor had been covered over, when a new tower was being used or the signal system was given up (see earlier discussion of this study).

Structure III-30

Halfway between Structures 14 and 22 was a narrow cave (Structure 30) with nooks and crannies opening off it in all directions. Each, of course, was explored. The finds were few but interesting: 6 widely scattered bones, rib, jaw, pelvis, tibia, and humerus, apparently all from deer. In the surface debris were 1 rose and white chert semicircular knife with lunate burin features, 1 pink chert side- and end-scraper, 3 unworked flakes (1 of chert and 2 of obsidian), and the long skinning pry-knife (24.5 x 6.5 cm and 2 cm through at the thickest point).

This "knife," originally a tooth-like piece of dark-gray flow basalt oxidized to a brownish shade, duplicates the shape of wooden paddles with sharpened tip made by Rio Grande Pueblo men within this century to use while cutting and pulling the skin away from a deer's carcass. Our basalt specimen had been given an irregular but sharpened outline by knocking off some wide flakes from both edges and the point. The wear on all edges for the foremost 13 cm indicates long use of this practical tool.

A partly charred log 6 inches long was taken from the cave for tree-ring study but like all the other wood from the mountain sites was found to be too complacent for dating. No sherds were present.

The small cave, we would surmise, was a place for working on hides and meat and for temporary storage.

The Western Half of Site III

Structure III-8

This semicircular structure with piled rock walls 2-3 feet high, measured 11 feet north-south by 12 feet east-west. It stood at the base of a cliff at the south end of the basalt ridge with the northern 3 feet of the room under an overhang. There was no evidence of a surface-level entryway or of postholes. Removal of 2 feet of loose rockfall from the walls brought us to a "bottom" of large flat rocks, but if there ever had been a clay floor, it had washed away.

On the southeast, a low curved wall extended out into the room from the main wall, and as charcoal was found within this small circle, it may have been a fire place or, more probably, a heating area. The very similar room, Structure III-7, adjoining domicile III-8 to the east, was not excavated.

Structure III-10

Structure III-10 was a roughly circular room 35 feet southwest of Structure III-8, about halfway down a broken tabular basalt talus slope from base of the basalt cliff. The walls of dry-laid masonry stood about 2.5 to 3 feet high; north-south measurement was 13 feet; east-west measurement was 11 feet. The fill consisted of soil and large rocks. Brush grew in the northeastern quarter.

No ground-level entrance opening was found and no actual floor or heating area remained. Five large and 78 small sherds were found in soft soil in the southeastern sector at depths of 6 inches to 2 feet. All were of Gallina Plain Utility ware and appear to represent two or possibly more vessels. As the lithic material (1 possible thick scraper of basalt, 1 long chert core possibly used as a scraper, 1 thin obsidian scraper, and 3 non-shaped small obsidian flakes used as blades) and a small amount of charcoal were found largely in crevices between rocks, it is possible that other items had been washed away. The sherds and lithic materials point to this structure originally having been a domicile.

Structure III-11 immediately adjoining it to the east was not investigated nor was Structure III-12 on its west side. A Gallina Plain Utility cook pot, with flat bottom and pinched decoration on the fillet a short distance below the rim, was found hidden near Structure III-11. Most of one side of this vessel was missing.

Structure III-13

Structure III-13 appears to have been a domicile in which construction used basalt boulders *in situ* with connecting dry-laid walls of small lava rocks. It lay about 40 feet west of Structure 8 among large basalt boulders on the west slope of the site. The walls, 3 feet and higher, enclosed an irregularly circular area 10.1 feet north-south and 9 feet east-west. There was no evidence of doorway openings, postholes, or a laid floor. Flat lava rocks made a base below the fill. Charcoal was scattered randomly through the bottom of the fill material, but more was concentrated toward the south wall. Three pieces of burned bone, 1 thin chert "arrowshaft tool," 1 jasper side-scraper, and 1 small non-shaped flake of chert used as a blade were the only artifacts found.

Structure III-14

This was another house, probably a domicile. It lay 55 feet north of Structure III-8 among large basalt boulders near the top of the west slope of Site III. In shape it can best be described as an oval polygon, utilizing large boulders *in situ* as far as possible. Two gaps between boulders were filled with dry-laid stone walls. A small cave led out from the north end of the east wall. The stone walls stood 3 feet or more high. The boulders, ranging from 6 to 8 feet high, provide us with some concept of original roof height. No laid floor was found; room dimensions were 15 feet north-south and 11 feet east-west.

Artifacts recovered from the fill consisted of 1 large side-notched obsidian knife intended to be hafted, 5 obsidian and 2 white chert nonshaped blades, 4 obsidian burin-blades, 19 small flakes used as blades, 1 small side-notched white chert Type 2 point, 1 very similar obsidian Type 2 point, 1 well-made Type 1 variant serrated side-notched point with a bifurcated base and flaring barbs, 2 broken Type 3 obsidian points, 1 of which may have been reworked for use as a scraper, 1 point of Type 6, 1 small obsidian snubnosed scraper, 19 unworked obsidian flakes used as knives or scrapers, and 7 flakes of obsidian debitage. Thirteen animal bone fragments, the jawbone, and 1 molar tooth of an animal were found. Close to the base of the more southern of the two boulders which formed the east side of the structure lay a charred log 62 inches long and 7 inches in diameter, possibly one member of the original roof. It was not datable.

Structure III-15

This was a semicircular room of tumbled, dry-laid tabular basalt, built against the edge of a cliff of the same basalt about 15 feet east-southeast of Structure III-8. The room measured 11 feet north-south and 12 feet east-west. The walls stood only about 13 inches high. Beneath the fill of humus, pine needles, leaves, and soft soil was some scanty evidence of a floor. In the fill were many animal bone fragments but only 3 pieces of charcoal and 1 triangular obsidian-flake scraper. As there was no evidence of a heating area or of other additions and so little sign of activity within these walls, this may have been a storage room.

The Animal Trap

By far the most curious feature of Site III was what appears to have been an animal trap, probably for deer. It lay in the woods at the top of the ridge approximately 100 yards to the north-northwest of the main part of the site. The trap consisted of a long trench (see Map 6), its walls being those of a natural fissure about 37 inches wide in the lava rock, with a dry-laid stone wall 41 inches long closing the trench at the western end and a large boulder, 31 inches across, set into the trench near its center to provide an east end. This left an open trench 10.2 feet long. From the boulder placed as an eastern terminal the fissure gradually sloped upward for 8.5 feet to ground level. That section originally may have been filled to the surface. The depth of the "trap" trench at the west end was 3 feet. When found, it was partly packed full of needles, leaves, and soft soil, but contained a few charcoal bits. These presumably had resulted from some of the forest fires known to have burned sections of this mountain area.

A long narrow pit of this type had been described to me by living Pueblo elders as their old-type deer trap, customarily dug into the soil or volcanic tuff and, if possible, across a deer trail. The trap was intended to be little longer or wider than the animal. A sharpened stake usually was set upright in the floor. The top of the trap was covered with light poles, soil, and needles or leaves which would serve as camouflage but give way under the weight of an animal. The creature, in falling, immediately was impaled on the stake. Hewett (1906:22) describes a related structure on the Pajarito Plateau used by men of San Ildefonso Pueblo.

We cannot prove that our deer trap was constructed or used by the Gallina people of the Dulce Springs site, for there is no question but that other peoples also came to this mountain for hunting and gathering at various times. One immediate piece of evidence for this was the single sherd of red-and-black-on-orange Gobernador Polychrome found in a small crevice 20 feet southwest of what was to be designated Bain's House, Structure III-13. This pottery is well known as having originated in the early 18th century when numbers of the Pueblo people left the Rio Grande, and even some of the Pueblo villages farther to the west, to join the Navajo as refugees. They had recently (1680) driven the Spaniards out of New Mexico, but the latter returned in 1692, and disruption of Pueblo life, even through the first ten years of the 1700s, was drastic. Some of the Navajo, who themselves, as far as we have evidence, had not reached New Mexico until very shortly before the first Spanish incursion, were living in the Gobernador Canyon area at least by the early 1700s. The Gobernador is only about 35 miles across country from the Dulce Springs site. There is evidence, we believe, in the series known as AR sites on Ghost Ranch (where we did several excavations in 1977) that a group of the Pueblo refugees brought the sheep they had aquired from the Spaniards and lived here for several years. Curt Schaafsma of the Laboratory of Anthropology in Santa Fe, who had conducted some AR excavations slightly earlier, felt that the inhabitants might have been Navajo of that period. Regardless of who built the AR structures, it is probable that Navajo and Pueblo refugees came into contact here, as in the Gobernador. Everyone agrees that the Navajo learned a great deal from the Pueblos of what later would become characteristic patterns in Navajo culture, though in modified form, including the making of painted pottery.

Our sherd of Gobernador Polychrome could have come from a vessel carried into the Dulce Springs area by Navajos and broken while they were involved in mountain hunting or gathering, or it may have been lost by Pueblo refugees, the first to produce this ware. We can say only that its presence strongly suggests that one or the other visited this site in the early 18th century, more than 400 years after the Gallina people had left for the last time.

Summary of Site III, Dulce Springs

Again we are struck with the fact that many of the people who came to spend summers hunting and gathering in these mountain sites deliberately elected to live on the lava. Why? We already have noted the important matter that heat absorbed by the black lava during sunny days would have been felt even at night, a point of comfort. Our further surmise is that two major points were ease and speed of building. The people obviously cared little about whether the camp house was polygonal or circular in shape if they could manage its construction by filling spaces between boulders with walls quickly laid up of the basalt slabs readily at hand. Clay was not so easily available and our guess is that many houses never had other than a relatively level floor of the lava itself. That, of course, would eliminate fire pits. One could have a heating place or area, with or without an encirclement of stones for coals brought in from a cooking hearth outside. Roofs carried much less of a clay or soil topping than at home, if we may judge from the shallow fill in every house, though the presence of some small lumps of clay in fill material seems to testify to at least a thin clay cover in some instances.

There is no evidence of bins in these houses. They would have been little needed by seasonal occupants. The finding of only one broken metate and two manos in all of the four mountain sites is reason enough to conclude that the diet of these summer campers concentrated primarily on locally available wild foods which did not require grinding. Trash or ash deposits are few and small even in the Gallina home villages and we have none for the mountain area. Whatever existed has been totally washed away. We know that the people boiled much of their food because the cook pot, like the water jar, was ever present. But on the matter of proportion of meat to vegetable food we have no data. Paucity of bones in the mountain villages probably results from the open nature of the sites, for the number of projectile points, blades, and scrapers is ample evidence of successful hunting.

One is tempted to try to make something out of the grouping of structures, including probable storerooms. The several groups at Site III could represent related families or close friends as in historic pueblos, but one has no basis on which to be more specific. The walkway ties six structures together, all of which appear to have been domiciles. The three others beyond the northeastern corner of the tabular basalt flow, also hypothetically domiciles, were but a few feet across soft soil from the trail's end. Other structures in the eastern section of the site give the impression of having been for storage, but without excavation any conclusion becomes guesswork. The six structures west of the lava may have been built after all the best lava sites had been appropriated.

Whether the unnumbered and unexcavated northwestern outlier, 12 feet in diameter and hence probably a domicile, carried any special function such as association with the deer trap 180 feet distant, we do not even guess.

Lack of evidence of any ground-level entryways and of floor postholes into which roof supports would have been placed checks similar negative data from the Turkey Spring

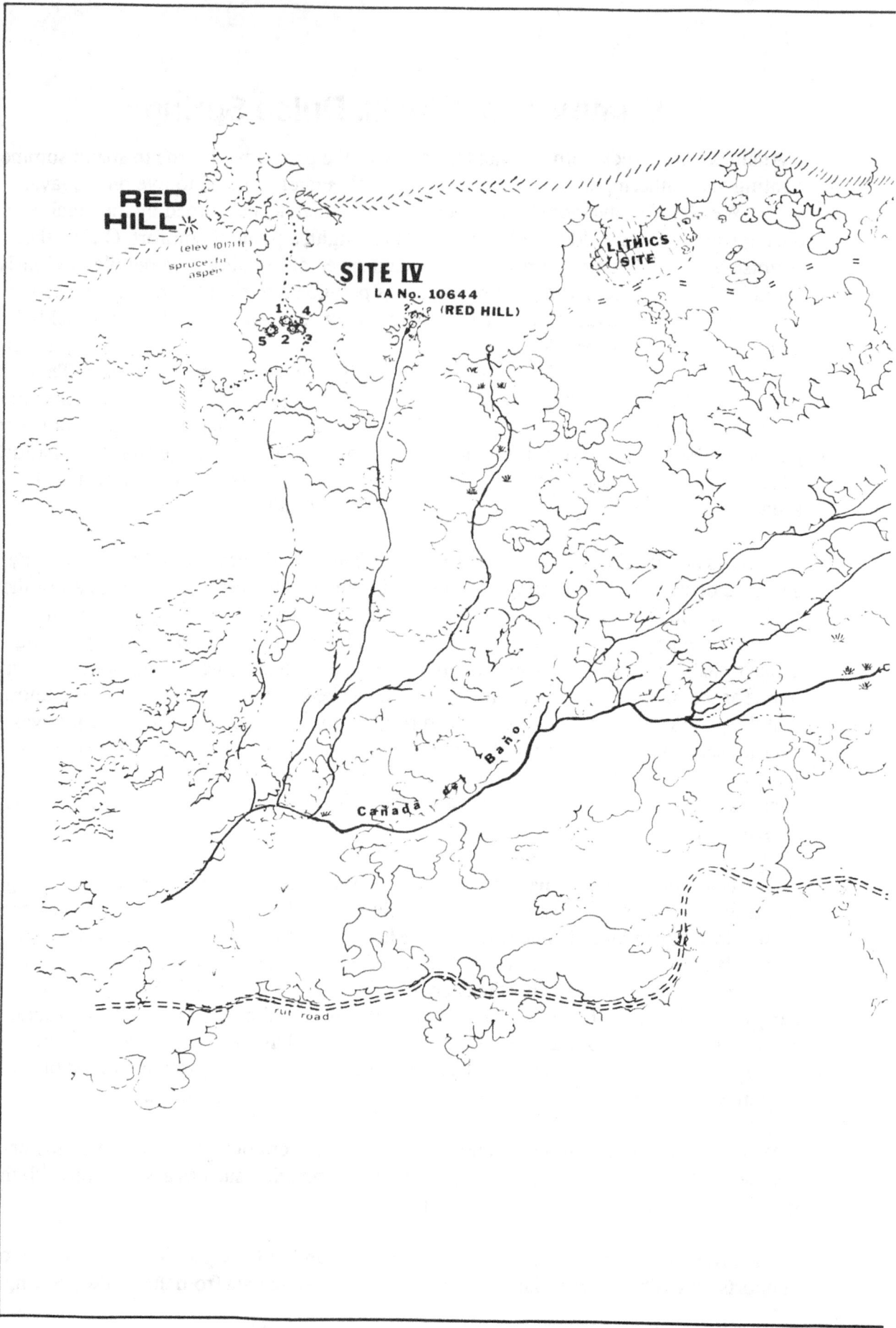

RED HILL
(elev 10171 ft)
spruce-fir
aspen

SITE IV
LA No. 10644
(RED HILL)

LITHICS
SITE

1   4
5 2   3

Cañada del Baño

rut road

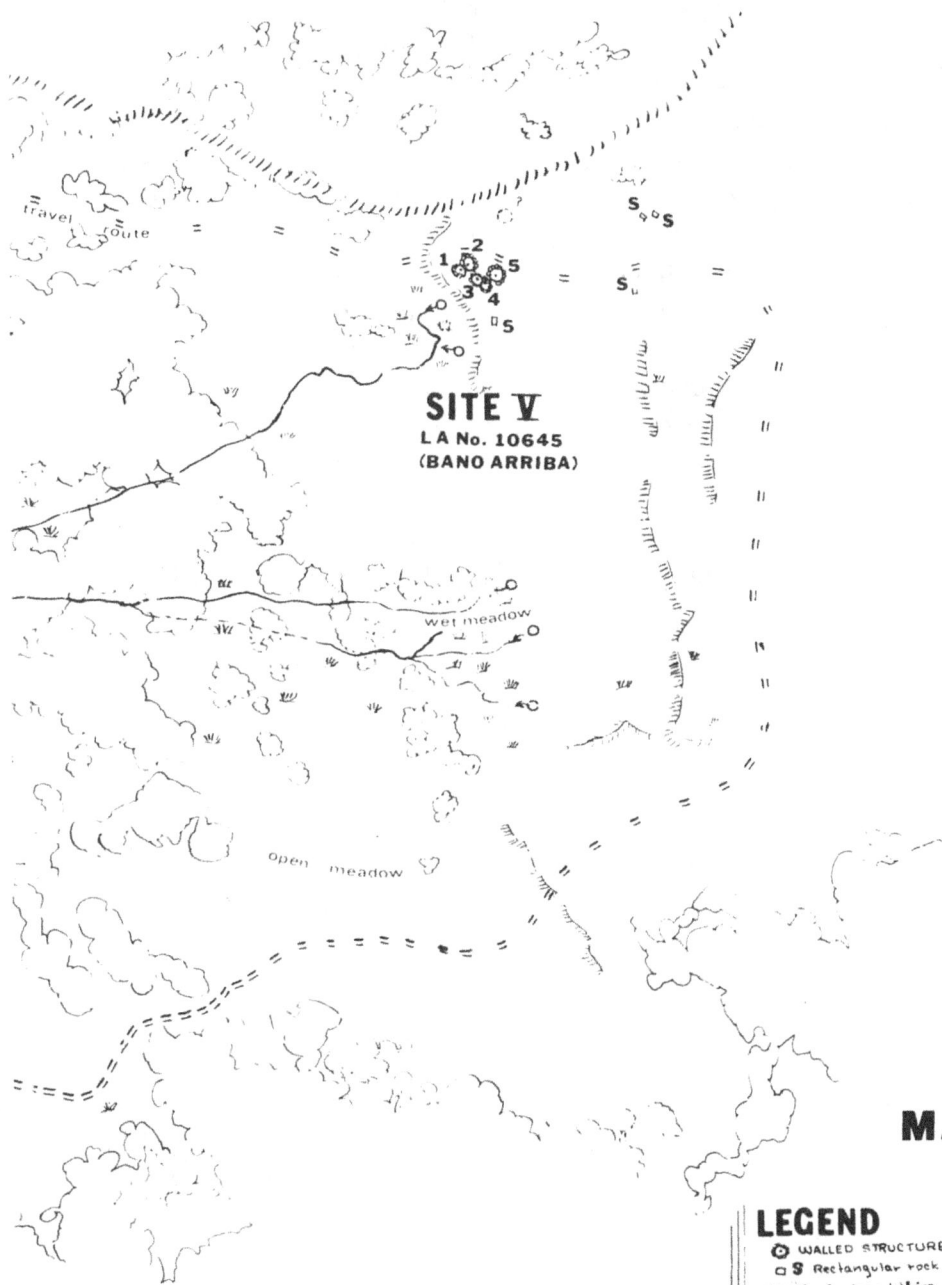

SITE V
LA No. 10645
(BANO ARRIBA)

travel route

S o o S

S

wet meadow

open meadow

MAP 7

LEGEND

- ⊚ WALLED STRUCTURES
- □ S Rectangular rock arrangements
- Surface lithics
- ◔ SPRING ── WET MEADOW
- Live Stream ─ ─ Intermittent Stream
- (((((RIDGE))))) RIM or Steep slope (break)
- ✳ HILL ••• Extent of volcanic surface rock
- Timbered Areas ==== Rut Road = = Travel Route

TURKEY SPRING ARCHEOLOGICAL AREA				
Site IV RED HILL		Site V BANO ARRIBA		
Site IV	NW₄ NW₄ SE₄ Sec 14 T27N R5E	SCALE	DRAWN BY J. S. HAYDEN	
Site V	SE4 SW4 Sec 13 " "	1in = 370ft approx	REVISED	
	DATE 11/74	APPROVED BY		DRAWING NUMBER

121

sites. Even the domicile, Structure III-1, undoubtedly built by one of the most conservative of the Dulce Springs families, shows its Gallina background only in the 6-foot thickness of the roughly laid walls at their base, as was common at home. The mountain dwellings must have had roofs which rested on the walls and were pierced by a small hatchway for entrance by ladder. There is no evidence of a ventilator opening through or within any wall, so we may conclude that sufficient ventilation to keep the little indoor smoke rising toward the hatchway-smokehole was expected to filter through the loosely constructed walls. A corollary to this comment is that we do not have actual evidence of fires having been used inside these houses. If occupation was limited to summer, as is quite certain because of the extreme cold of these elevated mountain slopes in winter, and if construction obviously was not planned to conserve heat, the warmth held and reflected by the lava of which the houses were built and surrounded may have largely handled the small heating problem except in brief periods of storms. A shallow heating pit or "place" where a few coals brought in from outside could be laid would have made these houses comfortable without a clay or slab-lined fire pit.

That our campers were Gallina people continues to be proven by the shapes of their projectile points and, most of all, by Gallina pottery left as sherds and as vessels hidden by housewives who decided not to add that extra bulk and appreciable weight to the toilsome homeward journey.

V

Red Hill, Site IV (LA 10644), and Baño Arriba, Site V (LA 10645)

Red Hill, our Site IV, is located in the northwest quarter of the southeast quarter of Section 14, T27, N. Range, 5E NMPM, in Rio Arriba County, New Mexico. Its altitude of 10,000 feet, only 171 feet less than that of the "recent" cinder cone of Red Hill itself, places it in a special category. Very few archaeological sites at such an elevation are known for the Southwest. Red Hill was the source of the lava flow which extends 3.5 miles in a west-southwest direction down to where we find the two Turkey Spring sites constructed in the scree. Much of the high area is patchily forested, with some interspersed meadows of moderate dryness but more which are wet, and a number of source springs at the upper end of the many tributaries of the Cañada del Baño.

Site V, located very near the two headwater source springs at the upper end of long Baño Canyon, lies one mile or slightly more to the east of Site IV.

Site IV, Red Hill (LA 10644)

The campsite at Red Hill is on the Lewis Formation, in an opening in aspen, spruce, and fir growth south and a little east of the lava flow which had left a field of red cinder rock from 50 to 200 feet wide. An intermittent stream which runs from slightly south of the camp to where it joins Cañada Baño may have provided water at times. The permanent spring at the head of the next watercourse to the east still is a dependable source, and a third spring lies at the head of another permanent water course only slightly farther eastward. This area is reminiscent of that around Mt. Redondo near the southern end of the Jemez Mountains, where today every headwater spring is sacred to the people of Jemez and Zia Pueblos.

The wall outlines of the four and possibly five circular structures of Site IV all projected from 1 to 2 feet above the present ground surface. As there were no boulders *in situ*, construction necessarily had been entirely of cinder rock picked up from the flow. There was no evidence in any one of these structures of a ground-level entrance or of mud mortar between stones which formed the walls.

After a preliminary survey it was decided to excavate the three structures spaced in a triangle across a shallow depression from the foot of the Red Hill cone.

Structure IV-1[*]

The center of Structure IV-1, apparently a domicile, lay on a line slightly north of east, 68 feet from the center of Structure IV-3, largest of the rings. North-south and east-west mid-wall to mid-wall measurements at the top of remaining walls for House IV-1 were each 12 feet. The fill, as in all the houses, was overgrown with heavy grass and aspen saplings. At all levels it contained bits of charcoal and the rock that had fallen from the walls. Floor level was found 31 inches below the present surface. The floor was uneven and saucer-shaped; it could be defined only by the difference in soil color. The only interior "built-in" was a crude U-shaped storage bin with walls of small rocks laid up without mortar. Its depth was 15 inches, which brought its wall height to 15.5 inches below the present surface. The top opening to the bin measured 7.5 x 11 inches, but at the bottom its floor widened to about 12 x 18 inches. A slab fallen partially inside the bin could have served as a cover but more probably merely had slipped down from the wall.

Beneath a rock near the west wall a concentration of seeds was found in an area of 4 x 6 inches. Most of them were identified by Mollie Streuver of the Castetter Laboratory for Ethnobotanical Studies at the University of New Mexico (May 14, 1976) as "Polygonum sp., three-faceted and of shiny mottled brown color. They ranged from 2.1-3.9 mm long and 1.0-1.9 mm wide for a single facet". Although they gave the appearance of having been spilled from a container, it is possible that the seeds had been brought in by rodents. Polygonum bistortoides (American Bistort, Western Bistort), a species common in wet mountain meadows at elevations of 8,500 to 11,000 feet, shows the most similarity to the seeds found in House IV-1.

A lesser number of seeds, fragmented and difficult to identify, from the cache in House IV-1 were tentatively placed as of Scirpus type. They are two-faceted and average about 4 mm long and from 1 to 2 mm in width. The Scirpus or Bulrush also is a wet-area plant. It is known to have been used as food, the young and crisp shoots consumed as they are, the seeds made into meal, and the fleshy fibrous rootstalks peeled and eaten raw or cooked. Some Indians used the tough fibrous leaves as material for matting (Harrington 1976:195-198).

Structure IV-2[**]

This house lay 34 feet west of House IV-3. It was circular, measuring roughly 15 feet in diameter, mid-wall to mid-wall at surface level. The stone walls were like those of House IV-1 in composition and type. Charcoal bits were scattered through the 29 inches of fill above the rough saucer-shaped floor. Its only "built-in" feature was a storage bin against the east wall, just as in House IV-1. (Dimensions of this bin most unfortunately

---

[*]   Supervised and reported by Frances R. Kenney.

[**] Supervised and reported by Frances R. Kenney and William Perret.

were lost; its size was close to that of the other bin.) Except for this house being slightly larger than House IV-1, the two could be said to duplicate each other.

A quartz crushing stone (9.9 x 9.0 cm), with a 4 x 4 cm very smooth end and two surfaces possibly somewhat used, was found 12 inches below ground surface in this house.

Structure IV-3*

This was the largest of the rock-ring structures near Red Hill. It lies 24 feet northeast of House IV-2 and 68 feet east of House IV-1. Before excavation, the evidence for this structure consisted of an almost circular ring of water-washed cobbles and cobble- to boulder-size blocks of red cindery lava which stood 1-2 feet above the surrounding terrain. Computations made on the basis of rockfall scattered out from the remaining wall indicated that the original height was 5 feet or slightly more.

The walls, like those of the other structures, consisted of rocks of random sizes piled in place without thought of coursing or chinking. The fill surface, 25.5 inches below datum, included more rocks scattered in a matrix of washed-in silt and clay. These rocks ranged in size and included chunks brought from the nearby Red Hill lava flow. The north-south diameter of House IV-3, taken from estimated wall centers, was 17 feet; the corresponding east-west diameter was 18 feet.

Several small aspens up to 2 inches in diameter grew in the fill near the north wall and were removed before excavation could begin. Loose surface rocks also were removed and a shallow north-south trench 3-4 inches deep and 2 feet wide was excavated across the center as a test. At 2 feet below fill surface small rocks and bits of charcoal roughly .25 inches across were distributed randomly through the soil. A possible hammerstone (little used if at all) was found close to the surface near the south wall. Near the north wall the trench was deepened to 41 inches below datum (15.5 inches below surface) to remove an ants' nest and the aspen stump. About 1 foot out from the wall, and 40.5 inches below datum (15 inches below fill surface), was a 5-inch piece of splintered lava covered with fine ash and charcoal. This suggested that a fire hearth or heating pit might be present. The area was refilled for protection, to be excavated on the morrow.

Heavy rain the next day prevented our reaching any of the mountain sites and left the end of the trench above the possible fire pit full of water and soupy mud, so this area was not disturbed when we resumed work on the third day. Excavation was altered from trenching to uniform lowering of the interior fill. Several large blocks of lava, including one 15 inches across which presumably had fallen from the walls, were removed. One lava boulder more than 2 feet across and extending well below levels reached in this excavation was not disturbed.

Digging continued down to a tentative "floor" 36 inches below datum (10.5 inches below the original fill surface). At this level, the north-south diameter, wall to wall, was

---

*   Supervised and reported by William Perret.

125

10.7 feet and the corresponding east-west diameter, 9.9 feet. Neither lithic nor pottery artifacts were found.

Throughout the excavated area small pieces of charcoal were encountered in wholly random distribution both horizontally and vertically. During the trenching the upper end of a log without bark and without present evidence of charring was found 27 inches below datum (1.5 inches below fill surface), resting against the inside south wall. It sloped westward at an angle of 20 degrees to a maximum depth of 44 inches below datum (18.5 inches below fill surface) at its western end. At its upper end the log was 7 inches in diameter; its lower end included a branched fork. It was taken for tree-ring study but the growth record was too short and complacent to permit dating. The fact that depth of the lower end of this log was very close to that at which the possible evidence of a fire hearth or heating pit had been found suggests that the log belonged to the period of house use, possibly as one element of the roof.

Work was terminated perforce by the end of the excavation program for 1974 and included partial refilling of this structure. There is no question that it should be totally uncovered at some later date.

A rectangular pile of water-worn quartzite cobbles measuring 3 x 9 feet lay to the northeast of the house circles of Site IV and, with the thought that it could have been a grave, a shrine, or even the covering of a cache, we put a trench 2 feet deep across it. At that depth, the disruption of a great anthill made further work impractical for the little excavation time remaining, but our trench definitely was sterile. It seems that the slump and flow action on the unconsolidated conglomerate of the Lewis Formation may have been responsible for this ridge and for others of similar appearance on the terraces between Site V and Canjilon Peak.

Site V, Baño Arriba (LA 10645)[*]

Site V consists of the remains of one rectangular and five circular structures, with three more rectangular rock arrangements a short distance farther to the east on the slope of Canjilon Peak and another possible circular structure to the north. These ruins are just above the rim of a short west-facing volcanic slope. Because of time limitations no excavations were made at Site V. One wonders about these rectangular platforms. Were they places for drying meat or plant items? Could they have been shrines? Were the circular structures shrines, as we are inclined to surmise?

Approximately halfway between the two sites but a little closer to Site IV is a lithics chipping station measuring 455 feet east-west and including some forested but more open area below (south of) the long south-facing lava rim. Surface samples show gray obsidian from Polvadera Mountain, glassy obsidian from the Jemez, and chalcedony from the Pedernal (identification by Helene Warren), but the small amount of debitage implies that no great amount of knapping ever was done here. Presumably the labor represents

---

[*]   Reported by William Perret.

reworking and replacement of points during a hunting season, and from the debris we know that the hunters carried with them a supply of their favorite raw materials. Considering the distances covered on foot, that extra weight certainly indicates strong selective preferences in minerals.

Summary of Sites IV and V

The structures, if we may judge from our small collection of data from Sites IV and V in the Red Hill area, were houses or shelters rather than storerooms. The two in each of which a small interior storage bin had been constructed against the east wall give the impression that food was being set out of the way of persons using the room. Lack of evidence of a fire hearth in those houses would have us believe that food was being cooked out of doors. Lack of any vessels or potsherds brings the suggestion that women may not have been present, and that when food was cooked it was roasted instead of boiled, but it is also possible that vessels were brought and eventually carried homeward or hidden at a little distance from camp.

The Pueblo men of the historic period constructed simple camps when they expected to be out in the mountains for several days. Before the recent years when camper-tops for pickups became available, the chill and general discomfort to be expected from mountain storms made shelter construction highly advisable, and what was built could be reused over a period of years. The men carried supplies of food, but cooking was no more elaborate than necessary. The women of a family were expected to provide their men with small cornhusk-wrapped tamale-like packets which contained sustaining food of a cornmeal base flavored with herbs, whether their trip was for hunting or for warfare. Thinly sliced dried meat weighed little. An even simpler food was corn flour (or cornmeal) carried dry and eaten mixed with a small amount of water. Fresh meat, when obtained, of course provided further nutrition. The primary need for a fire at 10,000 feet would be to provide warmth. Carrying vessels and foods certainly was reduced to a minimum. A hike of 3.5 miles up the lava flow from the Turkey Spring sites would not have been hard, even though the terrain was rough. We know that at least two types of seed food were available from the wet meadows near Red Hill, whether the small hoard we found in House IV-1 actually was carried in by man or rodents. We also know that edible fresh shoots from the same plants were valued and that other vegetable foods were available. (See Hayden's list in Chapter 1.)

But were the men who used these high-altitude hunting lodges of Gallina culture? This we cannot say positively because we lack any evidence of distinctive pottery; the total collection of artifacts from the Red Hill area is not large. There was a crushing stone with small grinding surface and the possible hammerstone. A large Type 1 obsidian point (Figure 35) which may have been hafted as a knife was found on the south slope of Red Hill. A fine obsidian triangular knife with burin, much like one from Bain's Cave but smaller, also came from this surface. There was 1 basalt chip from the edge of a house, half of a small Type 1 obsidian point from the forested area northwest of House IV-1, and the central portion of a serrated obsidian point from west of Site V. Near the bottom of the drainage area, a fragment from a fine chert point was found on an upper terrace near the "possible shrine" above Site V. A thick red and white circular knife (Figure 31c) came from the brow of the lower terrace, far from any habitations and between the two sites. From the chipping station we had 1 obsidian scraper and 1 chalcedony knife with burin. As far as one can determine, the points appear to have been of Gallina types, but they were not directly associated with the structures. The other stone items are not distinctive of any specific culture.

It seems unquestionable that the people who were living within 3.5 miles of Red Hill, and who, as we know from the Turkey Spring and Dulce Springs sites, favored the same minerals and shapes for their points and knife-scrapers as those flaked at Red Hill, did come to this upper elevation on temporary treks to hunt and collect high-altitude plants and their products. Our hypothesis is that the houses were theirs, inasmuch as construction shows similarities to that in the lower camps on this mountain. Later native peoples, and probably earlier as well, also may have come here to hunt and to gather.

The problem of the bits of charcoal found scattered throughout the fill of the excavated Red Hill houses needs further investigation which could be done very simply. If roof-burning provided the charcoal, as seems to us most likely here and for the Turkey Spring and Dulce Springs structures, a pit or two excavated out in the open to the depth of the house floors but away from the houses should show no random scattering of charcoal bits. If the charcoal found in house fills came from forest fires, the charcoal should appear in sterile soil even as it does in house fills. We did not have time for this experiment.

The possibility of old shrines near Canjilon Peak has been mentioned, and we do know that, historically, Canjilon has been a sacred mountain to the Pueblos. We know that both Jemez and Zia Pueblos still deeply venerate shrines where offerings are placed on Redondo Peak, the highest peak anywhere in their area. There also are shrines at the headwater springs of the streams which originate in that high mountain area. It would seem possible, then, that a parallel case may have existed on Canjilon Mountain centuries back. We have noted the several rectangular cobble-and-soil raised platforms, about 4 x 4.5 feet across, just below Canjilon Peak and the one of these found not far from Red Hill. Were they shrines or what was their purpose? We know of no historic parallel in shape or size to these structures. That they should be further investigated is clear.

VI

Pottery From the Canjilon Mountain Sites

The 48 largely whole or restorable vessels retrieved from hiding spots in the lava near seasonally occupied houses at the two Turkey Spring sites and the single site at Dulce Springs make up the largest collection yet obtained from a limited Gallina area. Data on the vessels have been organized into brief tables (Charts 1, 2, and 3) to permit easy reference while considering what information this pottery can provide on the lives of its users.

Pottery Types and Their Shapes[*]

The types represented are Gallina Black-on-white ware, which Hibben (1948) described as Gallina Black-on-gray, and Gallina Utility ware, most of which is plain, though for occasional pieces we find individual attempts at enhancement by simple texturizing.

Gallina Black-on-white actually is of medium-to-light gray background, like almost all the "whites" of prehistoric Anasazi pottery. Its paste is fairly fine, dense, and hard; it is tempered with fine sand. The surface is either slipped with the same clay and then polished or merely left unslipped and polished to a lower luster. For some years it has been recognized that this ware, like wares of the other Anasazi peoples, was constructed by the coil-scrape technique rather than finished, as originally surmised (Hibben 1948), by use of paddle and anvil. The carbon paint was applied as a plant juice which turned to deep gray or black when the vessel was fired in a reducing atmosphere. The black designs are simpler, as a whole, and much more carelessly applied than in most of the other areas of the prehistoric Southwest. An undecorated sherd from such a vessel can be identified by the paste and finish, feel, and sound when dropped.

Gallina Utility ware varies from light to dark gray in color. The temper is sand and the texture of the vessel more friable than that of Gallina Black-on-white. When dropped on a table, a sherd of Gallina Utility ware gives out a much lower-pitched sound ("plunk!"), in comparison to the Black-on-white's "ping." The feel of Utility ware in one's fingers similarly is coarser and more grainy than the feel of the smooth, hard Gallina Black-on-white.

The Utility ware, however, ranges from coarse (which Hibben places in a separate class) to a relatively fine paste and finish which occasionally may leave one puzzled in attempting to separate it from Gallina Gray ware, which presumably bridges the gap between decorated and Utility ware but is difficult to separate from fine-paste Utility ware.

---

[*] See plates at end of chapter.

One and occasionally two fillets frequently were added to rim exteriors of Gallina Plain Utility ware, not for decoration, as Hibben suggests, but to strengthen the orifices of these daily-use vessels. Hibben goes farther in stating that this fillet does not completely encircle the rim but is broken to leave a gap or "spirit opening." This appears questionable. None of the vessels with rim fillets (and they are common) in our collection shows any gap whatsoever. Rims with fillet are much less commonly chipped or broken than those without.

The exterior surface of this ware frequently was finished by stroking it vertically or at an angle with a dried corncob from which the kernels had been removed.[*] This technique, used on some Pueblo IV cooking vessels (after indented corrugated ware had largely run its course), lasted on into historic times in the Rio Grande. The exterior surfaces of Gallina Utility and Gray, however, sometimes show semismoothed or even unsmoothed (but not indented) coils, especially on the neck and to a lesser extent on the upper body. Some pieces of the Utility ware had the edge of each coil further emphasized by being outlined with a sharp instrument such as a splinter or a bone awl — but this modification was not found on any of our vessels from the mountain sites. A series of fingernail indentations, coarse incisions, punch-marks, or pinched-up projections decorated occasional vessels of the Gallina Utility ware, but these, too, were absent from most of our mountain vessels. As the several possible modifications, except for overlapped and sometimes outlined coils, are quite variable, description usually seems a more realistic approach than elaborating type designations.

The shapes of pottery vessels (Chart 3), though more difficult to describe than texture and paint, are of definite importance both as identifying characteristics and as our cue to use. From the three mountain sites where we found hidden vessels, in the category of Gallina Black-on-white only 1 canteen, 1 narrow-necked water jar, and 3 bowls (including one of which only some fragments remained) were retrieved. The water jar would have been typical of Gallina Plain Utility or Gray (the two grading into each other) except for a meandering simple double-line design on one side of the lower body. The bowls were fairly deep (two measured 8.9 and one 9 cm high with greatest diameter at the lip: 14.5-16.0 cm). Rims were direct, lips relatively square and several ticked. Exteriors were scraped but left unslipped. Interiors were slipped and given a simple and usually rather carelessly painted design.

Two of these three bowls came from Turkey Spring Site I; the other was from Dulce Springs. L71.2.20 is 15.9 cm across its opening and 8.9 cm high. The simple decoration consists of a series of 4 lines which cross at the center, a common Gallina motif but usually with little accuracy (as in this case) of execution. L72.2.2 is slightly smaller (14.5 cm rim diameter and 9.0 cm high). A very unusual addition to this bowl consists of two vertically pierced lugs placed opposite each other on the rim. In reflecting on the intended use of the vessel, the statement of a Jemez Pueblo elder comes to mind: "In the

---

[*] The Museum of New Mexico has a set of pottery-finishing tools from historic Picuris Pueblo, including a cob scraper bent to a curve by the pull of a tough string, for use on vessel necks and interiors.

past they placed everything they wanted to safeguard in vessels hung from the ceiling beams." We have heard this before in relation to the little vessels known as "kiva jars," but a suspended bowl is of another ilk, though in 1987 a bowl made from the base of a broken larger Black-on-white vessel, with ground upper rim and 3 drilled holes for suspension was found at Rattlesnake ridge in BG-3N. Perhaps for food intended to be protected from dirt and the rodents which must have been a constant trial to mountain housewives? Or for items used in ritual?

The bowl from Dulce Springs (L72.2.4) is 16.1 cm in diameter and 8.9 cm high. The interior border design of black parallel lines (the bottom line edged with dots) shows a "ceremonial break" or gap at one side. The design in the center bottom of this bowl is of two triangles joined at their peaks in what sometimes is referred to as a "bow tie." This symbol, fairly common in the center of Gallina bowls, has been explained by some modern Pueblo consultants as the war god symbol, but whether it carried that significance in the past is a question.

An incomplete nondecorated small bowl (L71.2.41), only 13.5 cm in diameter and approximately 10 cm deep, differs enough from the other vessels that we hesitate to include it in general statements. It appears to have been intended for Gallina Black-on-white, though never painted. Much of the slip, if it had one, has disappeared. The interior (bottom missing), below the thickened edge of a white deposit, apparently was filled. up to that line with a solution of gypsum, or burned gypsum chunks or ground powder,[*] which went into solution when water reached its hiding place in a cave. A paste of burned gypsum is used by Pueblos today to seal metates into their bins and to patch cracks around a fire place or in a wall. The type of use in a camp is unknown.

Hibben (1948) gives a series of olla (jar) outlines for Gallina Black-on-white ware which largely correspond with those known from our Llaves home sites. The upper body tends to be bulbous with a short flaring neck. The widest area is a little below mid-height, and the underbody often curves in with enough constriction to produce a slightly concave effect between the point of greatest diameter and the base. This can give the center area of the jar a slight overhang effect, though not of the "spare tire" type characteristic of so much of 18th-century Pueblo decorated wares. For Gallina Black-on-white jars the base itself may be a rolling curve or flattened, its area about a third or less of the greatest width of the vessel. From overall shape and the fact that the jar necks he shows are not narrow, I would infer the function of the majority to have been storage. Although we have found no such vessels associated with our mountain sites, we had two small vessels of Gallina Plain Utility ware which approximate Hibben's jar shapes and were very close to those of the preceding Rosa Phase.

Gallina Plain Utility ware comes in as many shapes as Gallina Black-on-white and today is recognized as a Pueblo development, but its history is clouded.

---

[*]   Analysis by Raymond N. Rogers, Research Chemist at Los Alamos National Laboratory.

Kenneth Chapman and B. T. Ellis (1951:257-269) succinctly summarize the foofaraw. Mera (1935:9-10) early emphasized the "very obvious popularity of [Gallina] conical-bottomed utility vessels" which bore "a striking resemblance...to pottery later made by the Navajo." In his conclusions (1935:34-35) he proposes that the "conical-bottomed pottery developed either autochthonously" or carried "a trait taken over from a non-puebloan source" such as the so-called Plains pottery of the San Luis Valley of southern Colorado. Hall (1944a:100-103) commented on lack of the conical-bottomed pot and of the "line break" in the painted vessels of Rosa Phase sites of Gobernador Canyon though two centuries later both features were well established in its direct descendant, the Gallina culture, 40 miles distant. Linton (1944:379) suggested that the Gallina people were migrants who might have come in contact with ancestors of the Navajo or others who carried a tradition of northern type conical-bottomed cook pots.

Jenness (1934:371) long before had pointed out that none of the early Indians of Canada (whence came the Athapascan Navajo and Apache ancestors) made pottery. Strong (1935:188) found Navajo Plain ware sharing more traits with the Sterns Creek Gray ware of western Nebraska than with any other. Some persons since have attempted to tie Navajo Plain ware to that of the Ute-Paiute and certain Utah and Colorado wares. None of these proposed ties seems to fit with the later finds of Reed (1963) and of Mackey (n.d.) indicating that the Gallina people were of Pueblo physical type and, as already discussed, came out of the upper San Juan Basin to seek a home along the Continental Divide, probably because of long-decreasing available moisture, headward stream erosion, and the ruination of formerly cultivated croplands.

Hibben (1948:197-200) shows seven shape-outlines for his Gallina Plain Utility ware and comments that Gallina Utility vessels "are universally conical-bottomed" with outlines which "vary from sharply pointed bases to others of truncated cone shape." But let us present our own findings from the whole or largely whole vessels of the Canjilon Mountain sites.

The count was 36 rounded, 5 pointed, and 3 flat-bottomed as found on the cook pots, water jars, bulbous canteens, and the small category of "submarine" shapes. All Gallina Utility vessels certainly did not have pointed bases.

In the Llaves area we have found a few truncated cone-shaped base sherds with a very thick basal tip. Undoubtedly such vessels would fit nicely into a fire pit containing "firedogs," stones set into the ashes to securely support a cooking vessel. But we have many more Gallina Plain Utility bottoms in sherds from the home sites which show gentle rounding. The majority of our cooking vessels have a tapered lower body (more so or less so) which culminated in a narrowed but gently curved base. The *base* does not include the sides of a vessel. Three of the bases shown in Hibben's illustration of shapes are clearly rounded. Our comment is that the term "pointed bottom" has been a confusing misnomer for "tapered lower body" or "underbody" and that examination of collections of culinary vessels from elsewhere in the northern Anasazi area (including Chaco and Upper Rio Grande) also show a fair number of Pueblo II and III vessels (A.D. 900-1300) on which the underbodies were tapered to a relatively small base.

The sharply pointed base, rare elsewhere in the Southwest, did actually appear in the Gallina, but not commonly. That development, I would surmise, was local, and its exaggeration tried out, with aid of firedogs, in the hope of keeping a vessel upright in a rather deep fire pit where heat could reach the contents through the sloping underbody as well as the base. In other words, the cook buried the lower half of the vessel in hot coals and ashes and thereby conserved heat, a matter of practical importance in a high altitude.

To those of us old enough for such memories, the sandstone slab lining and slab base found (though not invariably) in the Gallina home area fire pits are comfortably reminiscent of the "fireless cookers" of our youth. Two soapstone discs were heated in the oven of one's kitchen stove. One disk went into the bottom of an insulated metal tubular case. On top of this was set a food container which might contain a roast, vegetables, cake, pie, or bread. The second heated disc was set on top of the container, and an insulated cap topped the whole. One gratefully let the wood fire die out (or turned off the gas) in the stove, knowing that by the time lunch or dinner was called the savory dish entrusted to the "cooker" would be ready and the kitchen still cool. The Gallina cook lacked the second hot disc and the insulated cap, but her semisunken pot still would have produced a meal in much less time and with less fuel than required with an above-ground open fire which merely licked at the bottom of her stew kettle.

The two largest shape-use categories for Gallina Plain Utility from our three mountain sites are those of the narrow-necked water jar and the widemouthed culinary vessel. Sixteen of each were found. The 12 Turkey Spring I widemouthed cook pots (with possible exception of 2 which may have been used as small storage vessels),[*] the 2 from Turkey Spring Site II, and the 1 from Dulce Springs Site III (Chart 3) resemble in overall outline the long white grape we find in summer supermarkets. The mouth of the vessel is wide, as is necessary to get a morsel of food into and out of a stew pot, and it commonly is without any trace of flaring rim but may be strengthened by a lip fillet. The sides of this vessel flare out gently from the lip and the lower body tapers in gently. There is no neck.

Heights of Gallina Plain Utility cook pots in our collection from the mountain sites vary from 12.7 to 33 cm; diameters run from 12.4 to 25.1 cm, and outside lip diameter varies between 8.0 and 17.2 cm. Capacity ranges from 650 to 8,200 mls, with a mean of 2,489 mls, but when the extremes of range, as in this case, are widely apart as the result of but two exceptional specimens, the median capacity (1,960 mls) gives a more realistic concept of the usual size for these vessels. (There is no real mode within this category; see later discussion of the distinct grouping of these specimens and the probable reflection of family size as indicated by those groupings.)

---

[*] Finding the upper portion of one (L71.2.22) somewhat shouldered, with a slightly flaring rim, and a circular ground potsherd fitted to the orifice as a cover suggests possible storage use, and we have thus classified it. Two other vessels which would have been about equally usable as cook pots or storage jars we have tentatively placed in the former class, though they much resemble Rosa Phase storage jars.

The base of the Gallina cooking pot, like the bottom of the grape, may be smaller across than the wide mouth. On only 2 of our 16 cooking vessels is the base pointed. On 2 it is flat. For the remaining 12 on which the base still is present, it is rounded and neither sharply pointed nor of truncated cone shape. Two definitely rounded bases show a small protrusion pushing out from the center-base of the vessels. This is related to the pointed bottom and would have aided in keeping a vessel upright in a shallow fire pit.

It is possible that the style for bases could have changed through time in the Gallina area or that they varied geographically within that area. The concept of possible Navajo or Woodland associations with the Gallina, however, which originally had been derived in part from the concept of Gallina vessels presumably having pointed bases, long has been ruled out on the basis of time differences and the fact that the Woodland-associated cord-marked decoration supposedly found on 6 sherds apparently never was actual cord marking. It could have been the vague imprints of the coils of fine baskets, such as we have found very clearly delineated on the exterior of a number of sherds from the south Llaves home area. In the historic period, shallow bowl-shaped coiled baskets were among the supports used as a *puki* (Tewa designation) onto which the patted-out base of a vessel was set so that the whole could be turned around to be seen by the potter while she was adding the coils to maker the upper part of a piece. Basket-marked sherds from the lower portion of Black-on-white and, much less often, of culinary vessels are not unusual finds in the Rio Grande drainage, but when some of those from the Gallina area show the clear fine imprint of basket coils extending for 3 or more inches up the side of a vessel, we know that this was intentional decoration. Separation of basket surface from surface of the vessel carefully pressed into it would occur naturally as the clay mix shrank on drying. The 3 Gallina Plain Utility or Gray ware canteens from Turkey Spring Site I are of a single pattern. The first (L71.2.17) is a bulbous rounded vessel originally with lugs for suspension. It is now too incomplete for measurements. The second (71.2.26) is of similar shape, 19.1 cm in diameter and the same in height, with a narrow neck, filleted rim, and 4 vertically pierced lugs at the point of greatest diameter. The missing base makes capacity measurement impossible. The third (L71.2.11) also has 4 lugs and is similar to the first two except that with a height of 14.3 cm it is shorter for its width of 14 cm. The capacity is 1,250 ml.

The 3 canteens from Turkey Spring Site II show more diversity. One (L73.2.1), as already noted, is of Gallina Black-on-white. Although fundamentally a round vessel with rounded base, 4 corners have been pulled outward from the upper body. Each corner is enhanced by a pierced lug which angles upward. The narrow neck carries a band of black decoration, and the flattened upper body of the vessel has a band design of dots between line- and dot-filled triangles. Near one lug the band is left on which open in a definite "ceremonial break," the interuption of a circular or even rectangular design found in certain archaeological areas from Basketmaker II all the way to the modern period. This break seems best explained as symbolic of permitting the escape of the spirit within a vessel (Chapman and Ellis 1951) rather than imprisoning it by a solid line.

This canteen, with a diameter of 15 cm, height of only 13.5 cm, and a volume of 1,000 ml, is a little smaller than the smallest of the three from Site I. The second (L72.2.5) from Site II is of Gallina Plain Utility ware, bulbous (20.3 cm in diameter, and 23 cm in height), with 4 lugs at the widest diameter, a narrow neck, and rounded base. It is almost a duplicate of those from Site I in shape but somewhat larger, with a volume of 3,450 ml.

The third from Site II is of the same type and shape but slightly smaller (18.9 cm diameter, 21 cm high), slightly less bulbous, and with a wider and more sloping neck and wider orifice. The capacity is 3,050 ml. The 4 suspension lugs duplicate those found on the other canteens of this shape. Lips for this type of canteen range from 4.3 to 7.3 cm across, the orifice being in proportion to the general size of each vessel. The single bulbous canteen from Site III, Dulce Springs, is our largest, measuring 24.0 cm high by 27.0 cm in diameter, with a volume of 5,500 ml.

For our six bulbous canteens the range of volume can be summarized as 1,000-5,500 ml. This gives a mean of 2,611.6 ml which would be close to the median of 2,750 ml. However, with so much variation in half a dozen vessels, it is clear they must have been made to provide water for working or traveling parties of different numbers. We have 15 examples of the narrow-necked water jar, though some have breaks which make measurements impossible. One (L71.2.1) conceivably could have been a storage vessel. The water jars (with the narrow neck they would have been impractical for almost all other purposes) are of much the same shape and appearance as the Gallina Plain Utility canteens described above, though without suspension lugs. Water jars tend to be larger than the bulbous canteens. Our measurable vessels run from 15.2 to 23.8 cm in diameter and from 17.5 to 29 cm high. From these we can cite a range in capacity of from 1,720 to 6,500 ml, with quite even graduation. Mean volume is 3,241 ml. The diameter of orifices, often with "rolled lips" and strengthened by a lip fillet, runs from 6.3 to 10.5 cm. When we see the nicks and breaks in lips of historic Pueblo water jars, the advantage of this strengthening of the orifice becomes the more obvious.

In general, one could characterize the Gallina water jar as more amphora-shaped and with a more tapering neck than the bulbous canteens. The longer neck commonly shows rather rounded coils only half obliterated, whether left for decoration or to make the vessel less likely to slip in one's hands. One water jar (L71.2.32) shows the two scars where a handle reaching from neck to body has been broken off. This would have placed the vessel in the category of a pitcher shape. Another (L73.2.2) has a short horizontal projection from the neck to aid in handling the vessel while pouring. Still another (L71.2.7), which had been hidden at Site II, shows a depression in the center of the rounded base to make carrying the vessel on a woman's head easier. This type of basal depression was fairly common on water jars in the Chaco but less frequently seen elsewhere.

Like the bulbous canteen, these water jars perhaps should be classified as Gallina Gray in hardness and lack of friability of paste, though drawing any definite line separating them from the Gray Gallina Utility in most cases seems impossible. The surface of water jars has been floated (rubbing the surface repeatedly while wet, and thus bringing a "float" of tiny clay particles to the surface to make a fill between the larger particles of clay and temper), as seems to have been true also for the widemouthed cook pots, in order to make them less pervious to liquid contents.

The function of the submarine-shaped vessel, a speciality in Gallina Gray Utility ware but in one case decorated by pinching up the clay in a serrated single line, is something of a puzzle. As the four we found all came from Turkey Spring Site I, we might wonder whether they were the product of a single potter, but they have been reported by other archaeologists from Gallina home sites.

One example (L71.21.10) has 2 loops for suspension on the upper part of the flattened sides, so we can be fairly certain that it served as a canteen or at least was hung to protect whatever its contents may have been. It measures 13.3 x 18.4 cm in body diameters, 18.4 cm high, and 5.5 cm across the outside of the lip, which was reinforced with a fillet. Capacity was 1,420 ml. The flattened sides would have made this a more conveniently carried canteen than those with a bulbous body. The neck of each canteen, as in those of the historic Pueblo peoples, probably was plugged with a folded wad of grass during use. Although the submarine shape is known for other Gallina sites, it is not so common as to rule out the probability that relatively few women specialized in this pattern.

A much smaller submarine, found tucked away near a bowl at the end of a 5-foot tunnel in the lava, was appreciably smaller (8 x 15.5 cm, lip 4.3 cm, height 14 cm), with a volume of only 400 ml. This and our two others without suspension loops (one 13.7 x 21.3 cm and not otherwise measurable but apparently about the size of the submarine with 1,420 ml capacity, and the other larger, with 2,350 ml capacity) each could have been covered with a loose yucca-leaf or yucca-cord net, which would have made carrying easy. On the other hand, it is possible that canteens without suspension loops could have served as small storage vessels. We can appreciate these unusual forms (as no doubt the Gallina people did) better than we can explain them.

This leaves us with but a brief note on the last of the Gallina Plain Utility ware shapes: the single group of fragments making up a partial bowl from Site I. The one measurement possible was 16.0 cm for diameter, which is but .1 cm larger than the Gallina Black-on-white bowl L71.2.20 found not far distant. After the end of Basketmaker III, plain undecorated bowls became increasingly uncommon, but never entirely disappeared.

Functional Significance of the Canjilon Mountain Pottery Finds

What can we learn about family life in camp from the cooking-dining equipment they left behind?

First, it is clear that expectable household vessels consisted of the widemouthed stew pot, the bowl in which to serve food to groups of different sizes, a water jar in which to bring water to one's camp shelter or house, a bulbous canteen possibly used similarly but more likely carried by men or women on treks for hunting or gathering, and finally the strangely shaped and relatively small submarine vessels. Our finds in these categories were so consistent that I think we could safely postulate an assemblage of one of each, with exception of the submarine, as composing the standard set of household equipment other than baskets and stone, bone, antler, skin, wood, and reed artifacts. As sherd pottery-scrapers are quite common in home village houses but no pottery-making tools were found in the mountain camp sites, it seems certain that pottery fabrication did not take place on the mountain. This leaves us to suppose that all vessels used there were carried from the home villages. In contrast, we know that some stone implements were made and/or reworked when broken or dulled. We find knapping areas where the men must have congregated for companionship while they worked. There also is evidence for some such work in homes. All debitage, as well as scattered implements, is made up of materials brought from outside to this mountain slope. The continuous need for numerous flaked stone implements far outran that for pottery vessels in campsites established for hunting and gathering.

In the more conservative New Mexico pueblos the Pueblo concept of what should make up a meal and how it should be served still held through the 1930s but rapidly changed in the 1940s when their enlisted men returned from World War II (Hawley, Pijoan, and Elkin 1943). Stew long had been standard fare, a combination of fresh or dried meat, wild greens when available, wild potatoes at times, and dried kernels from roasted ears of corn. It was served with raised wheat bread or tortillas made according to recipes borrowed from Spanish neighbors, or, as in the old days, with corn cakes or "paper bread" (*guayaves* or *piki*), thinner than cornflakes, baked from a gruel of finely ground corn flour spread over a smooth stone griddle specially surfaced with tallow or with finely crushed sunflower seeds. When the gruel cooked enough for the edges to begin curling, the sheet was deftly turned over and given a moment or two of baking on the opposite side before being peeled off and either rolled into a cigar-like shape or folded. Color depended on selection of meal from red, blue, white, yellow or speckled corn, but could be enhanced by including powdered dried wildflower petals in the batter.

The cooked stew was poured into a bowl to be placed on the living room floor where family members sat around it, plucking out pieces of meat with their fingers and sometimes dipping up the juice with a small pottery spoon handed from one to another. More commonly the stew liquid was soaked up with the paper bread or, later, wheat bread. Good manners, as I recall from sharing such meals in Zia and Santo Domingo Pueblos in the 1930s, included careful neatness. The floor was swept with a short grass broom before and after the meal. As anything left must be saved, the precept of food conservation being strongly emphasized, the bowl used was intended to be of a size appropriate to the number expected to eat. Cushing (1974 reprint), who lived with the Zuni as an adopted member of that tribe between 1879 and 1884, provides our best survey of Pueblo foods, their preparation, and household customs. Among the latter was the invariable invitation given any visitor to eat, and food soon was brought out from what was on hand. In most cases it was appreciated but, as Cushing realistically noted, during his stay word was around Zuni that stopping in at a certain dwelling was not wise because the conservative housewife kept leftover stew so long that what was offered frequently had soured. The native cook who would prevent wastage before the modern period of electric refrigerators (not in every Pueblo household even yet) had to estimate expected consumption with some accuracy. Her measure was the size of her stew pot and her serving dish.

A housewife might have more than one bowl and cook pot, their sizes matched to their intended purposes, but there is little question that when vessels and implements had to be carried 20 miles or so to a mountain camp, the assemblage would have been kept to a minimum. This, as already pointed out, is affirmed by the consistency in shapes of vessels found. The size of these vessels is our best clue to the size of the household units which depended on them and thus is worth considering in some detail. In historic times Rio Grande Pueblo women expected to cook two meals per day for families busy with hunting and gathering. The three Gallina Black-on-white bowls we found all were close to the same size. The smallest has a volume of only 820 ml (Chart 2), almost 1.7 pints or 3.5 cups if filled to the brim.[*] To handle a bowl of food without spilling, one dare not fill it closer than .5 inch or more from the lip. This vessel can be thought of as having held no more than 3 cups of stew, which would provide approximately 1.5 cupsful apiece for each of two persons.

The second bowl, with a volume of 900 ml, 1.9 pints or 3.8 cupsful, was scarcely larger. It would have held slightly over 3 cupsful of stew, enough for two diners.

The third has a volume of 1100 ml, 2.32 pints, or 4.64 cupsful. This would hold about 4 cupsful of food when offered to the family. What size family? Certainly not more than 3 and perhaps only 2 if the diners were young workers.

One could argue that bowls could have been used otherwise than for serving food, though that certainly was their main function in the historic period, except for the big doughbowls used, after the Spaniards had introduced wheat, to hold bread dough during its stage of rising. But the size of the cook pot, for which there is no question as to use, can be taken as even more reliable than that of bowls in indicating the size of group intended to be fed from its contents. The concept of conserving food was so important to the Pueblos-on-their-own (pre-canned-goods era) that we find it incorporated in precepts repeated in religious rituals.

Our 12 measurable widemouthed culinary jars (Chart 2) came, as already noted, in a greater size range than any of the other shapes present, but they clearly were clustered into groups. With such an extended range, the mean of 2,020 ml really is not so significant in meaning as could be wished. If we hypothesize that the vessel size groups provide a clue to the number of persons a housewife expected to feed, we obviously should check the matter of volume per vessel group throughout the collection of cook pots.

The smallest one held only 620 ml or 1.31 pints (2.62 cups) when filled to the brim. To allow for bubbling during boiling and for handling an open vessel in removing it from the fire, we will subtract a minimum of about half a cup. This leaves a maximum of 2 cups of prepared stew, which happens to be a cup less than the volume we computed

---

[*]   1 pint (2 cups) = 473.167 ml. We can beg pardon for reverting to lowly kitchen measure, but in terms of eating this is a more comprehensible unit than milliliters to most readers.

for our smallest serving bowl. The jar could not have held more than enough for one meal for 2 very moderate eaters or for one hungry individual.

The next larger cook pots have volumes of 1,100 and 1,200 ml respectively. The first translates into 2.34 pints or 4.68 cups, and the second into 2.54 pints or 5.06 cups. After cutting each volume a minimum bit to prevent boiling over or slopping in handling, we have about 4 cups left for the first and less than 4.5 for the second. If we estimate moderate averages of 1.5 cupsful per person,[*] the first pot would provide one meal for 2 plus a cup extra for the man of the house, a child, or leftovers, and the second would feed 3 persons. (There is, of course, the probability that all cook pots were not always well or equally filled.)

The next two larger vessels each have capacities of 1,400 ml or 2.96 pints, which gives 5.92 cups. We can conservatively count on 4 or 5 and a fraction cupsful of food. Certainly 3 persons and possibly even 4 could be fed at one time.

The single cooking vessel of 1,800 ml capacity would have held 3.8 pints or 7.6 cups, which should feed 5 persons for one meal.

The vessel of 2,120 ml capacity, or 4.48 pints which is 8.96 cups, might feed 6 persons skimpily but 5 more adequately. That of 2,200 ml, 4.63 pints or 9.26 cups, similarly would feed 5 persons but could be stretched for 6. The vessel of 2,300 ml, 4.86 pints or 9.72 cups, would feed 6 persons.

We jump to the next category with the first at 3,700 ml, 7.81 pints or 15.62 cups which should feed a group of 10 at maximum. The second vessel holds 3,800 ml, 8 pints, or 16 cups, and would feed a group of the same size.

Our single big cooking vessel of 8,200 ml, 17.39 pints or 34.78 cups, is reminiscent of the large cook pots common in Pueblo IV sites and represented in the living pueblos by oversized metal containers purchased for use in preparing meals for an extended family and friends at some celebration such as a saint's day or to provide a meal for members of a religious society at the time of its retreat. Twenty-three persons could have been fed one meal from our single big Turkey Spring Site II culinary jar.

If we add the number of persons who could have been fed at one time from the moderate-size cook pots, we can account for 54 diners grouped in 11 households, 10 of which would have been in Turkey Spring Site I and the others in Turkey Spring Site II. Some of those, such as the two units of 2 diners apiece, may have been related and lived in some of the pairs of houses built contiguously or at least very near each other. The

---

[*]   Santo Domingo Pueblo friends say that early in this century a certain one of "grandmother's" pottery serving bowls (5.75 x 3.75 inches or 14.6 x 9.7 cm) was regularly filled twice to feed a family of 6 at a meal. According to our measurement, when filled to within 0.75 inches (2 cm) of the rim, it holds 4 cupsful. This allowed 1.33 cupsful per person.

number of known dwellings (and others unexcavated) for which we have no vessels indicates that we are not giving a total population estimate.

For the group of 23 presumably fed from the big vessel, we can hazard three suggestions. One is that an extended family made up of 4 or 5 biological or primary families actually was being fed by one person acting as cook. This is unlikely.

The second suggestion is that at least one religious society was represented in these mountain sites and did go into retreat in connection with customary summer rituals. The objection to this hypothesis is that religious society retreats customarily — but not always — have been held only in or near the home village during the historic period. As all members are required to participate, if they are scattered out in farm villages or private field houses, a messenger summons them to their home center at the proper time. This, of course, may not always have been the custom.

Our third, and less esoteric suggestion is, perhaps, most easily given tentative acceptance. If plant foods were being collected for winter use, some may have been boiled as part of their preparation. Here we are caught with inadequate knowledge of early use of the wild plants, and most of today's Pueblo women would be little more knowledgeable. We do know that the Rocky Mountain beeweed (not found in the high altitude of the sites with which we are concerned) was boiled down and the thick juice poured into corn husks and put away, dried, to be used later as a pottery paint base or as food in times of considerable need. The juice from cactus fruit in some areas and the root and fruits of one or more types of yucca elsewhere were cooked and stored for winter use. These would not have been native to our mountain area, but one may think in terms of wild berries, bulbs, and tubers. We have data on a type of blood sausage flavored with juniper berries and stuffed into cases made from cleaned intestines, much as in other parts of the world. All such products require cauldrons for preparation and our cooking pot of 8,200 ml volume certainly would classify thus. It is possible to argue that even the cook pots which would have served 10 persons at a time may have been intended primarily for preparation of foods to be taken back to the home villages. True. We can only say that the several examples of two structures built to adjoin each other or very near to each other could have housed about 5 persons apiece, and in the Pueblo scheme the occupants probably would have been relatives who cooked and ate together.

The amount of water which a person or household should be expected to use per day would be difficult to determine without some specific figures on historic pueblos before water systems were put in. Capacity of the narrow-necked water jars found in the mountain sites, like that of the cook pots, stretched over a wide range (4,780 ml difference in volume between smallest and largest) and similarly was concentrated in groupings. The smallest stood alone at 1,720 ml (3.63 pints). The next 4 clustered between 1,880 and 2,300 ml (3.97 and 4.86 pints). Then came the two at 3,100 ml and 3,200 ml (6.55 and 6.76 pints), followed by one at 4,000 ml (8.45 pints), one at 5,630 ml (11.9 pints) and one at 6,500 ml (13.73 pints).

As water from the household jar would have been used for little other than drinking and cooking (Pueblo ablutions commonly being made at springs or rivers in the historic past and dishes scraped clean more frequently than washed), we can guess that those amounts represented approximately daily household use. It thus looks as if household units of six different sizes may be represented by the water containers.

Our 6 bulbous canteens showed approximately the same range of difference in capacity (4,400 ml) between smallest and largest as the water jars, though the actual volumes for the canteens were lower (1,000-5,500 ml or 2.1-11.62 pints). Their mean of 2,611.6 ml is close to their median of 2,750 ml.

The 3 measurable submarine vessels are far too few to warrant mean or median estimates. Their only contribution to present considerations lies in their capacity range (400-2,350 ml or .845-496 pints) being great, just as we found for all other shape-categories except bowls. We must set aside our sample of 3 as not necessarily representative of an entire category.

Either all the pottery vessels used in these mountain camps were not hidden away when the people left or they have since disappeared. The number of apparent domiciles is appreciably larger than the number of either the cook pots or the water jars retrieved.

Had we a larger sample of vessels within each shape-use category, we could be more sure of conclusions, but it seems safe to surmise from the data on those two groups, generally corroborated by water jar and even canteen data, that the units which came to the hunting-gathering camps consisted of from 2 to 10 persons per home area family. The majority of those units, we suggest from these data, included only from 3 to 5 persons. These numbers also would be reasonable for the floor space found in most mountain houses.

From what we know of native peoples of the world and Pueblo people of the historic period, we would expect the women to have done most of the gathering and the men most of the hunting. This economic specialization of labor, responsibility, and resultant respect between the sexes continues to the present day.

CHART 1: POTTERY VESSELS FROM LAVA BEDS GROUPED ACCORDING TO LOCATION
TURKEY SPRING SITE II (LA 10643)

LOCATION	NUMBER		TYPE		SHAPE						BASE		SIZE			VOL.	REMARKS
	Field #	Catalog #	Gallina B/W	Gallina Plain Utility*	Bowl	Canteen	Submarine	Narrow neck water jar	Wide mouth culinary jar	Shouldered possibly storage	Rounded	Pointed	Diam. in cms.	Lip in cms.	Height in cms.	Vol. in mls.	
Alley I	72/II/II-4	L72.2.7		xG				x			x		21.3	7.3	22.0	4000	Base indented to carry on head. Lip fillet.
	73/II/ 1/A1	L73.2.1	x			x					x		15.0	4.5	13.5	1000	4 lugs. Good example Gallina B/W. Rim fillet.
Alley II	72/II/II-5	L72.2.1		x					x			Flat	13.0	9.3	20.0	1400	"Vase shaped".
	72/II/II-5a	L72.2.5		x		x					x		20.3	5.0	23.0	3450	4 lugs for suspension. Found in deep crevice near L72.2.1.
Feature 28	73/II/ 8/A-II	L73.2.3		x				x				x	-	-	-	-	Incomplete
Alley III	72/II/II-8	L72.2.3		x					x		x		25.1	16.2	33.0	8200	Lip fillet. Largest pot from mountain sites.
	72/II/II-1	L72.2.4		x		x					x		18.9	7.3	21.0	3050	4 lugs.
Alley IV	72/II/II-12	L72.2.8		x		x						x?	18.7	-	-	-	4 lugs. Small cave near trail to cave 12
	72/II/II-2	L72.2.6		x				x					18.1	-	-	-	Partially missing.
	73/II/ I/A-IV	L73.2.2		x				x			x		18.2	5.0	16.5	2000	Protrusion from neck for handle. Probably originally one on opposite side.
SUB TOTAL FOR SITE II			1	9	0	4	0	4	2	0	6	2?					

CHART 1: POTTERY VESSELS FROM LAVA BEDS GROUPED ACCORDING TO LOCATION

DULCE SPRINGS SITE III (LA 10642)

LOCATION	NUMBER		TYPE		SHAPE						BASE		SIZE			VOL.	REMARKS
	Field#	Catalog #	Gallina B/W	Plain Utility*	Bowl	Canteen	Submarine	Narrow neck water jar	Wide mouth culinary jar	Shouldered possibly storage	Rounded	Pointed	Diam. in cms.	Lip in cms.	Height in cms.	Vol. in mls.	
Feature 11	74/III/5	L74.2.5		x					x		Flat		14.2	-	20.8	-	Fillet below lip with pinched design. Almost 1/2 missing.
"Helm's cave" west of Feature 14	74/III/2	L74.2.3		x				x				x	24.0	10.5	31.0	6500	Lip fillet. Neck coils visible to just above shoulder.
	74/III/1	L74.2.2		x		x					x		24.0	8.5	27.0	5500	3 lugs 7.5 cm. below neck and 3 more lugs 5 cm. below main bulge of vessel.
25' NW of Feature III-25	74/III/3	L74.2.1		x				x			Flat		16.5	5.7	18.2	1720	
In Feature III-29 (cave) near Feature 23	74/III/4	L74.2.4	x		x						x		16.1	-	8.9	900	Interior decoration
SUB TOTAL FOR SITE III			1	4	1	1	0	2	1	0	2	1					

* May show partly obliterated coils

143

CHART I: POTTERY VESSELS FROM LAVA BEDS GROUPED ACCORDING TO LOCATION

TURKEY SPRING SITE I (LA 10641)

LOCATION	NUMBER		TYPE		SHAPE						BASE		SIZE			VOL.	REMARKS
	Field Gmt #	Catalog#	Gallina B/W	Plain Utility*	Bowl	Canteen	Submarine	Narrow neck water jar	wide mouth culinary jar	Shouldered possibly storage	Rounded	Pointed	Diam. in cms.	Lip in cms.	Height in cms.	Vol. in mls.	
Near House #3	71/I/11	L71.2.29		x				x			x		23.8	8.8	29.	-	
	71/I/11a	L71.2.30	x					x			x		-	-	-	-	Not all present.
	71/I/12	L71.2.2		x				x			x		23.3	9.4	28.3	5630	Rolled lip. Coils left showing on entire upper body, especially neck
Near House #2	71/I/5	L71.2.13		x					x		x		14.0	8.3	20.0	1830	Rim fillet.
	71/I/6-1	L71.2.18		x					x			x	17.2	11.5	21.0	-	1/4 missing.
	71/I/6-5	L71.2.14		x					x		x		17.5	14.	26.0	3800	Very similar to 6-1 except has rim fillet.
Near House 1	71/I/2	L71.2.19		x				x			x		15.2	7.2	22.5	1880	Some coils still visible.
	71/I/3	L71.2.17		x		x					x		18.1	-	-	-	Top broken, lip fillet. 2 vertically pierced knobs for hanging, originally may have had 4.
	71/I/1	L71.2.7		x			x				x		15x23	9.7	20.3	2350	Largest of this shape.
	71/I/4	L71.2.22		x						x			-	11.8	-	-	Upper portion of culinary or possibly storage jar, orifice fitted with sherd lid.

CHART I: POTTERY VESSELS FROM LAVA BEDS GROUPED ACCORDING TO LOCATION

TURKEY SPRING SITE I (LA 10641)

LOCATION	NUMBER Field Gmt #	NUMBER Catalog #	TYPE Gallina B/W	TYPE Plain Utility*	SHAPE Bowl	SHAPE Canteen	SHAPE Submarine	SHAPE Narrow neck water jar	SHAPE Wide mouth culinary jar	SHAPE Shouldered possibly storage	BASE Rounded	BASE Pointed	SIZE Diam. in cms.	SIZE Lip in cms.	SIZE Height in cms.	VOL. in mls.	REMARKS
Near House 1 continued	71/I/4a	L71.2.25		x				x?					-	-	-	-	Less than 1/2 present.
More or less opposite "possible Tower 1" base (?) watchmen's area(?)	71/I/8a	L71.2.12		x			x		x		x		12.4	9.4	19.7	1200	Bias corn cob scraper grooves on surface, upper right to lower left.
	71/I/9	L71.2.3		x			x				x	x	13.7x 21.3	-	-	-	Neck and part of upper section missing. Body encircled by finger-pinched decoration.
	71/I/10	L71.2.28		x				x			x		31.8	-	-	-	Upper portion missing.
	71/I/3-4	L71.2.6		x					x		x cp		17.8	17.2	22.9	3700	Rounded bottom but center protrudes. crude rim.
Opposite Garden plot 1 but not definitely associated with any specific house	71/I/14a	L71.2.32		x				x			x		-	8.0	22.9	3200	Rolled lip with fillet. Scars show loop handle from lip to shoulder originally existed, making it a big pitcher.
	71/I/6	L71.2.26		x		x					x		19.1	5.6	19.1	-	Lip fillet, 4 vertically pierced knot lugs(1 now missing.) Roughly smoothed coils visible

CHART I: POTTERY VESSELS FROM LAVA BEDS GROUPED ACCORDING TO LOCATION

TURKEY SPRING SITE I (LA 10641)

LOCATION	Field #	Catalog #	Gallina B/W	Plain Utility*	Bowl	Canteen	Submarine	Narrow neck water jar	wide mouth culinary jar	Shouldered possibly storage	Rounded	Pointed	Diam. in cms.	Lip in cms.	Height in cms.	Vol. in mls.	REMARKS
Near work area and Garden 2 Continued	71/I/3-3	L71.2.37		x					x		x		14.0	9.8	17.8	1400	Lip fillet.
Near the 3-house complex which we described under house 4	71/I/3-15	L71.2.20	x		x								15.9	-	8.9	1100	Largely complete
	71/I/3-15a			x	x								16.0	-	-	-	Fragmentary, similar in size to 3-15.
	71/I/5-1	L71.2.9		x			x				x		8.0 x 15.5	4.3	14.0	400	Neck fillet, vessel found at end of a 5 ft. tunnel, near #3-15
Near skull cave	71/I/13	L71.2.31	x				?		x		x		-	-	-	-	About half missing
	71/I/15	L71.2.33						x			x		20.3	8.7	24.1	3100	Coils left showing on upper body but very simple painted design on lower body
	71/I/15a	L71.2.34		x					x		x		15.9	11.5	20.6	2300	Rim fillet
Near Bain's Cave,#1	72/II/A (Pot A)	L72.2.2	x		x								14.5	-	9.0	820	2 vertically pierced lugs, most unusual for a bowl.
?	71/I/3-6	L71.2.21		x					x		x		-	-	-	-	Half missing
?	71/I/3-14	L71.2.40		x		?		?			x		18.4	-	-	-	lower half present
SUB TOTALS FOR SITE I			4	31	3	4	3	8	12	3?	28	3					

cp= center base protruding

146

CHART I: POTTERY VESSELS FROM LAVA BEDS GROUPED ACCORDING TO LOCATION

TURKEY SPRING SITE I (LA 10641)

LOCATION	NUMBER		TYPE		SHAPE						BASE		SIZE			VOL.	REMARKS
	Field Gmt#	Catalog #	Gallina B/W	Gallina Plain Utility*	Bowl	Canteen	Submarine	Narrow neck water jar	Wide mouth culinary jar	Shouldered possibly storage	Rounded	Pointed	Diam. in cms.	Lip in cms.	Height in cms.	Vol. in mls.	
Opposite Garden plot 1.... continued	71/I/7	L71.2.27		x					x			x	16.2	11.	20.3	2200	Lip fillet,
	71/I/3-8	L71.2.4		x				x			x		17.2	6.3	17.5	2080	Double row of incised angled lines encircles shoulder.
	71/I/3-9	L71.2.1		x				x?		?	x		16.5	6.5	20.2	2300	Neck coils quite clear. Found with L71.2.10.
	71/I/3-10	L71.2.10		x		x--	x				x		13.3x 18.4	5.5	18.4	1420	Submarine with 2 vertically pierced knob lugs. Lip fillet.
	71/I/3-11	L71.2.11		x		x					x		14.0	4.3	14.3	1250	4 vertically pierced knob lugs. Lip fillet.Found near L71.2.9 and L71.2.1 Vessel contained 9c. unpealed stick with charred end and fiber cord(?) around middle.
Near work area and Garden 2	71/1/8	L71.2.8		x					x		x		14.3	12.5	21.9	2120	Double rim fillet
	71/1/3-2	L71.2.36		x					x?	?	x		12.7	8.0	12.7	620	Short with shoulder unusual in cook pot
	71/1/3-1	L71.2.5		x					x		x		13.0	10.3	16.2	1100	Shorter than usual Found with L71.2.36 Look to be by same potter.

CHART 2: RANGE OF DIMENSIONS PER SHAPE CATEGORY FOR VESSELS FROM GALLINA MOUNTAIN SITES

	TURKEY SPRING SITE I (LA 10641)				TURKEY SPRING SITE II (LA 10643)				DULCE SPRING SITE (LA 10642)			
	Diam. in cm.	Lip in cm.	Ht. in cm.	Capacity in mls.	Diam. in cm.	Lip in cm.	Ht. in cm.	Capacity in mls.	Diam. in cm.	Lip in cm.	Ht. in cm.	Capacity in mls.
Narrow neck water jar	23.8	8.8	29.0	---	21.3	7.3	22.0	4000	16.5	5.7	18.2	1720
	23.3	9.4	28.3	5630	18.1	---	---	---	24.0	10.5	31.0	6500
	15.2	7.2	22.5	1880	18.2	---	23.0	2000				
	---	8.0	22.9	3200								
	17.2	6.3	17.5	2080								
	16.5	6.5	20.2	2300*								
	20.3	8.7	24.1	3100*								
Total: 13 (10 measurable)					*Could be "shouldered jar possibly for storage"							
Wide mouth culinary jar (cook pot)	14.0	8.3	20.0	1830	13.0	9.3	20.0	1400	14.3	---	20.8	---
	17.2	11.5	21.0	---	25.1	16.2	33.0	8200*				
	17.5	14.0	26.0	3800								
	12.4	9.4	19.7	1200								
	17.8	17.2	22.9	3700								
	16.2	11.0	20.3	2200								
	14.3	12.5	21.9	2120								
	12.7	8.0	12.7	1100								
	13.0	10.3	16.2	620(?)								
	14.0	9.8	17.8	1400								
	15.9	11.5	20.6	2300								
Total: 14 (12 measurable)	1 more of this shape found but upper section missing.				*Largest vessel from mountain sites.							
Canteen	18.1	---	---	---	15.0	4.5	13.5	1000	24.0	8.5	27.0	5500
	19.1	5.6	19.1	---	20.3	5.0	23.0	3450				
	13.3x18.4	5.5	18.4	1420*	18.9	7.3	21.0	3050				
	14.0	4.3	14.3	1250								
Total: 8 (6 measurable)	*Submarine type canteen, also listed under "Submarine".											
Submarine	15.0x23.0	9.7	20.3	2350								
	13.7x21.3	---	---	---								
	13.3x18.4	5.5	18.4	1420*								
	8.0x15.5	4.3	14.0	400								
Total: 4 (3 measurable)	*Submarine canteen with 2 suspension loops.											
Bowl	15.9	8.9	8.9	1100					16.1		8.9	900
	16.0	---	---	---								
	14.5	9.0	9.0	820								
Total:4 (3 measurable)												
Base shapes: Rounded	28				6				2			
Flat	0				1				2			
Pointed	3				2				1			

CHART 3: RELATION OF TYPES TO SHAPES

Sites:	Turkey Spring I		Turkey Spring II		Dulce Spring		Total per Shape
Pottery Types: / Shapes	Gallina B/W	Gallina Culinary	Gallina B/W	Gallina Culinary	Gallina B/W	Gallina Culinary	
Bowl	3	1	-	-	1	-	5
Canteen	-	4x	1	3	-	1	8
Submarine	-	4x	-	-	-	-	4
Narrow neck water jar	1	8xx	-	4	-	2	15
Wide mouth culinary	-	12xx	-	2	-	1	15
Totals per Type	4	28	1	9	1	4	46

x 1 submarine also is listed as a canteen and must not be counted twice in computing total

xx For Site I: number includes 1 narrow neck water jar and 1 presumed wide mouth cook pot which possibly could have been storage jars.

CHART 4: EXAMPLES OF POINTS OR POINT-LIKE BLADES FROM THE CANJILON MOUNTAIN SITES

Site	Structure or Area	Type 1 Point Size	M	2 Point Size	M	3 Point Size	M
TS I	Bains Cave (Cave 1) (5 broken not listed)	2.6x1.6 cm. at b.b. 4.0x ca. 1.7 cm. at b.b. ca. 3.0x ca. 1.3 cm.	obs. obs. obs.	2.3x1.3 cm. across stem	obs.		
	Feature I-1	6.5x ca. 2.8 cm. (bifurcated)	ch.			ca. 4.7x ca. 2.5 cm.	obs.
	Feature I-2 (house)						
	Feature I-4 (house)	1.9x1.0 cm. 2.1x1.2 cm. 2.0x1.3 cm.	obs. obs. obs.				
	Surface					ca. 4.6x ca. 2.6 cm.	obs.
TS II	Feature II-3 (house or storeroom)			4.0x2.5 cm. (largest)	obs.		
	Feature II-12			ca. 2.3x1.2 cm.	obs.	ca. 4.0x ca. 2.4 cm.	obs.
	Feature II-13					ca. 2.1x ca. 1.2 cm.	obs.
	Feature II-14 (house)			1.8x1.0 cm.	ch.	(reused as blade)	obs.
	Feature II-19 (house)	ca. 2.2x1.5 cm. ca. 2.0x1.5 cm. 2.2x1.0 cm. 1.7x0.9 cm.	obs. obs. obs. obs.	ca. 2.0x1.2 cm.	obs.	ca. 4.0x2.8 cm.	obs.
	Feature II-26 (house)			1.5x1.2 cm. (our smallest)	Qtz.		
	Surface, Alley 1						
DULCE SPRINGS (III)	Feature III-14 (house)	3.5x1.8 cm. at tangs. Serrated, with bifurcated base	obs.	2.1x1.0 cm. across stem 2.1x1.6 (bunt)	ch. obs.	ca. 3.5x2.0 2 - lower part only	obs. obs.
	Feature III-1 (house)	3.4x1.6 cm. 2.8x2.5 cm. ca. 2.5x1.5 cm. (two notches taken from one side)	obs. obs. obs.	2.7x1.2 cm. 2.0x1.3 cm.	obs. obs.	2.6x ca. 2.5 cm. (reworked?) ca. 3.0x1.5 cm. (1 edge shows 1 notch removed)	obs. obs.
	Feature III-3	ca. 3.0x1.5 cm.	obs.				
	III-2						
	III-22			1.8x ca. 1.4 cm.	obs.		
	Surface III	ca. 3.6x2.1 cm.	ch.				
RED HILL		5.0x2.6 cm.	obs.				
TOTALS		18		11		9	

All measurements are in centimeters. The first dimesion given is length, the second is width.
ca. = approximately (estimated because of break)

4. Knife or Blank? Size	M	5. Point Size	M	6. Point Size	M	7. Point Size	M
ca. 4.3x1.6 cm.	ch.	3.5x2.4 cm.	Qtz.	ca. 4.0x1.8 cm.	obs.	ca. 5.5x2.1 (1 edge noched) ca. 5.0x2.2	B. ch. B ch.
				ca. 3.2x ca.1.3 cm	obs.		
2.0x1.8 cm. 3.0x2.0 cm.	obs. obs.						
				2.8x2.3 cm.	dull obs.		
2.6x1.7 cm.	obs.			ca. 2.8x1.3 cm.	obs.		
3.1x ca. 1.7 cm.	fl.					ca. 1.9x1.1 cm.	obs.
		ca. 4.5x ca. 2.8 cm.	obs.	2.5x1.7 cm.	obs.		
				ca. 3.3x1.9 cm serrated	obs.		
4.7x2.3 cm.	obs.	ca. 2.7x ca. 2.4 cm.	obs.			ca. 2.4x1.4 cm 2 notches on 1 edge. None on other. ca. 2.0x1.1 cm.	obs. obs.
				ca. 4.5x2.2 cm.	obs.		
6		3		7		5	

M   = Material   ch.   = chert   B.ch. = brown chert
bb   = base of blade   ch.   = chalcedony   Qtz.   = quartz
obs.= obsidian   fl.   = flint

Gallina Plain Utility
Submarine-shaped vessel
L 71.2.7 Diam. 15 x 23 cm.
Ht. 20.3 cm.

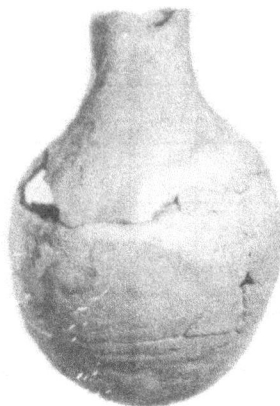

Gallina Plain Utility
Narrow Neck Jar
L 71.2.19 Diam. 49.2 cm.
Ht. 22.5 cm.

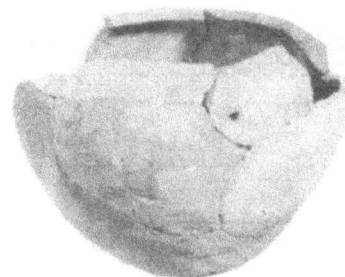

Gallina Plain Utility
Narrow Neck Canteen
with 4 lugs (2 missing)
L 71.2.17 Diam. 18.1cm.
Ht. 14 cm.

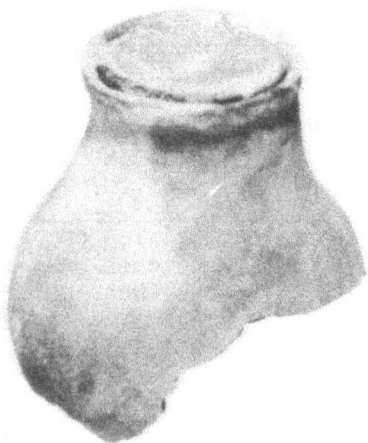

Gallina Plain Utility
lidded jar.
L 71.2.22

Gallina Plain Utility
Wide-mouth pot with
rim fillet.
L 71.2.13 Diam. 14 cm.
Ht. 20.0 cm.

Gallina Plain Utility
Canteen with rim fillet
and lugs. L 71.2.26
Diam. 19.1 cm.
Ht. 19.1 cm.

Plate 1

Gallina Plain Utility
Wide-mouth jar with rim fillet.
L 71.2.27. Diam. 16.2 cm.
Ht. 20.3 cm.

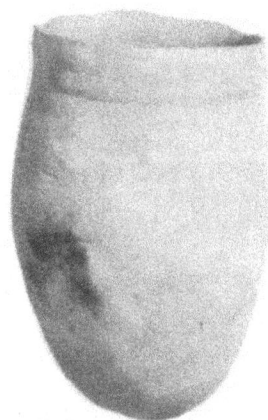

Gallina Plain Utility
Wide-mouth jar with
double rim fillet.
L. 71.2.8. Diam 14.2 cm.
Ht. 21.9 cm.

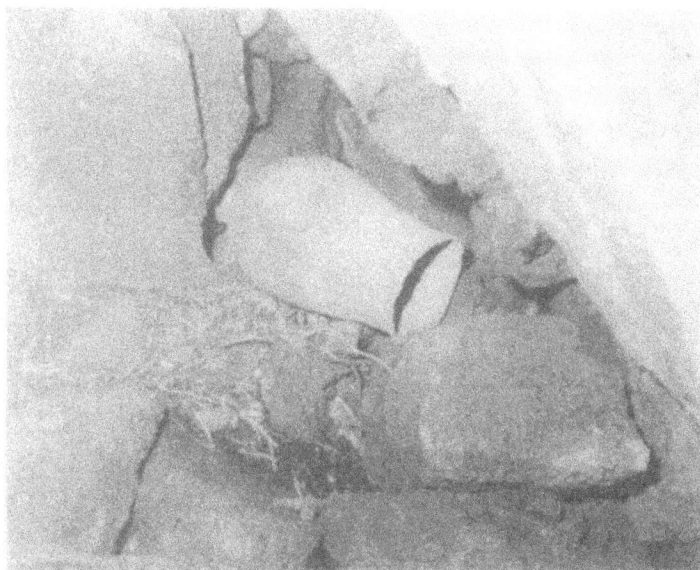

Gallina Plain Utility Wide-mouth jar
in situ.
L. 71.2.12. Diam. 12.4 cm.; Ht. 19.7 cm.

Plate 2

Gallina Submarine-shaped
vessel with finger pinched decoration.
L. 71.2.3.   Diam 13.7x21.3 cm.
Ht. ?

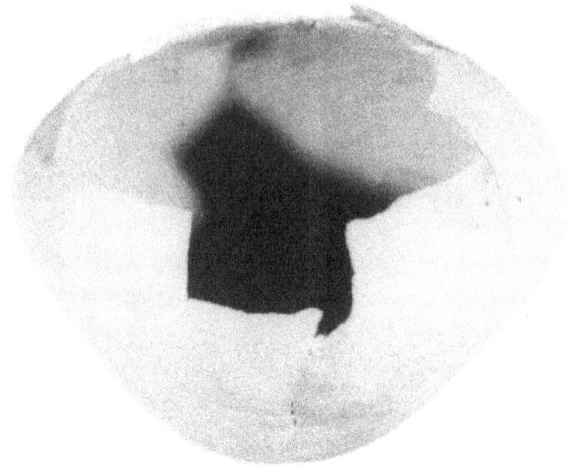

Gallina Plain Utility
jar fragment.
L. 71.2.28   Diam. 31.8 cm.
Ht. ?

Gallina Plain Utility
narrow-neck jar.
L. 71.2.29.   Diam 8.8 cm.
Ht. 29 cm.

Gallina Plain Utility
narrow-neck jar with "rolled
lip". L. 71.2.2. Diam.
23.2 cm. Ht. 28.3 cm.

Plate 3

154

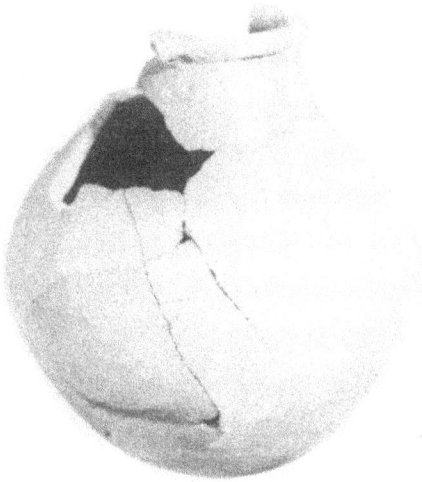

Gallina Plain Utility
Narrow-neck jar with loop
handle (missing).
L. 71.2.32. Diam._____
Ht. 22.9 cm.

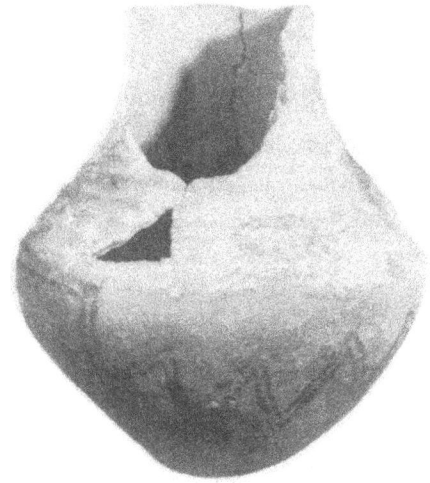

Gallina Black on White
Narrow-neck jar with accented
corrugations and lip fillet.
L. 71.2.33. Diam. 20.3
Ht. 24.1 cm.

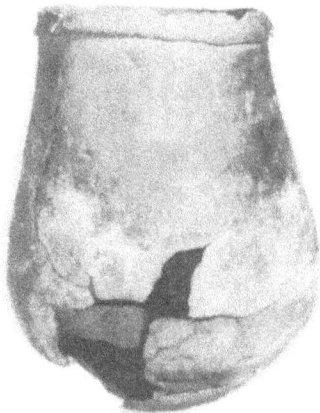

Gallina Plain Utility
Wide-mouth jar with rim
fillet. L. 71.2.34.
Diam. 15.9 cm. Ht. 20.6 cm.

Gallina Plain Utility
Wide-mouth jar.
L. 71.2.36. Diam.
12.7 cm.; Ht. 12.7 cm.

Gallina Plain Utility
Wide-mouth jar.
L. 71.2.5. Diam. 13.0 cm.
Ht. 16.2 cm.

Plate 4

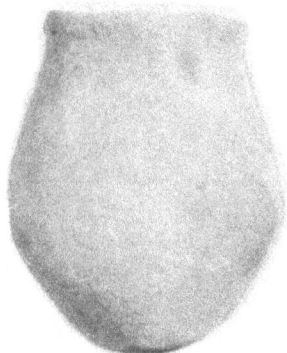

Gallina Plain Utility
Wide-mouth jar.
L. 1.71.2.37 Diam. 14 cm.;
Ht. 17.8 cm.

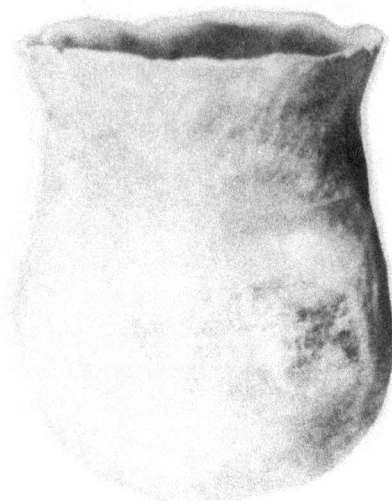

Gallina Plain Utility
Wide-mouth jar.
L. 71.2.6 Diam. 17.8 cm.;
Ht. 22.9 cm.

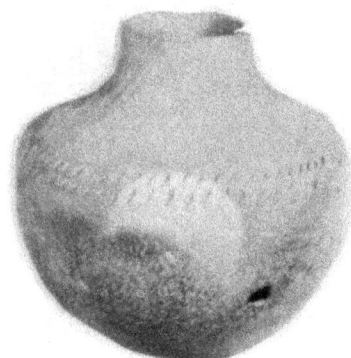

Gallina Incised Utility
Narrow-neck jar.
L. 71.2.4 Diam. 17.2 cm.
Ht. 17.5 cm.

Gallina Plain Utility
Narrow-neck jar.
L. 71.2.1 Diam. 17.2 cm.
Ht. 17.5 cm.

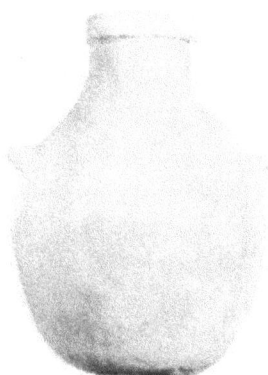

Gallian Plain Utility
Submarine-shaped
canteen with rim fillet
and 2 lugs. L. 71.2.10
Diam. 13.2 cm.
Ht. 18.4 cm.

Gallina Plain Utility
Submarine-shaped vessel.
L. 71.2.9
Diam. 8x15.5 cm.
Ht. 14 cm.

Plate 5

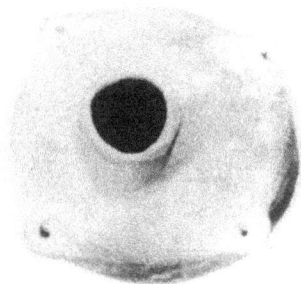

Gallina Plain Utility
Small canteen with rim fillet.
L. 71.2.11. Diam. 14 cm.
Ht. 14.3 cm.

Gallina Black on White bowl
L. 71.2.20. Diam. 15.9 cm.
Ht. 8.9 cm.

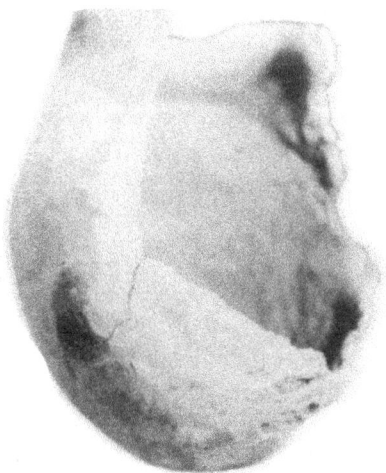

Gallina Plain Utility
Wide-mouth jar.
L. 71.2.18. Diam 17.2 cm.
Ht. 21 cm.

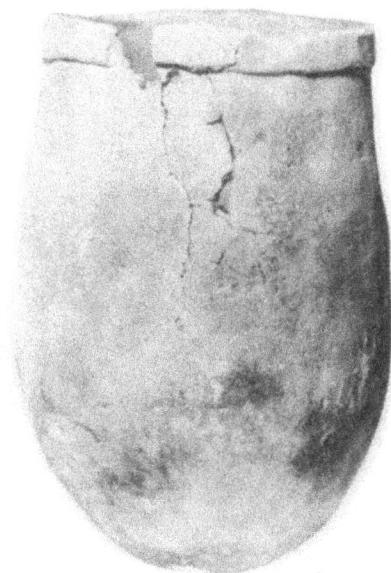

Gallina Plain Utility
Wide-mouth jar with rim
fillet. L. 71.2.14.
Diam. 17.5 cm. Ht. 26 cm.

Plate 6

Gallina Black on White
Bowl with 2 lugs for
suspension.
L. 72.2.2.   Diam. 14.5 cm.
Ht. 9 cm.

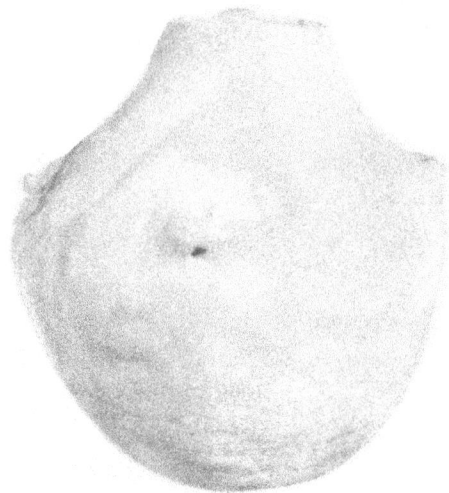

Gallina Plain Utility
Narrow-neck jar with
4 lugs for suspension.
L. 72.2.4.   Diam 18.9 cm.
Ht. 21 cm.

Gallina Plain Utility
Narrow-neck jar.
L. 72.2.6.   Diam. 18.1 cm.
Ht. ?

Gallina Plain Utility
Narrow-neck jar with rim
fillet and indented base.
L. 72.2.7.   Diam 18.1 cm.
Ht. ?

Plate 7

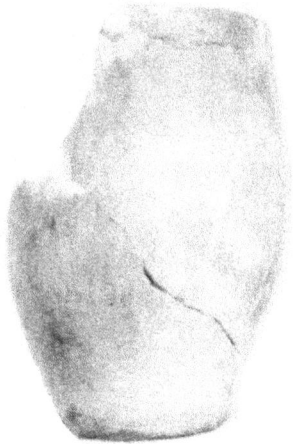

Gallina Plain Utility
Vase-like wide-mouth jar
with rim fillet, and flat bottom.
L. 72.2.1. Diam. 13 cm.
Ht. 20 cm.

Gallina Plain Utility
Wide-mouth jar with rim
fillet. L. 72.2.3
Diam. 25.1 cm. Ht. 33 cm.

Gallina Plain Utility
Canteen with 4 suspension lugs
(2 lugs missing).
L. 72.2.8 Diam 18.7 cm.
Ht. ?

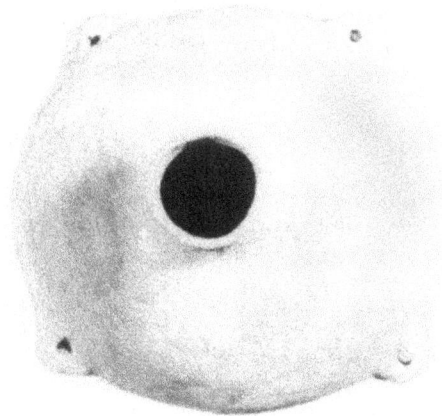

Gallina Plain Utility
Canteen with 4 suspension
lugs. L. 72.2.5
Diam. 20.3 cm.
Ht. 23 cm.

Plate 8

Gallina Black on White
Canteen with 4 suspension
lugs.
L. 73.2.1. Diam. 15 cm.;
Ht. 13.5 cm.

Turkey Springs Site II
Gallina Plain Utility
Narrow-neck jar, partial with
flat spur-like handle on neck.
L. 73.2.2. Diam. 15 cm.;
Ht. 13.5 cm.

Plate 9

CHOPPERS

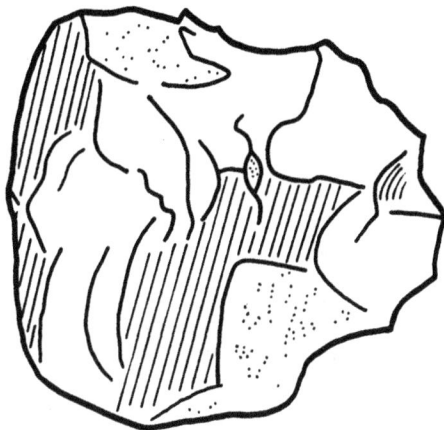

28A TURKEY SPRING II ALLEY 3 Surface Quartz chopper.

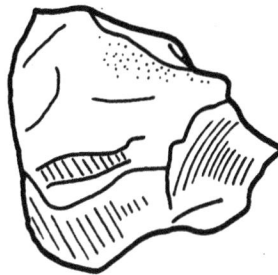

28B TURKEY SPRING II ALLEY 3 Surface Quartz chopper.

Figure 28

Metate:

Basalt block
length 18 in.
width 8-1/2-11 1/2 in.
thickness 4-7 in.

Trough
length 14 in.
width 8 in.

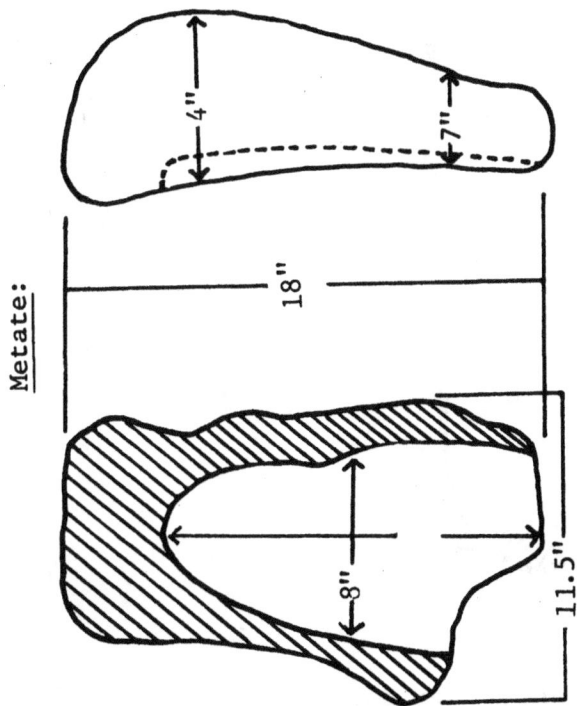

18"   11.5"   4"   7"   8"

▬ = 1-1/2 in.

Figure 26

Polisher (?):

Tanning Stone

length 3-1/4 in.
width 1-5/8 in.
thickness 1 in.

Work Surfaces

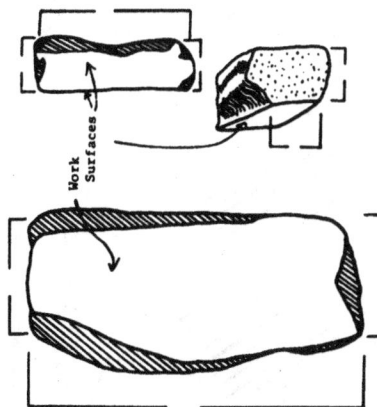

Figure 27

161

— = 1/2 inch

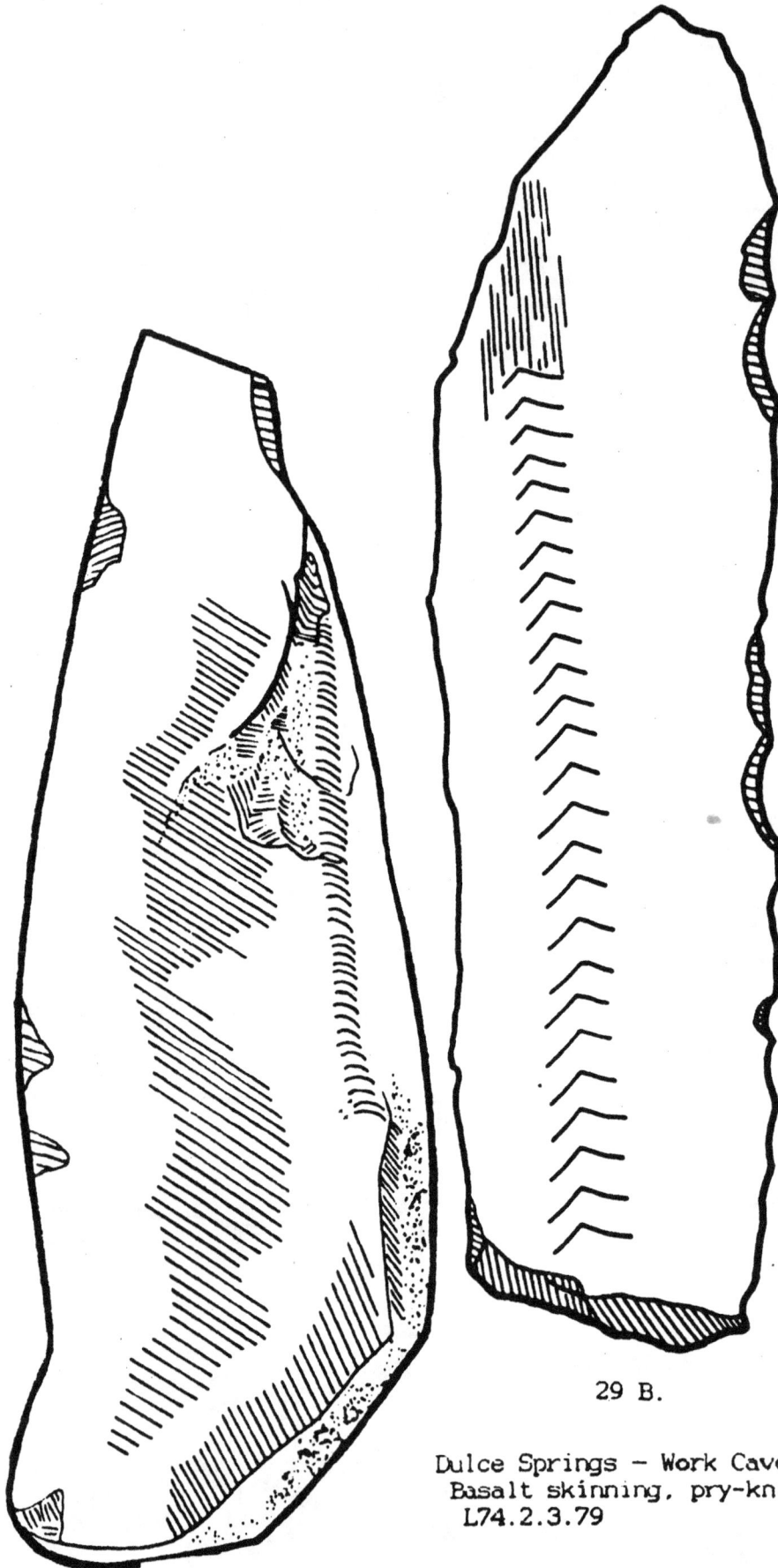
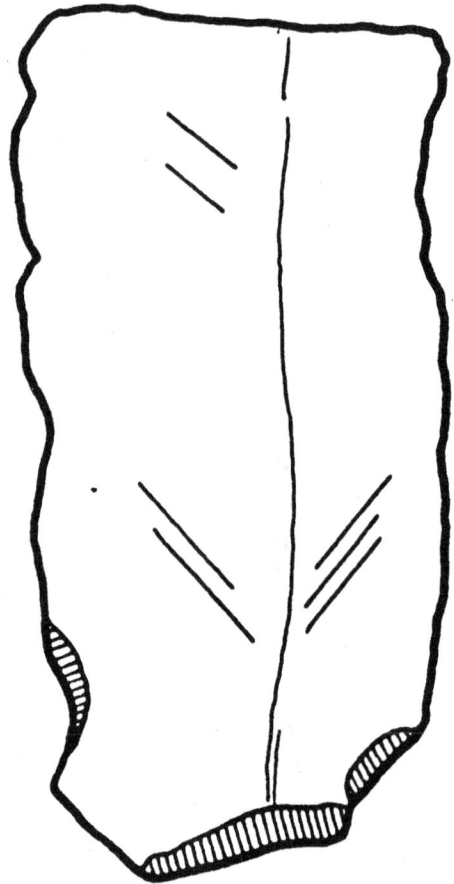

29 C.

Dulce Springs, -- Work Cave 30.
Basalt Saw
L74.2.3.78

29 B.

Dulce Springs — Work Cave 30.
Basalt skinning, pry-knife
L74.2.3.79

29 A.

Four Corners,
Black Diorite, skinning pry-knife

VII

Stone Implements and Mountain Site Economy

In going through the stone implements retrieved from the hunting-gathering campsites of the four groups of Gallina villagers, our first reaction was the realization that chipped stone items were proportionately more numerous per average structure than those found in the home sites of the same people. The majority of these mountain site implements had to do with hunting and processing the resulting meat, skins, and, to a much less extent, bone and antler. One's first conclusion, then, is that the Gallina people must not have been accustomed to handling much large-game hunting, with its attendant activities, from their permanent home sites as base, even though the sites were not far different in altitude from Turkey Spring Site I. We and others (Holbrook and Mackey 1976; Mackey and Holbrook 1978) have pollen evidence that even the now much-eroded and relatively arid territory of the south Llaves district supported pines, Douglas fir, and other vegetation of a biome which may have been more similar to, than different from, that of the mountain sites, but the countryside around home villages probably would have been largely hunted out during the early years of occupation. Moreover, the sights and smells of such occupation would have discouraged an influx of new animals. As field crops became increasingly undependable in the 13th century, an answer to the Gallina need for greater hunting activity could have been the establishment of such hunting camps as we have been investigating.

Our concern with stone implements, as with pottery, takes two major lines. One concentrates on how they were made and of what, but the other, at least as important, looks to the type of use and the economic complex within which such use occurred. As an aid to hypotheses, we have brought to the study what could be learned from Pueblo relatives and descendants whose emphasis on traditional conservatism minimizes the likelihood of change in overall patterns even though details shift. It is with this broader picture in mind that we already have noted for various examples of houses and caves the occurrence of specific stone implements left together with other artifacts as a complex. What we found would not include everything the family used, some items probably having been lost or deteriorated to dust and some carried away by their owners, but the picture remains predictably constant.

Stone work customarily is divided by archaeologists into two large categories, the artifacts made by grinding (pecking and abrasion) and those produced by chipping (chips removed by concussion) and flaking (flakes removed by pressure). Ground stone items required less precise technique but more hours of labor. Fewer types of stone could be used and, fortunately for a sedentary people who must have found themselves very busy at best, fewer ground than flaked implements figured in daily life. Replacement was less of a problem because wear and breakage were slower. The careful conservation of ground stone implements is apparent in almost all such items found in the abandoned

163

houses of home villages being broken or badly worn. Those in good shape had been carried on to a new site even though the weight would have been considerable.

Ground Stone Artifacts

The major ground stone implements of all the historic Pueblos were the metate and mano (a basal stone carrying a pecked grinding area, and a handstone with which to grind), used by women to crush corn first roasted in its shucks and then dried and shelled. As we know that the staple for the prehistoric Pueblos was maize and that they, too, used metates and manos, it is probable that preparation was similar.

Corn flour has been basic to the Pueblo diet at least since the first few centuries after the time of Christ. Maize, originally domesticated in southern Mexico, had been introduced into our Southwest by Mexican Indian traders two to three thousand years earlier, but time was required for the change in overall life patterns imposed by the necessity of becoming sedentary if the people were to be farmers. They also had to learn how to farm. During this period new varieties of corn, again from native Mexico, were introduced. These had been developed to withstand enough cold so that maize cultivation became possible at relatively high altitudes.

The Pueblo people and others of the prehistoric Southwest did not entirely give up their old standby, grass seed, customarily ground in a basin-shaped metate, nor did they forget the numerous wild greens, root crops, fruits, berries, seasonings, and medicinal plants long important. Even within the 20th century some of these still have a place of their own in Pueblo life, but corn became of such primary importance that the religious concept of Corn Mother was made synonymous with that of Earth Mother.

Corn remained the staple until the Spaniards introduced wheat, domed outdoor ovens, and the recipe for raised bread when their first Southwestern settlement was established in San Juan Pueblo in 1598. Since that date corn and wheat have shared first place. We know that cornmeal and corn foods wrapped in cornhusks in the past were prepared for the treks of hunters and warriors. We also know that corn flour and shelled corn from which to grind flour were carried when 20th-century families went out to camp for several weeks or even months of piñon-picking in the mountains. Each family took a metate to camp so that they could grind not only the corn but also herbs used for medicines. The collecting of mountain herbs for medicinal use was one major concern of campers, and they took the plants in amounts intended to last over a lengthy period. The heavy metates were not carried back to the pueblo after each season at the camp but, like other implements brought from home, were hidden somewhere nearby for future use. It is worth remembering that even within the 20th century when Pueblo religious leaders made trips of a few days length to collect medicinal herbs, the plants commonly were dried and ground on a metate concealed in the collecting area. Piñon camps and brief collecting activities provide our closest parallels to what must have taken place in the ancestral hunting-gathering mountain sites.

We found but one metate in our four Canjilon Mountain sites. As it lay on top of the debris of House I-4 at Turkey Spring I, it must have been left on the flat roof of the structure. We actually do not know whether corn was or was not grown in the "gardens" at Turkey Spring I because although no corn pollen was identified in our single soil sample, it is possible that the topsoil in which planting would have taken place on the crest of this ridge could have totally eroded off, leaving only the clay which we found under a thin covering of more recent humus. The campers may have ground shelled corn they had brought from home, or herbs they had collected, or they may even have used the metate for crushing seeds, fruits, berries, or vegetal foods collected in the area.

Our metate, fashioned from a slab of volcanic scoria 45 cm long by 29 cm across, may have been old when brought to the camp. It is of the one-open-end type common in Basketmaker III and Pueblo I sites but also illustrated for the Rosa Phase in Gobernador, ancestral to Gallina culture (Hall 1944a: Figure 33). The pecked grinding basin was long and shallow, 20.3 cm at its widest (Figure 26). At the upper end this basin terminated in a neat oval curve. A corner at the opposite end of the metate had been broken off but the grinding basin extended at full width to the end of the slab (40 cm). To facilitate grinding, this metate was made thicker (17.7 cm) at one end than the other (10 cm) so that it stood by itself at a slant and need not have been used in a bin or with a prop. A big sherd or flat basket or even a piece of tanned skin could have been placed beneath the open end to catch the ground material.

Two fragments of small manos or crushing stones were found in House I-4. Both were of coarse pink quartzite. One fragment (7.5 x 6.5 cm) was 5 cm thick, with the gently curved edge necessary for work in a basin metate or one with a narrow oval at one end, such as ours. This mano had been used on only one flat side (as was frequent for one-hand manos particularly in the Gallina home sites). One edge also appears to have been intended for grinding, possibly for smaller lots of food or medicine. The facet is only 5.3 cm across but exceedingly smooth, again similar to some of the narrow facets found on manos in the Rattlesnake Ridge site.

The second fragment of a mano (?) or crushing stone (11.5 x 6.5 cm) from this house was worn smooth on two faces, and both edges of the side seen on the fragment were gently curved. Exposure to fire (presumably from a burning roof) has left the fragment friable and discolored.

Another mano fragment (11.5 x 7.5 cm, 3.7 cm thick) was found in House II-8 at Turkey Spring Site II. It is of pinkish quartz which appears to have been shaped at the side and even more obviously on its steeply rounded end. From the shape of that end we can see that the implement had split lengthwise not far from its midline, which gives us an estimate of original width at approximately 12 cm. Four centimeters of this were lost to use by the oblique rather than vertical sides. The other break, which ran across the implement, may have lost half or less of its length. One wonders, in looking at the chipped end, whether this rather wide mano may not have been used on top of a grinding surface without raised sides. Otherwise the end should have been worn toward a vertical line instead of each chipped face tapering downward until they met. We see a few of these manos especially those with 3 grinding surfaces, worn to pointed instead of rounded ends in the Rattlesnake Ridge site.

A quartzite grinding or crushing handstone (9 x 9 cm and 6 cm thick) which cannot be classified as a mano came from House 3 at Red Hill, the most elevated site on which we worked. Its rather small base had become much smoothed in grinding, and two angled side surfaces possibly may have been slightly used.

The other manos, one whole and one a fragment, came from House II-21 at Turkey Spring Site II, but, considering their small size, we probably should refer to them merely as "grinding stones." Both are of quartzite, like the others. The fragment presents what appears to be a cross section (8 x 4 cm). The other stone is whole (7.5 x 7.5 cm) but of irregular shape which fits nicely into the palm of one's hand. Both stones show use on but a single face, which had become very smooth.

Our one heavy mano or crushing stone is of volcanic scoria (15.5 x 8.3 cm at the large end and 6.4 cm at the smaller end). It is shaped much like a small loaf of bread, even to the rounded top. The bottom is flat from grinding, but of course far from as smooth as the quartz surfaces we have described. The smaller end is quite flat; the other is irregular and possibly could have been used for pounding. This implement, just large enough to have been used in two hands, was found in Skull Cave toward the southern end of Turkey Spring Site I, probably intentionally hidden. A number of heavy loaf-shaped manos were found in the 2 home sites we dug.

The loaf-shaped scoria mano would have been an efficient corn grinder. The same could be said of the quartzite manos of which we have fragments, though the surfaces of all really are too smooth to have been efficient.

One notable artifact which falls under ground stone implements but never could have been a mano is what until our recent observation would be called a somewhat irregularly shaped polisher with two worked surfaces (Figure 27), one of which gleams. The object is of fine-grained stone, 8.2 x 4.1 cm, with ends 3.2 and 3.5 cm across. The piece resembles some of the finest of the stones which have been known as prehistoric "floor polishers," supposedly employed to compress and harden clay wall or floor surfaces, but it is little more than half their size. One cannot picture anyone bothering with an elaborate finish on a floor or partial floor for these mountain camp structure. It is too large for a pottery polisher. A much more tenable suggestion stems from seeing hides in a modern Rio Grande Pueblo being rubbed and stretched during tanning. A stone similar to the one we recovered is held in the palm to protect the heel of the hand used to stretch and soften the leather.

Another artifact which technically falls into the ground stone category is a small single-grooved arrowshaft polisher (7.8 x 3 cm; 1.5 cm thick) of coarse sandstone. It was picked up on the surface at Turkey Spring Site I, near the cluster made by Structures 17, 18, and 19. The groove .7 cm wide runs lengthwise down the center. This neat little object in itself suggests that these Gallina people were using the fast cane arrows for warfare, as their descendants did in historic times. The nodes of the reed were removed by abrasion with such an implement. It also could have served to remove the bark and smooth the sides of slender branches of local shrubs for the foreshaft of such arrows and for the entire shaft of the slower arrows of wood used to kill game. Cane large enough for arrows, as far as we know, would not have been growing closer than the Chama Valley some 12 miles distant. To young Indians trained, as in the past and even today in Jemez Pueblo, this would not have been a long junket, but wood usable for arrows certainly grew closer. The contrast between the sandstone grooved arrowshaft smoother and the finely shaped and polished "crested arrowshaft polishers" of which we found two in the bin of a Gallina house in the south Llaves district and which sometimes are thought of as distinctive for Gallina culture, presumably rests on a matter of special functions, possibly concerned with use of wood versus cane or reed.

Throughout much of the Southwest, stone axes were made by pecking and grinding, but this was only partly true for the Gallina area where some were shaped from river cobbles by knocking off large flakes to produce sharp irregular edges. No axes at all were retrieved from our mountain sites. Used as weapons as well as for the many purposes an axe might serve, they undoubtedly were carried home by their owners.

Chipped and Flaked Implements

Choppers

In the overall category we think of as largely covering delicately fashioned objects, our only chunky artifacts are the choppers. The shape is roughly conical, though sometimes the cone is partially flattened. In general, choppers are somewhat reminiscent of the cruder of Old World hand axes and probably served many similar purposes. They are longer than wide, and wider than thick. Our mountain campers who showed such preference for quartz cobbles, ranging in color from white to rose, for possible grinding implements, selected the same hard and heavy stones as material for their choppers. Such implements would have been used for chipping other stones, perhaps for knocking flakes off a core, for digging, breaking animal bones and firewood, and probably for macerating some plant materials. At close range one would have been a dangerous weapon.

The upper portion to be clasped in the fist usually is the rock in its natural form, but some chips may be removed so that it fits the worker's hand comfortably. Our largest specimen (Figure 28A), found on the surface in Alley III of Turkey Spring II, is a deep rosy quartz cobble left almost unmodified at the top but with big chips struck off by percussion to form a jagged edge down the two sides and across the rounded point. With this heavy artifact, a man's implement (9.8 x 10.5 cm; 6 cm thick), one easily could kill an enemy or an animal, chop branches, take a yucca plant apart, dig cattail rootstalks for food, break away protruding pieces of lava, or excavate a roasting pit.

Our chopper next in size is of white quartzite (7.0 x 6.8 cm; 4.2 cm thick), a cobble unworked on one face but flaked entirely over the other. It was found in Structure 30, a cave in the Dulce Springs community, and I am inclined to think of it as a woman's implement because it fits a woman's hand, though we must remember that most of the Pueblo men of today have much smaller hands and feet than their Anglo counterparts. This chopper looks as if it had lost a once-sharper tip through use.

Our other small chopper (Figure 28B: 6.7 x 7.0 cm; 3.5 cm thick) was found in the cave (Structure 30) adjacent to Houses III-17 and III-18 in Dulce Springs. It is a piece of pink and white quartz cobble worked over much of its surface. It fits well into a small woman's hand. The tip is a sharp point. It is easy to picture the housewife using it to break bones for marrow and to make them short enough to go into her stew pot.

Skinning Pry-Knife, Saw, and Stone Pot Lid

These three unusual categories, each represented by a single specimen from the mountain sites, assure us that the Gallina people were open to new thoughts on useful equipment and observant of materials from which to make the artifacts they envisioned. Let us hasten to add that although none of these three items is unknown elsewhere in the Southwest, nowhere are they at all common. According to contemporary Jemez accounts, Pueblo hunters often disjointed the limbs of a freshly killed deer but left the tendons in so that the legs could be brought together to make carrying the animal easier. First the carcass must be hung, well out of reach of animals, to bleed and briefly cure. A deer might be carried home whole, after hanging, if killed fairly near living quarters. Otherwise, only the heart, lungs, liver, and both hind legs were brought home initially to be eaten shortly. The remainder could be left hanging until later. The work of skinning was done in the hunting camp, which in the case of those we have described on Canjilon Mountain would have been moderately close and convenient. Slicing up the meat to dry for jerky also would have been done there, and our guess is that the women may have been expected to handle much of that task.

The skinning pry-knife (Morris 1939: Plate 169c, d) (Figure 29A) for which our identification depends on some bits of fortunate information from Pueblo men of the living Rio Grande Pueblos, measures 24 x 6.5 cm, with approximately straight sides tapering to an oval tip. Originally it had been a tongue of basalt which showed the wrinkled lines left as the surface had cooled. The hunter who picked it up recognized that with a minimum of labor he could make himself an instrument to separate the skin from the flesh of deer or elk when the hide was to be used and should show no welts.

In this century Pueblo men often have cut flat wooden paddles with oval tip for the same purpose. Navajo women sometimes use the dull backside of a butcher knife to push into difficult areas while skinning an animal, especially around its head, and Pueblo men find that a folded jackknife can serve the same purpose. For prehistoric comparisons we can look at a black diorite skinning pry-knife from the Four Corners area, a somewhat uncommon implement usually erroneously tossed into the category of chamahias (stone hoe blades especially characteristic of Mesa Verde culture). This diorite specimen measures 25.3 x 7.3 cm at its widest point (Figure 29B). It has an angled beveled (but not greatly thinned) tip and tapering handle. The Gallina basalt

Figure 30

Knives to be hafted (73% actual size)

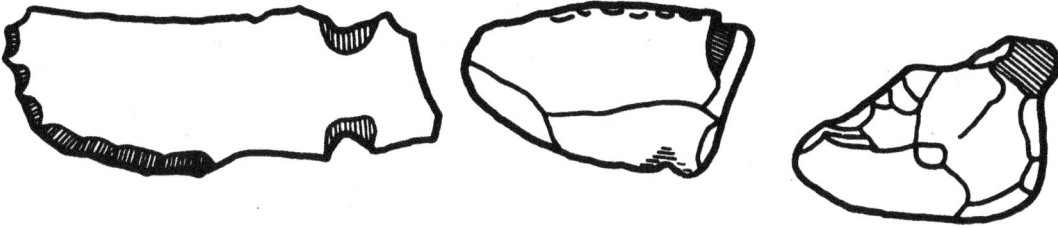

A. Dulce Springs, Feature 3
Obsidian, 7.5x3 cm.

B. Dulce Springs Feature 14
Obsidian, 4.9x3.2 cm.

C. Turkey Spring I, Bain's Cave
Obsidian 4.7x3.2 cm.

Non-hafted Knives)73% actual size)

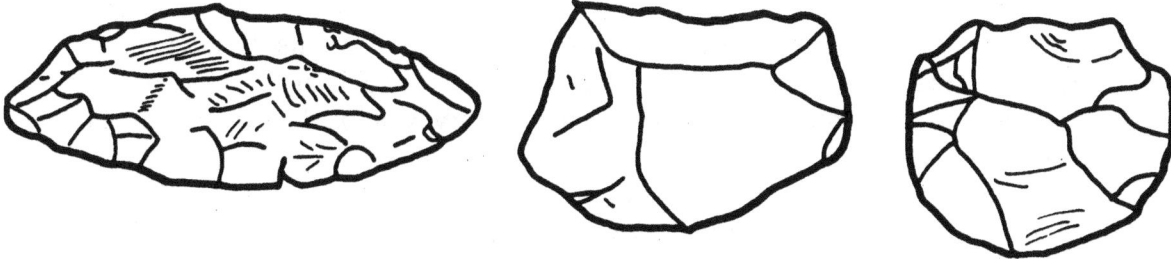

A. Turkey Spring I, surface
Gray Quartzite flake knife
8.3x3.3 cm.

B. Turkey Spring II, surface
Obsidian Knife, edges
dulled by use. 5.8x
3.8 cm.

C. Red Hill-Canjilon Mt. surface.
Heavy circular knife, rose and
white chert. 4.8x4.2 cm.

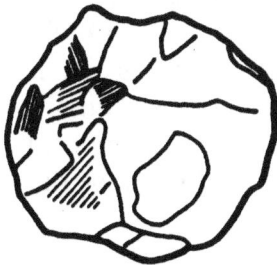

D. Turkey Spring II, Cave 12
Circular chert knife
4.7x4.8 cm.

E. Turkey Spring II surface.
Chert burin blade dulled
by use. 7x4.2 cm.

F. Red Hill-Canjilon Mt. surface.
Triangular knife with burin,
and cutting curve. 3.9x2.6 cm.

Figure 31

169

counterpart found in Structure 30, the work cave located a short distance from Houses 14 and 22 at the Dulce Springs camp, has a number of shallow chips intentionally knocked off its straight side and a few down over the curve of the angled tip. The edges of the front half of this Gallina pry-knife are noticeably worn; the chipped edges along the rear half where one would grasp the implement are appreciably sharper. In its lighter weight, more slender lines, and thinner well-shaped tip, this was much the better implement of the two.

On the floor of the cave with the pry-knife was a fine "snubnosed scraper" (Figure 34D) made from a flake of the rose and white chert (5.8 x 4 cm) so favored by this Gallina group. It was not surprising to find many deer bones and a few debitage flakes in the same cave.

Few saws are found in prehistoric sites, though they certainly would have been a convenience, and rarely are they as large as our specimen (Figure 29C 14 x 6.8 cm). It had been made from a natural flake of gray basalt with one flat side and a horizontal ridge on the other, the two planes sloping down to the edges. Uneven chipping was added to one edge to produce the jagged saw-like effect. A second glance shows us the lunate curve which so commonly appears on our mountain site cutting implements. Here, as in the other examples, it is near the end of one side and shows wear. Distance across the curve (2.1 cm) is close to the width of several of the lunate curves on blades. What may have been an aberrant attempt to produce such a curve is seen on a corner of the opposite plane on the saw front, but the stone was too thick at that point and the edge of the resulting flake scar is not sharp and does not show use. Two smaller pieces, 3 and 6 cm long, which could have come from the same original flake and had been used as scrapers or saws, were found in Bain's Cave, Turkey Spring I.

The stone pot-lid is an object of unusual interest because of its rarity in small size, though the larger flat stone lids worked from a sandstone slab or a large flat quartzite cobble for storage jars and large floor cists are not unusual in Gallina home sites. The small lid (10.5 x 9.7 cm) from House I-4 in Turkey Spring I is a large domed flake from a pink quartz cobble, chipped around the periphery to improve its more-or-less circular shape, and then somewhat ground on top of the chipping to rid it of sharpness. Final thickness at the edge varies from 3 to 9 mm. It is very reminiscent of the sherd pot-lid described in the chapter on pottery and would have fitted a small-to-medium cook or storage pot. The Jemez people of today explain that stone lids customarily were placed over the tops of jars in which cooked fruits or corn flour were stored. Elsewhere in the Southwest, jars with lids sealed on with clay at the edges have been found. Whether lids ever were used to speed cooking (as in our own kitchens) no one knows.

Blades and Scrapers

In one of the classic studies of Anasazi stone artifacts, Woodbury (1954:142) emphasizes that "most of the tools of the Indians of the Southwest were put to a multiplicity of uses" and that "many of the tools used for cutting and scraping formerly may have been used on projectiles."

Figure 32

A. Turkey Spring II, Cave 12
Obsidian flake knife, all edges
worked. Burin point near one
end, adjoining lunate curve.
5.2x1.7 cm.

B. Turkey Spring II, surface.
Obsidian burin flaked on
all sides to a thin edge.

C. Turkey Spring II, House 27
White chert burin blade.
3.4x1.3 cm.

D. Turkey Spring I, surface
Obsidian burin blade.
2.3x2.4 cm.

E. Turkey Spring I, surface
Obsidian burin blade
1.9x1.7 cm.

F. Dulce Springs 22
Obsidian burin blade
1.7x1.8 cm.

BURIN BLADES

A. Turkey Spring II, House 13
Beige color translucent
chert arrowshaft tool
with lunate curve and
burin. All edges finished
for cutting.
5x3.2 cm.

B. Turkey Spring II, House 26
Obsidian Arrowshaft tool
with lunate curve and burin.
6.5x3.2 cm.

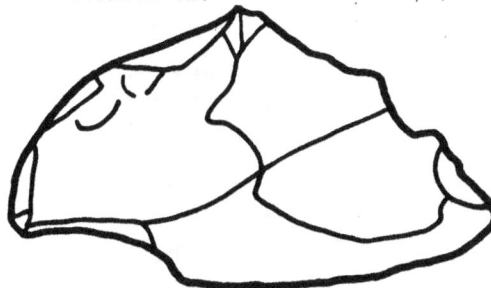

C. Red Hill
Obsidian blade with
lunate curve and
burin. 3.5x4.5 cm.

D. Turkey Spring II, Cave 12
Rose chert lunate-burin
Arrowshaft tool.
7.5x4.5 cm.

Figure 33

ARROWSHAFT TOOLS

The initial concept of separating implements by simple use categories thus becomes difficult and puzzling. When is a projectile point only a projectile point, and when is it a knife or a scraper?

Most of the mountain site implements do not show a great deal of wear which might aid our interpretation of use. Thinking of knives in our own kitchen, we quickly recognize that what has been purchased as a blade often takes on several functions. We peel the apple, scrape carrots, cut eyes from potatoes, cut up stew meat, strip celery, and sometimes even scale a small fish with the same implement because it fits the hand well. Larger and smaller specialized tools may lie for months unused in the drawer.

One can scan the edges of a stone implement with a 10-power hand glass or peer at them through a 30-power microscope. Both help. But the problem of interpretation of what one sees requires further understanding. Pick up a fresh flake and use it to cut a twig or to scrape a bit of wood or bone. Use another fresh edge of glass and cut into (as we did) a piece of cowhide a few months old. Use a third fresh edge to scrape an inside area of that hide clean. Magnification shows that employment as a knife results in edges becoming finely serrated by the horizontal wear. Use of the glass fragment or the stone flake on a hard material may mark the smooth surface of the implement with a minute scratch line or two crossing the many natural lines which stem from the bulb of percussion. If the flake edge has been used much and thereby dulled, that also will show in the series of once-sharp-edge cusps now being flattened. The edge may even feel dull when tried with one's finger.

A used scraper, in contrast, often has lost a series of small flakes leaving scars reminiscent of half bubbles along its edge, roughening it. This also can happen to a blade when cutting wood, but the scraper picks up no horizontal lines.

The point, in contrast to both blade and scraper, should not show wear or lines on its edges. Warm fresh flesh and even fresh hide are soft.

We still come up with use categories based on the preponderance of traits which appear to place the object according to its major function. Under "blades" we would list knives, scrapers, scraper-knives, and what we are thinking of at present as probably an "arrowshaft tool." This implement leads us into the subject of burins or gravers, which may be found alone or flaked onto the corner of a knife or an "arrowshaft tool."

The chipped and flaked implements, most numerous of all the artifacts here, were used primarily for slaying animals and preparing plant foods, but on the latter our data are minimal.

KNIVES: The classification problem, as already noted, at times becomes very real in attempting to separate knives, scrapers, and points. The Gallina people made some excellent knives, well shaped, well flaked, sharp, and generally pleasing to look at and doubtless to use. Scrapers obviously planned for that specialized use and very well fashioned also were made. But some of the scrapers would have done well for cutting and some of the less specialized knives would have worked well as scrapers. The most efficient of all the cutting edges actually were on small unworked thin flakes of obsidian which could have been used as scrapers on small skins or as knives if one were more interested in delicate cutting than hacking, but they would have required a flexible and skilled hand in manipulation. They also would have dulled rapidly, making replacement necessary.

Small knives, which at first glance look like points, also were made and some broken projectile points may have been reworked into knives or scrapers. We could wish that the implements showed heavier wear which might aid in our interpretations. Although some of our mountain site implements definitely were knives and some were scrapers of specialized type, we have designated a few as scraper-knives where it is clear that the artifact could have served both uses. Brief use and easy replacement are suggested.

In our Gallina home sites of the south Llaves district (excavated after the sites on Canjilon Mountain), chert was a common material for implements, but for some obsidian was used. In the mountain area obsidian implements were more common than those of chert. There is no question that the type of implement to be made largely but not entirely determined choice of material. The obsidian, ranging from almost transparent to gleaming black to dull gray (rare) was taken mostly from the famed deposits in the Jemez Mountains a little south of Los Alamos and perhaps 35 miles distant from the Llaves area home sites. Most, if not all, of the chert came from Pedernal Peak about 25 miles from Llaves, that conveniently located source of great beds, ranging from gray through white to attractive pink obviously was the most attractive to our mountain flint-knappers, as to us. Chalcedony, semitranslucent when flaked thin, also would be found there and was used for a few of the finest implements. Quartz ran a low fourth in amount chosen for flaked items.

Our four most sophisticated knives, each intended for hafting, are of obsidian. The first (Figure 30A) is extraordinary in that it so resembles our own knives. The glossy black obsidian of which it was made had been found as a natural, long smooth piece about 5 mm thick at the center, with a slight torque and thinning toward its sides. The hunter who picked up this little treasure removed a series of spaced flakes from each side to make a curving blade on one edge, with a tip tapered toward the opposite edge as in our kitchen table knives. About 1 cm from the proximal end he put a notch 8 mm wide in each edge. Thus he had a sturdy and sharp serrated knife with a tang and notches to permit efficient horizontal hafting. As both edges of the blade for 3 cm below the notches show grinding (abrading), it seems that the binding may have extended down that far, leaving a protruding blade of 3.5 cm.

A second knife (Figure 30B) obviously intended to be hafted is of gleaming black obsidian, a flake with no further work on the back but a small amount on the front. The edges have been flaked all the way around on both sides. In shape this knife has a somewhat narrowed but rounded point. On each edge, as close as might be to the proximal end of the knife, a notch has been made so that a haft might be lashed to the blade. The shank or tang is so short that the assemblage would seem not to have been very strong,

173

though for a distance of 9 mm below each of the two notches the side of the blade has been ground to prevent cutting of the binding which evidently reached that far.

It is possible that the shank to this knife originally was longer but has been broken. The blade projecting beyond the ground areas is only 3.3 cm long but appears to have lost a bit off its tip. This specimen came from the fill of House 14 in Dulce Springs.

The third obsidian knife made for hafting is triangular (4.7 x 3.2 cm), worked over both surfaces and all edges but with a rough knob left at one upper corner (Figure 30C). It came from Bain's Cave in Turkey Spring I. The flat knob was the tang provided for hafting with two thin pieces or even a single piece of wood or bone split at one end to permit insertion of that projection. Another possibility is that the haft consisted of two flat pieces of wood or bone, the whole secured by sinew bindings and possibly some piñon gum. As the haft necessarily took an upward angle, the whole would have been less strong than the horizontal knife described above. The fourth (6.5 x 4.0 cm) with an asymmetric blade serrated on one side and a irregular protruding base to carry the haft came from the floor level of House I-1.

The items we categorized as "projectile point-like blades or knives to be hafted or not" came in some individualistic variations but also in type groups.

One is a little keeled blade (3.2 x 2.1 cm) of dark brown flint, its back humped, its front somewhat concave, with most of the retouching done on the front edges which come together in a sharp tip. The back has been thinned on one side but the natural shape of the flake prevented a neat outline. This implement, with back keel, found in House II-13, Turkey Spring II, would have been easier to hold in the fingers than one of the thin unretouched flakes. The blade still is sharp though some minute use-flakes on the edges prove that it saw service.

A small (3 x 1.6 cm) leaf-shaped knife from House III-1, Dulce Springs, is no more than a thin piece of almost clear obsidian, retouched mostly on one side. It differs from a piece of debitage picked up for use only in that it has been retouched.

An appreciably larger and more sturdy knife, also from House III-1, Dulce Springs, is a slightly asymmetrical blade of obsidian (4.7 x 2.3 cm) without notches. Some dulling of the edge can be felt and also seen under a glass.

From House I-2 came two nonnotched triangular obsidian flake items which may be blanks (preforms) from which to fashion points but quite possibly were knives. (See Type 4 in Figure 35.) One measures 2 x 1.8 cm and the other 3 x 2 cm (one lower corner missing). These and 4 others have thin worked edges and give the impression of a fine serration though no individual barbs are visible. The peak of the triangle is sharp. They might have been hafted with the aid of gum but could have been held in the fingers.

The category of "knives never hafted, with and without burins" is best represented by a fine gray leaf-shaped quartz blade (Figure 31A) measuring 8.3 x 3.3 cm. This was picked up on the surface at Turkey Spring I. The knife had been flaked all over on both sides; all edges were retouched. Ends were moderately pointed. A much simpler obsidian knife (Figure 31B) found below what appeared to be the floor of House I-1 at the same site was merely a flake showing three large scars on the front and with lower edge retouched on both sides. This knife (6 x 4.5 cm) had been used enough in cutting for its edges to have been considerably dulled.

A contrasting shape for what appears from use evidence to have been a knife rather than a scraper is approximately circular, the basis being either a thick flake with domed cortex surface on one side or a piece of stone worked on both sides into such a shape. Our first example in this group (Figure 31C: 4.8 x 4.2 cm; 2.0 cm thick at center) is of rose and white chert with a central ridge down the worked side. The circumference edge has been worked where necessary on the front and the scars from miniature use-flakes give the effect of minute serration in some parts. At one point a small burin may have been left. This artifact was found on the surface at the brow of a terrace between Canjilon Peak and Red Hill. A second example (Figure 31D: 4.7 x 4.8 cm; 2 cm thick at center) is of rose and gray chert with inclusions, worked on both sides and with an area of cortex still showing. A small burin apparently was intentionally chipped to project from one side, though making a smoother circle would have been easier than shaping this projection. The specimen came from Cave 12 in Turkey Spring II.

Another knife (Figure 31E) found on the surface at Turkey Spring II had been made from a large thick flake of rose and white chert with only a few flakes removed from the back but the entire front flaked and the lower curved edge serrated. This piece (7 x 4.2 cm) could have served as a scraper if one wished. It legitimately can be referred to as a combination tool, for extending upward .5 cm above the top is a sharp little burin or graver. Had we not found projecting burins as a common addition to various shapes of mountain knives or knife-scrapers we might have overlooked this example as merely an indication of uneven finishing.

In what activity does one use a burin? As with a knife tip, this small protruding point can be used to inscribe bone for cutting reeds or a slim branch of hardwood cut for arrowshafts, cattails gathered for roof covering, and foods or medicines sliced. One can trace a pattern into buckskin or make small slits to accommodate lacings of tanned skin. Against the sharp side of a burin one can cut through strands of yucca fiber or sinew, the makings for a bowstring, the twine for wrappings, the thread for sewing. Jemez men today buy a hooked knife, actually a shoemaker's tool, to cut sinew and tendons.

In the old days, explain Jemez Pueblo people, the Gallina ancestors lived in too cool a climate for raising cotton, so clothing was made from skins. Not necessarily buckskin, which became uncomfortable on one's body when wet and did not hold up well. A man wore a short kilt of hide tanned with the fur still on the outside. Yucca strips or fiber provided a belt to hold it in place. In cold weather a man's shirt was a piece of skin tanned with the hair still on.

175

A. Turkey Spring II, House 26
    Triangular obsidian scraper.
    Part of cortex remains.
    All 3 edges used.

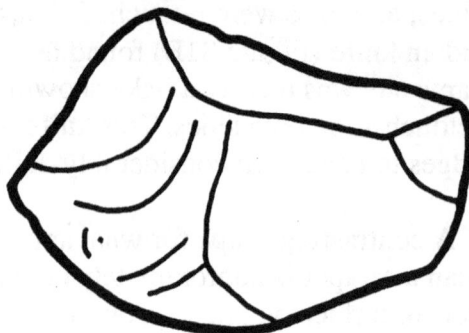

B. Turkey Spring I, House 1
    Obsidian scraper.
    6x4.3 cm.

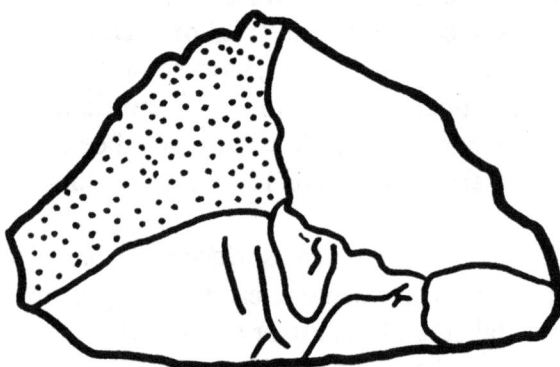

C. Turkey Spring II, House 15
    Obsidian scraper.
    7x4.5 cm.

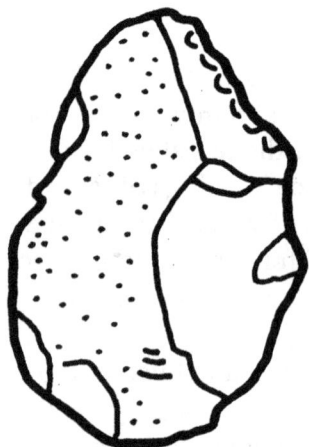

D. Dulce Springs, Cave 30
    Rose and white chert.
    5.8x3.5 cm.

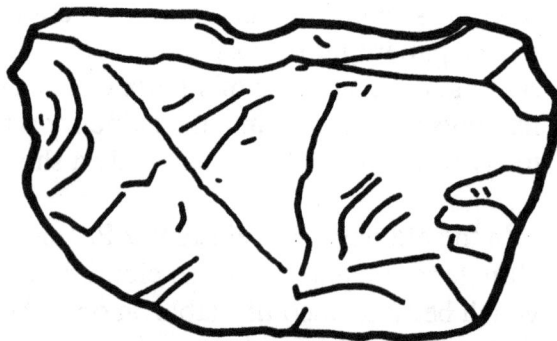

E. Turkey Spring I, Surface
    chert.   7.3x3.9 cm.

Figure 34

POINT TYPES (actual size)

Point types found in the Canjilon Mountain Sites

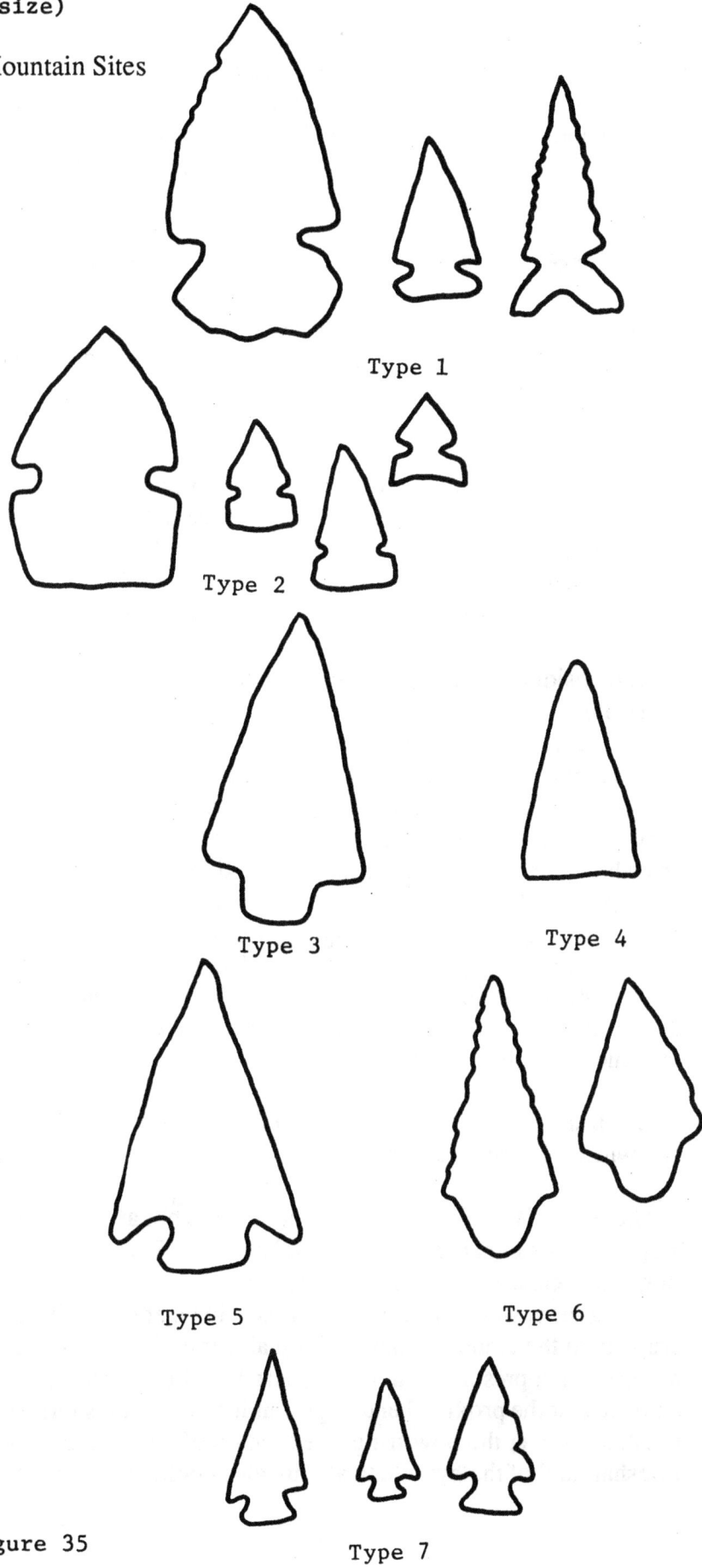

Type 1

Type 2

Type 3

Type 4

Type 5

Type 6

Type 7

Figure 35

177

It went over one shoulder and under the other, like the top of a Pueblo woman's woolen dress in post-Spanish times. When the shirt was tucked under the belt or into the kilt, it was allowed to blouse enough in front to form a pouch in which implements and food (including the turkey eggs to be relished should a clutch be found) could be carried. A woman's dress was of the same pattern but, whether made in one or two pieces, was longer than the kilt. Men wore sandals; women frequently went without.

Another obsidian knife (3.1 x 2.6 cm) with burin addition was triangular and worked all over, including its edges (Figure 31F). The burin at one corner is just beyond a sharp, shallowly curved depression in the edge, a knife blade intended for rounded surfaces. The opposite corner of the implement was so sharply pointed that it could have been used for shallow reaming or even for graving. This knife was found on the surface in the little group of structures at Red Hill.

Still another obsidian burin-knife consisted of an elongated flake blade flat on one side but with two opposing planes forming a ridge down the center of the other. All the edges had been delicately worked, and protruding out from the side at one end was a small beak-shaped burin (Figure 32A). The whole measured 5.2 x 1.7 cm. The implement had been left in the floor fill of Cave 12, Alley IV, Turkey Spring II.

One obsidian flake burin as such (Figure 32B), found on the surface in Alley III of the same site, had been chipped all over and to a thin edge on all sides. It could have been used for cutting, but none of the edges was straight. The main use of the instrument may have depended on the burin which angled up like a small truncated pyramid. The overall size of this flake was 3 x 3.2 cm. Another, a thin white chert flake (Figure 32C) which shows working and may have been used as a knife is so small (3.4 x 1.5 cm) that it is probable the beaked-hook burin at one end indicates its primary use. A small obsidian knife (Figure 32D: 2.3 x 2.4 cm) with burin at one corner was found on the surface at Turkey Spring I and another (Figure 32E: 1.9 x 1.7 cm) at House 22, Dulce Springs. An even smaller piece (Figure 32F: 1.7 x 1.8 cm) of worked obsidian which seems to have been made intentionally as a burin knife also was found in the fill of House 22. Many of the burin projections are shaped like birds' heads, and in some examples one can easily imagine the entire bird (Figures 32C, 33C).

This brings us to an implement which appears to have been intended for arrowmaking and which also bears a burin.

Hitherto this implement was without name but after we had spotted at least four examples, we designated it the "arrowshaft tool." It was used primarily, we surmise, in cutting reeds, cane, or slender branches from shrubs to become shafts for arrows and in scraping them where necessary. This would be at the nodes of reeds and where twigs had erupted on the branch. A neat section also must be cut from the distal end of a reed shaft to receive the presumed short foreshaft of wood which carried the stone point, and possibly also at the proximal end to permit insertion of a short wooden plug carrying the notch to fit over the bowstring. Preparation of the short and slender elliptically shaped foreshaft and of the hypothetical plug also could have been done with this instrument.

The most beautiful of our "arrowshaft tools" (Figure 33A) was made from a thin piece of slightly pinkish translucent chalcedony (5.0 x 3.2 cm). The front side and all edges of this flake have been worked. At the bottom is a wide concave lunate curve which by shape and sharpness of the edge would have served very well in cutting reeds or slender branches or have scraped a foreshaft into shape. At the end of this curve is a burin which, with the thinned edges making up the other sides, would have been useful for cutting sinew with which to secure feathers and point to foreshaft and for notching the proximal end of the shaft to take the bowstring and splitting the foreshaft tip to take the point. This specimen came from the fill in House 13, Turkey Spring II.

A second tool of this type (Figure 33B: 6.4 x 3.9 cm) is of clear-to-black obsidian with small-dot inclusions. All edges are thin and show use. The two roughly curved spaces on top may have served for cutting something tough enough to have produced a shattering effect along the thin edge; we would guess they had been used across reeds or wood with a sawing motion. The burin, which shows use across its small top, projects just at the end of one of the cutting-curves, as frequently is seen. The lower long edge has been dulled as well as a little shattered probably by sawing and/or cutting. With its two ends lower than the long center area, it would have made anything but a good scraper, for those projections would have cut into a hide.

A third example, smaller and simpler (Figure 33C: 3.5 x 3.1 cm), is of dense rather than clear obsidian, worked on both sides. Most of the top is a wide smooth curve, the edge adapted to cutting. This lunate curve apparently had been achieved by a single firm tap on a pointed instrument (of antler?) held against the flake. Extending out from this curve is a burin. The entire lower edge of the flake has been sharpened by removing small flakes from both sides.

One other possible example (Figure 33D) is of rose and white chert (7.7 x 4.5 cm) with hollow back. This, ostensibly, is a triangular scraper in shape, with a somewhat curved lower edge, obviously worn, but the last 2.5 cm of that lower edge is in a shallow concave, slightly irregular curve, and it shows use which could have to do with cutting bone, reeds, or wood. It could not have served for scraping on a flat surface because its own curvature stands above the down-curving remainder of the lower edge. At the outer corner of the shallow curve is what appears to be a small burin.

Fine gray quartz is the material for another large and thin blade (6.7 x 4.3 cm), its lower edge and one small end rough but used. The most interesting edge on this implement is somewhat concave, thin and sharp (the edge of a large flake scar), and definitely has been used for cutting if we may judge by the series of minute use-flake scars which cover its full length (2.2 cm). Once again we suggest reed- or slender branch-cutting as a major use, and if this is so, the implement was an arrowshaft tool. An approximation of a burin was made on its smaller end.

SCRAPERS AND SCRAPER-KNIVES: This category includes instruments which have been intentionally fashioned according to pattern and a great many more which actually were debitage picked up for use. One of the former (Figure 34A: 5.1 x 3.7 cm) from

STONE ARTIFACTS - POINTS

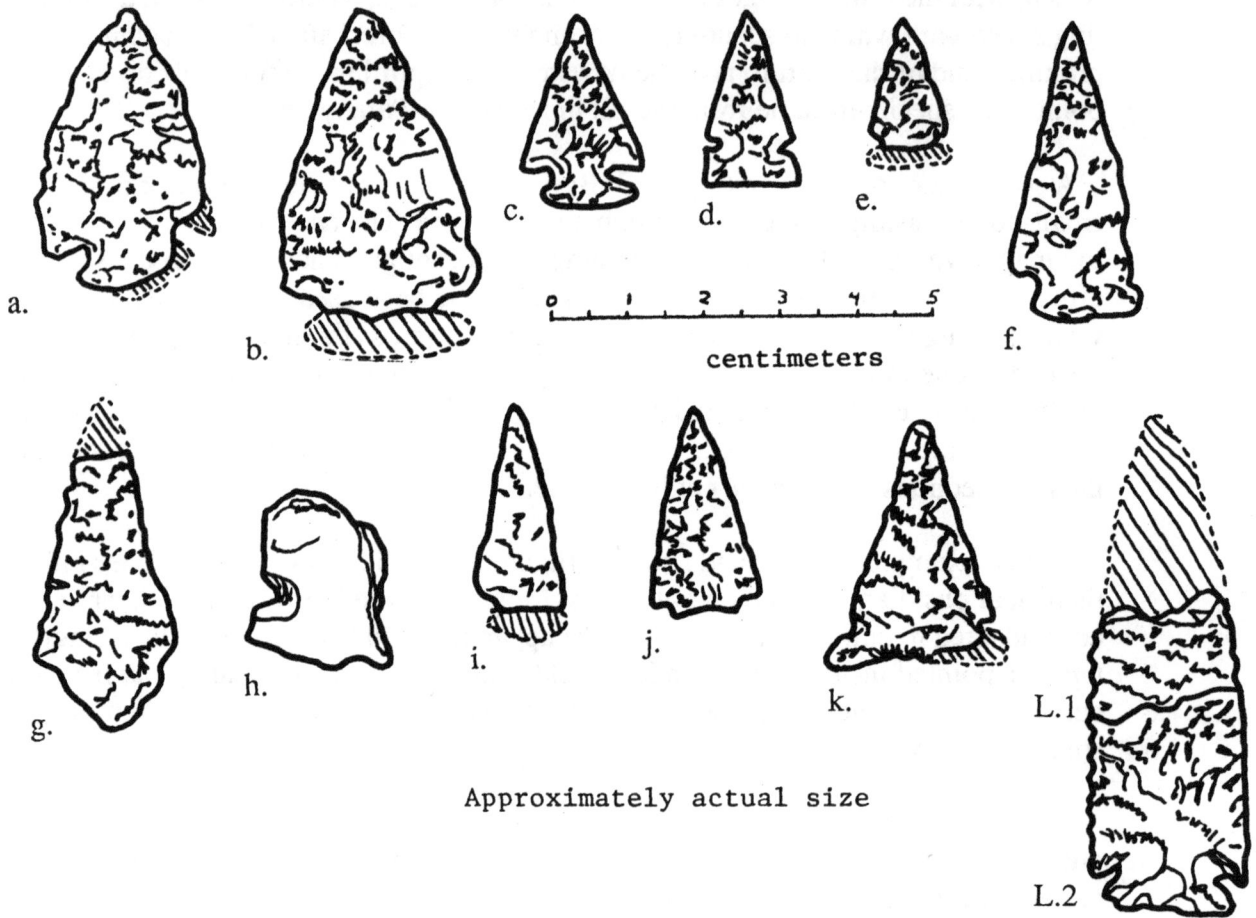

a. through g. - obsidian points.
h. Obsidian with inclusions; possibly a fractured point.
i. Basalt point.
j. & k. White Quartz points.
L.1 & L.2 Chert points (material not recognized but not a local chert).

Figure 36

House II-26, Alley II, at Turkey Spring II is a triangular obsidian flake with concave back retouched with only a little flaking at the edges but showing three major flake scars and an area of the original cortex on the front. The cortex area has been ground near the edge to thin that periphery. All three edges were retouched on the front. This implement with its major edge in a convex curve would have made an excellent scraper and shows dulling from use. It certainly could have been used as a knife as well.

A rather similar triangular obsidian knife-scraper (Figure 34B: 6.0 x 4.3 cm) was found on the surface at Turkey Spring I-1 (House). It shows some retouching of the long curved edge on both sides and some tiny use-flakes missing from the more-or-less straight opposite edge.

Another triangular scraper (Figure 34C) of obsidian, much like those just described but a little larger (7.0 x 4.5 cm), was picked up on the surface about 1 meter from the possible roasting pit, Structure 15, at Turkey Spring II. The back shows no retouching but only a few tiny use-flake scars. The front has two large flake scars and an area of original cortex. Two edges, side and long bottom, show some use-scars; the bottom appears to have been retouched in part.

A rose and white semitranslucent chert scraper (Figure 34D: 5.5 x 3.7 cm) and 2 unused flakes were found with the skinning pry-knife in the work cave (Structure 30, by function) at Dulce Springs. Part of the cortex is present on this approximately triangular implement.

A contrasting shape is that of a rose and white chert scraper (Figure 34E), in rectangular form (7.3 x 3.9 cm) flaked on both faces, the three edges worked on both sides, and only the thick tip (1.6 cm across) left in its original state.

Some small scrapers and scraper-knives were intentionally shaped, the most common form being the small end-scraper (not "snubnosed") of obsidian, perhaps 2 cm high by 1.5 cm wide. Use of the lower end is obvious. The most exotic of these, with about the same measurements but with its greater dimension being in width rather than height, is a piece of red chert, with a few dark flecks and dots on its interior. The surface and lower edge have been worked. This colorful piece from the surface of Turkey Spring I no doubt was a much-prized possession.

Because the shapes were accidental and use evidently brief for most, the little scraper-knives do not warrant lengthy description. Their presence and that of the lesser number of debitage flakes (usually smaller) found unused give us one important insight, the practice of flint-knapping in the camp houses and work caves, as already noted. From such a special area as we have described between Sites IV and V at Red Hill, we know that the men also gathered to work together in the open.

Gallina Type Points

The most interesting of all artifacts to some persons is the projectile point, and many tend to think of a specific type as the unquestionable identification mark for a certain tribe or culture. Though this is relatively true for pottery, it is much less so for point types. One even may find that several point types were produced by a single culture group, and similarly shaped points by different culture groups. This quite certainly was the case for our Gallina mountain-camp people (Figure 35). Though we cannot at present state that every type found was a Gallina product, at least five were. If we further subtract the one type which may have been a knife rather than a point, or possibly even a blank carried into the area so that points could be completed when needed, we still have our people making and using four types of projectile points.

Seven types of points and/or related blades were found on the surface or in house or cave fill in these mountain sites. All but three types were side-notched. A flake was removed at right angles to the edge of the blade near its base. The edge of that notch was ground by rubbing it with something abrasive so that the point could be bound to a foreshaft without the sinew binding being cut.

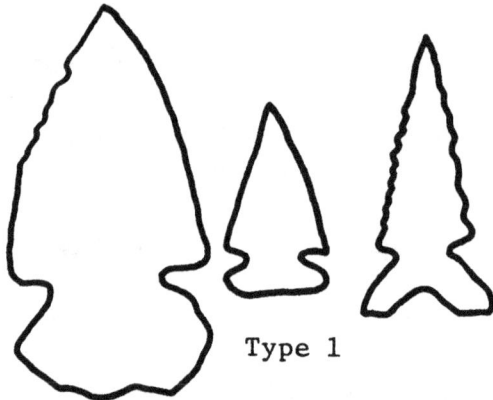

Of the three remaining types, two were corner- or diagonal-notched; the notch was put in at an angle which separated stem from blade. These may not be of Gallina workmanship. The other type was without notches and, as already stated, could have been a knife rather than a projectile point, but it appears to belong to the Gallina complex.

Type 1

GALLINA TYPE 2 POINTS: The points which we have gathered under the designation of Type 1 can be described technically as triangular, side-notched, with stem wider than the shoulders and straight, slightly convex, or even intentionally concave base. This type of point with straight base was widely distributed in the Southwest from Pueblo I through Pueblo III.

Two of the variations within this type have been given names in the past. "The Pecos variety of side notched triangular point with concave base, is much less commonly reported" (Woodbury 1954: 126). However, it has been found at the Riana Ruin (a Pueblo III ancestral Tewa site on the Chama now mostly under water a short distance behind the Abiquiu dam), at sites of the Rosa Phase which are recognized as ancestral to Gallina culture, from certain distant areas in northern Arizona, and in the majority of our Gallina sites. The "Awatovi variety of side-notched triangular point" (Woodbury 1954:126-127) is distinguished by its notched base and has been reported in widely scattered areas including Riana Ruin, Rosa Phase sites in New Mexico, in Utah, and elsewhere. In our specimens the basal variations run easily into each other, though the remainder of the point is unchanged. (See Figure 35 for comparison drawings of the

Type 2

points.) One could designate subvarieties of our Type 1, but except in drawing a clear picture there seems little to be gained. Any two or all three of the variations are found together in our mountain sites, whether in domiciles or caves. In other words, the variations in the basal finish are not significant of time or regional or cultural differences but apparently merely indicate personal preferences with, perchance, a small basis in some factor of performance.

In size, our obsidian Gallina Type 1 points from the mountain sites range from 1.7 x 0.9 cm to about 4.0 x 1.7 cm.

GALLINA TYPE 2 POINTS: These were the second most popular in our mountain camps. They look more different than they turn out to be when analyzed. They are triangular and side-notched, with base broader than shoulders. The two major differences between Types 1 and 2 are that in Type 2 the stem is at least twice as long, vertically, as it would be on a Type 1 point of the same total length, and that the Type 2 stem usually has straight and approximately vertical sides and a thin horizontal base rather than rounded sides and a convex, moderately straight, or even concave base. This gives the effect of a short blade coming out of a solid-appearing large rectangular stem. The result is eye-catching, with stem almost as long as blade and, as for Type 1, as wide or even wider than the blade. The point actually looks much as if it were simply a preform which had been prepared and then, when needed, quickly given the two side notches which make it into a simple point. Other types of points could have been fashioned from the same preform but would have required shaping of stem and base, and those with downraking barbs or corner notches would have taken much more time and care for their finish.

Its marked simplicity, we would suggest, could have been the "reason for being" of the Type 2 point. This at once brings the realization that although we have ample evidence of knapping done on Canjilon Mountain, cores from which flakes were struck are not found in mountain houses, and the flakes recovered, both used and as debitage, are far from sufficient in number or in representative materials to indicate that the major work of such implement production was handled here. Materials used are not local. Blanks must have been prepared either where the basic selected material was obtained or at some of the "chipping stations" found scattered across the basin below the mountain slopes. Little cultural evidence other than debitage is left for their identification; we cannot at present pick out Gallina chipping stations as such. The final shaping of implements, reworking broken pieces, and retouching edges when necessary — those were the tasks for a rainy day at home in camp.

Green (1962:150) notes that in 1940 Hibben listed the "basal tanged knife" as an implement distinctive of the Gallina Phase, explaining that haftings he had found in place indicated that the pointed end of this artifact actually was a basal tang and the blunt end was the blade. If so, we submit that any evidence of hafting could have pertained to late use of this individual implement as a knife after its discard as a Type 2 point.

Careful examination under 30-power magnification of our own largest specimen of a Type 2 point, which duplicates Hibben's point as shown in Green's Figure 5 except for being more carefully made and slightly wider in proportion to length, offers no evidence whatever of its "basal tang" having been used for cutting, scraping, chiseling, or any other active purpose. Its edges and those of the seven smaller examples of Type 2 are identical in appearance to those of the "stem" on other points, and as the edges and surfaces of the "tang" do not differ from those of the blades of other Gallina points, we suggest that the "basal tanged knife" is no more than a Type 2 projectile point seen upside down. Our conclusion is that if Hibben's example was, indeed, hafted with the blade as a tang, this had to do with eventual reuse of the artifact.

The smaller, like the larger, examples of Type 2 points are distinguishable primarily on the proportion of height of stem to length of blade being not far from equal. Bases of the smaller examples are more likely to make a neat concave line, and sides of the stem may be quite exactly flaked with their edges vertical or even with removal of an extra flake at each lower corner, slanting toward the center. Between these two finishes we find variations toward the rounded outer edge of Type 1 points, the difference between types then going back almost entirely to the variation in height of stem and its noticeably greater proportion in comparison to length of blade. Type 1 and Type 2 point shapes can and do merge into each other, though 2 was somewhat less popular than 1 in our counts. The greatest width of Type 2 is across the stem rather than across the shoulders. Size range is from 1.8 x 1.0 cm to 4.0 x 4.5 cm.

Type 3

Type 4

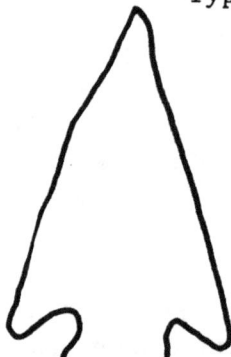

Type 5

GALLINA TYPE 3 POINTS: These points are distinguished by their stems being considerably narrower than the blade and with more or less vertical sides. The area below the side notch made on the preform was removed to the depth of that notch. This eliminates the point from the triangular category. The Type 3 shape is more commonly found in, but not limited to, large points up to about 4.7 cm long by 2.6 cm wide, but it also is recognized in a point measuring only 2.1 x 1.2 cm. It appears to have been approximately as popular as Type 2.

GALLINA TYPE 4 POINTS: The Type 4 "point" characteristically is without stem and hence may be a blade, though, as others have noted, stemless points can be hafted, especially if gum is used as an aid. It even is possible that the Type 4 pieces were preforms, their triangular shape permitting modification at will. Base and edges on our examples are

184

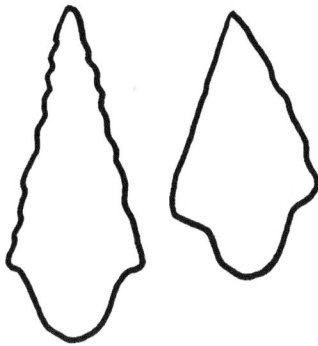
Type 6

likely to be thin and to have fine serration. In this collection they are only about half as common as Type 3 points. The Type 4 specimens range from 2 to 3 cm high and from less than 3 to at least 2 cm wide.

GALLINA TYPE 5 POINTS: Type 5 points are still more rare than Type 4. These were made from a wide-based triangular preform but corner notching produced downraking barbs which, at least in some cases, have had their sharp points squared off. Greatest width is across the barbs. Our examples appear to have been thinned across the base rather than carrying a stem, but we cannot be certain. The overall size is about that of Type 4.

GALLINA TYPE 6 POINTS: Type 6 is an "old-fashioned"-appearing point with an oval base at the end of the stem which tapers in a gentle curve from the bottom of the side notches. When Wendorf and Miller (1959) found some points of this shape in the high-altitude hunting sites of the Sangre de Cristo Mountains north of Santa Fe (see comparison of those Sangre de Cristo surface finds as discussed in Appendix), they suggested that these could represent the Archaic stage of culture, when points of this shape commonly were made of cloudy gray obsidian. Archaic sites are not rare in the Ghost Ranch region, and our Type 6 points similarly are of the cloudy gray obsidian. The Canjilon Mountain site examples, however, were found in association with all of the other types in the lithic complex uncovered on the floors of our mountain structures. It is, certainly, quite possible that the Type 6 points had been picked up here and there by prehistoric collectors whether for use or as curiosities. It also is possible that this shape could have resulted from reworking a broken Type 2 point, but that would not explain the material. Thinking of Type 6 points as Archaic remains tempting, but we do not know. The size range of our four examples is from about 2.3 x 1.3 to about 4.1 x 1.8 cm.

Type 7

GALLINA TYPE 7 POINTS: We have defined the rare Type 7 as a corner-notched point with stem narrower than blade. Shape of stem is similar to the rounded-edge variations found in Type 1. Two of our examples (broken) showed that one edge of the blade portion but not the other had been notched, which gave an interesting asymmetric appearance. The notches were large enough to weaken the whole, and both points are broken. This type perhaps should be considered a variant of Type 1, even though the basic notching (side vs. corner) for hafting differs. Type 7, in our examples, runs from about 1.9 x 1.1 cm to 3.6 x 2.2 cm for obsidian specimens.[*]

---

[*] The very few examples of chert points are not here given in comparative dimensions. Chert is tougher and definitely less subject to fracture than obsidian, but obsidian was lighter and easier to work. The few chert samples of points vary little from the proportions of obsidian samples.

Drill

A single stone drill point was found in Structure II-17. It differed from the points only in being long and slender (3.7 x 1.3 cm). The material is obsidian. As there were no notches for hafting, the implement must have been held by hand. The lower end from a distance of 1.2 cm up from the tip shows grinding, from use.

Summary

How should we sum up the stone implement complex and the economy of the Canjilon Mountain sites?

The economy, if we might start with a hypothesis based on what foods have been available in this area in the historic period, would have been a combination of hunting and gathering. For those who knew their plants, there was an abundance of plant food. For those equipped and trained for hunting, there was a plentitude of animals to hunt. What was hunted and what was gathered and in what proportions? Heavy evidence pertaining to hunting is provided by the stone implements left, whether lost, hidden, broken, or dulled, when the males who owned them departed. In contrast, relatively few implements pertaining to the collection and preparation of plants for food or other use have been found. To judge from what we know of native gathering in the historic period, that task was handled almost entirely by women. Their implements would have consisted of a digging stick and perhaps a stone chopper, with a burden basket for one's back. The digging sticks and burden baskets, if not returned to the home base, would have lasted but a few years with the little protection provided by small caves in an area of considerable summer rainfall and heavy winter snows. A flint knife or unshaped flakes used as knives made up kitchen cutlery. We already have described the choppers and blades found.

Our best evidence pertaining to plants gathered is a combination of direct data, from pollen analysis, and tangential data, from a combination knowledge of plants growing on this mountain and plants reported by Pueblo peoples to have been important to their ancestors.

In 1935 Castetter published a list of wild plants formerly or then still used for food according to a few historic references and the statements of a number of informants. His study was made just in time, for acculturation, which had been a slow process for 340 years, took a leap ahead in the 1940s. Pueblo men who had glimpsed something of the outer world as soldiers in World War II returned with a new desire for modern furnishings and modern menus. As the trading post, the grocery store in town, and, finally, the supermarket supplanted mountains and valleys as sources to supplement corn, beans, squash, and chile from the planted fields, upcoming generations learned little of the old dietary. Today very few Pueblo persons can talk of the old foods or recognize the old food staples.

If we check Hayden's admittedly incomplete list of plants used by various South-western Indians (largely Pueblos) at the end of Chapter I, we find duplication in 22 examples. These should be — as far as we can know — the plants most likely to have been utilized by the Gallina families which came to exploit the area with which we are concerned. The people needed, first, plant food for their own present subsistence and, second, plant foods which could be ground or dried and, with dried meats, carried back to the home villages for future use, though the time of use must have depended on how much crops planted at home produced as a return in that year. Many of the plants gathered by the various tribes living in different geographic areas were expectably different, but they fall into approximately parallel groupings: those valued for their seeds, those with nourishing roots, greens which when dried still provided enough nutrition to permit slim survival, small bulbs or shoots carrying some food values but valued chiefly as flavorings, and those used for medicines.

One of the three most important categories was that of wild grasses which produced seeds, small but opulent in numbers. When ripe these could be brushed from the seed-heads into a basket and later ground into meal to be cooked as gruel, mixed with liquid for drinking, eaten dry in pinches, or baked into some type of breadstuff. June grass and Indian millet (Castetter 1935:22) are two in our mountain area likely to have been garnered. Several other seed-producing grasses still are found there and, though not in Castetter's list, quite certainly would have been used. All would have required crushing or grinding whether on metates brought from home or on suitable stones *in situ*, and the several broken small handstones we found well may point toward the latter explanation.

Acorns from Gambel oaks comprise the second category known to have been used extensively by Pueblo peoples even in the historic period. They could be ground into meal or simply boiled, and among their virtues, according to local belief, is increased sexual potency (Castetter 1935:47; Ellis 1959:17). This small oak, more a shrub than a tree, is plentiful in the mountain area.

Third is the *Yucca baccata* which, like its larger relatives elsewhere, was important to most of the native peoples of historic times in our Southwest and Mexico. The crown, young leaves, and sometimes the upper tender portion of the stem of this short-leaved yucca and its close but smaller relative known as *Yucca glauca, amole*, or soap-weed, were baked in a pit, especially in times of food shortage (Castetter 1935:14). Short-leaved yuccas today are found in numerous large patches on the mountain and may have been one of or even the specific food plant for which the roasting pit in the Turkey Spring I site was constructed.

Piñon nuts (Castetter 1935:40-42) are known to have been exceedingly important to the Pueblos, who continue to gather them today though primarily as a relished delicacy. In the past they were roasted and eaten from the hand, or ground into flour to mix with corn flour. As many as possible were stored in hidden crypts in house walls or set away in storerooms as a major resource kept on hand to help preserve life in times of drought and crop failure. As they mature in mid-October or later, we may hypothesize a second visit to the mountain for this purpose in years when trees in this specific location were observed to be bearing well.

Into this century, berries of the one-seed juniper and also of the Rocky Mountain juniper have been eaten eagerly, fresh or boiled, and also used as meat seasoning by Pueblo peoples. We know that the Zuni (and hence probably others) also ground the berries into meal for cakes (Castetter 1935:31-32; Ellis 1959:16). Serviceberries were an important food-in-hand, sometimes known as "apples," which formerly were collected in the mountains (Castetter 1935:16), and the chokecherry was eaten raw, made into preserves, or even ground and pressed into cakes to be dried for future use (Castetter 1935:46). The fresh leaves of the currant (*Ribes*) were eaten in spring and the berries consumed fresh or made into preserves (Castetter 1935:49). The red raspberry also was a favorite when found (Castetter 1935:49), and we can add the wild strawberry, which Castetter missed. The Buckthorn berry also was eaten.

Rus trilobata, the three-leafed sumac unpleasantly referred to by some as the skunkbush but by others as the lemonade shrub, produces a tart small red fruit which can be eaten as it is or crushed to flavor a drink. The fruits contain a seed which, with the flesh, formerly was ground to produce meal (Castetter 1935:48, 49). The young and flexible stems of this shrub were the major material used in Pueblo coiled basketry.

The stems of *Rumex* or dock were cooked by some much as we cook rhubarb, or boiled with the fruit of the prickly pear cactus to add flavor (Castetter 1935:50). Roots of dock (*canaigre*) also are known to have been used by the Navajo (and probably others) in coloring the red-brown buckskin for moccasin uppers. The considerable amount of tannin in these roots may have given aid in the tanning. *Canaigre* also was an herbal remedy.

Bulbs of the Sego or Mariposa lilly still are eaten raw in spring. The flower buds of rabbitbrush were salted and eaten, and wild rose hips were a tidbit when found. Young dandelion provided greens, wild onions and celery were eaten raw or used as flavoring in stews, and the fruits of various cacti offered sweetening (Castetter 1935:19, 24, 49, 53; Ellis 1959:17). Entire small cactus plants sometimes were cooked after singeing or rubbing off their thorns, and the young leaves (pads) of the prickly pear cactus remain favorite additions to stews in some of the pueblos of today.

Even the inner bark of the Western yellow pine "and other conifers" was chewed or eaten by many Southwestern Indian peoples when other food was scarce (Castetter 1935:42), perhaps an explanation for the mysterious removal of bark slabs from the "squaw trees" reported for several mountain forests in the Southwest.

We had hoped to gain from pollen studies some information on wild or cultivated food plants used by our native campers, but the results were entirely disappointing. As stated in Chapter II, little pollen could be found in the samples, and that found merely represented flora as of the present forest and nothing of food plants, wild or tame.

The overall picture of stone implements retrieved from domiciles, possible storerooms, work caves, and surface of the five mountain sites in which we did surveys and (in the first four) excavations, clearly illustrated hunting as the dominant interest of the camp inhabitants.

Chart 5
<u>Chipped Stone Artifacts, Gallina Mountain Sites</u>

Site	Shaped or big flake blades.	Lunate burin blade, burin, or arrowshaft tool.	Unshaped small flakes used as blades.	Points whole or broken.	Scrapers or scraper knives.
TS I	10	8	13	20	11

Total artifacts:62.
Also present: 1 pot-lid, 2 fragments rubbing or crushing stones, 1 volcanic scoria mano, 1 volcanic scoria metate, 1 fine polisher or tanning stone.

TS II	14	24	32	21	11

Total artifacts:102
Also present: 2 choppers, 1 arrowshaft smoother, 2 broken cobble rubbing or crushing stones, 1 fragment of mano, 1 long basalt saw, 1 small obsidian serrated saw, drill or point.

Dulce Sprgs. III	18	19	43	24	14

Total artifacts:118
Aso present: 2 choppers, 1 long basalt skinning pry-knife, 1 three-sided chert core-scraper.

Red Hill IV, V	3	2			2

Total artifacts:7
Also present: 1 crushing stone.

Total artifacts :	45	53	88	67	36

Final Total: 289 artifacts.

The largest category of lithics is that of unshaped small flakes, actually debitage, which were sharp and hence, as we know from examination of their edges, utilized as blades, though not lengthily. They and the shaped blades and more common large flakes somewhat worked and often retouched as knives (usually triangular) would have had their main use in cutting meat. This would include butchering and slicing, either for immediate use or for jerky. Projectile points were more numerous than knives and arrowshaft tools almost as numerous as scrapers for working hides of the animals taken.

In thinking of the animals available to Gallina hunters in the Turkey Spring-Canjilon Mountain district, as in considering available plants, we had best start with Hayden's list at the end of Chapter I of wildlife to be found there today. We can picture some of the rodents and other smaller creatures being trapped, just as by Pueblos in the earlier part of this century. Some which lived in burrows may have been taken by thrusting a sturdy forked stick down the hole and twisting it in the hope that it would catch in the animal's fur and bring him as a captive to the surface. Birds, even in this century, were taken with snares tied from horsehair and attached to a dead branch laid upon the ground. Before Spaniards introduced the horse, single yucca fibers or human hair could have been similarly used.

Birds, which provided feathers for ritual offerings as well as food, also may have been shot down with arrows tipped with the smallest of the points found, but it is likely that these also would have been used for larger species such as wild turkey, grouse, eagles, and hawks. Other small-to-medium-sized points would have been appropriate for squirrels, raccoons, rabbits, beaver, fox, coyote, and porcupine. Jemez descendants say that all animals were served for food, even the mountain lion, a sacred animal hunted so that its skin could be tanned as material from which to make a quiver for one's arrows. The black bear also is sacred but hunted and its carcass treated ritually. The mountain lion, the bear, and deer would require larger points on an arrow, but not as large as those intended for the Wapiti elk, the most massive animal available on this mountain. Deer also were taken in pit traps, and it is probable that smaller animals were taken in traps of wood, stone, and sometimes cordage as in historic times.

The several types of projectile points complete enough for classification were found in the following numbers:

Type 1	18
Type 2	11
Type 3	9
Type 4	6 (possibly knife or preform)
Type 5	3
Type 6	7 (conceivably an Archaic point collected by Gallina late comers.)
Type 7	5

Types 5 and 7 quite possibly should be combined. Both are corner-notched. Type 5 could be merely a large Type 7 with narrower base than found in the smaller Type 7 examples. Larger points checked under a 30-power microscope to determine whether they could have served as knives showed no such use. Variants in type 7 are 3 points with notches down one edge of the blade. Most but not all of the points were finished with tiny edge serrations, but a few show larger precise serration. Other than by size, we have no means of associating individual points with the type of animal for which the hunter had prepared them. Nor have we any indication that certain point types were used for certain animals. Except for the large Type 5 points, various sizes are found in each type, the most common in all types being what one must refer to as "medium size."

The type divisions we have used are separated primarily on stem and base shapes. These hold to certain characteristics well enough for such a series to be established but there obviously is a tendency for types to run into each other. This is not surprising in that we find a number of the different types together in those structures where a considerable collection of artifacts, whole or broken, had been left. (See illustration of Stone Artifact complex found in Bain's Cave as examples: Figures 36, 37, 38.) Apparently one man or one man and his brothers or other close relatives were producing several types of projectile points at one time. Obsidian was the favorite material, probably because of its sharpness and the ease in flaking. Chert also was used and a few points were made from quartz. Preforms, possibly exemplified by what we have called the Type 4 point or knife, quite certainly were brought into the area to receive their final shaping here, as indicated by the lack of cores and presence of only a moderate amount of debitage.

As already explained, we have designated the arrowshaft tools as such because it seems that they were primarily adapted for such use, though they may have been picked up to cut or scrape other items as well. The lunate curve obtained through striking with a baton, probably of antler, held against the flake being worked would have been ideal in cutting reeds or cane for arrowshafts if one went down to the Chama along which such plants grew, but also would have worked on slender rods. The edge of the lunate curve, on the shaft tool, usually thicker than edges finished by retouch-flaking, often shows wear or even appreciable chipping from use.

Relatively little data on historic-period Pueblo bow and arrow are available. From Gifford's (1940:29-30) synoptic listing on the bows and arrows of four pueblos (Walpi, Zuni, Santa Ana, and San Ildefonso) we know that the bows of this sampling commonly were of oak or juniper, sinew-backed or self-bows, and often double curved. Strings were made from the back sinews of deer or other animals. All four pueblos used arrows of willow with a stone arrowhead but no foreshaft or of cane with a hardwood foreshaft with or without a stone arrowhead. Arrows with a thick blunt end were used for birds and rabbits. All four pueblos feathered their arrows with eagle, hawk, or turkey feathers. As discussed earlier, we have data on use of wood from other shrubs, as well, for arrowshafts.

The small burin or graver created by clever flaking at the end of the lunate curve, or even on knives without such a curve, is so frequently found on mountain implements that it must have proved of real convenience in scoring or cutting, especially in providing a slot for mounting the point. The thin edge found over most of the remainder of the "arrowshaft tools" presumably was to facilitate cutting and scraping the shaft into a neat and smooth line. As far as I am aware, neither the lunate curve nor burins have been reported to be common elsewhere in the Southwest.

Two other unusual implements found here are the basalt saw, made by irregularly chipping the side edges of a natural long flake of that volcanic material, and the skinning pry-knife from a fortunately shaped long basalt piece in modern knife form. A few flakes down the sides of this knife made its handling the more secure. The primary function of this implement was to pry and cut the skin from a carcass, especially in the skull area.

Other notable productions of these people were the four obsidian knife blades made to be hafted, one in triangular shape with a tang, one in the shape of a large and somewhat rounded projectile point, and the third in the shape of a modern kitchen or table knife, with spaced flakes removed on its lower edge to create a coarse serration. The second and third of these knives would have been hafted horizontally; the first carried its haft at an angle. The blade of the fourth was asymmetric and the protruding base to carry the haft was irregular in profile, the whole being a poor example of the type.

Local concern with serration is noted in three points with 2 to 3 notches removed from one edge of the blade, in another point or drill or possibly miniature saw with distinct small serration cusps down both sides, and in a long and beautifully made, similarly serrated point of foreign material which may have been obtained through trade. Although there is no question that some of the local knappers were not very adept (such as the males in House II-15, possibly because they were quite young), others were doing excellent work (such as the male of Bain's Cave and the other in House III-1). (See Figures 36, 37, 38.)

STONE OBJECTS

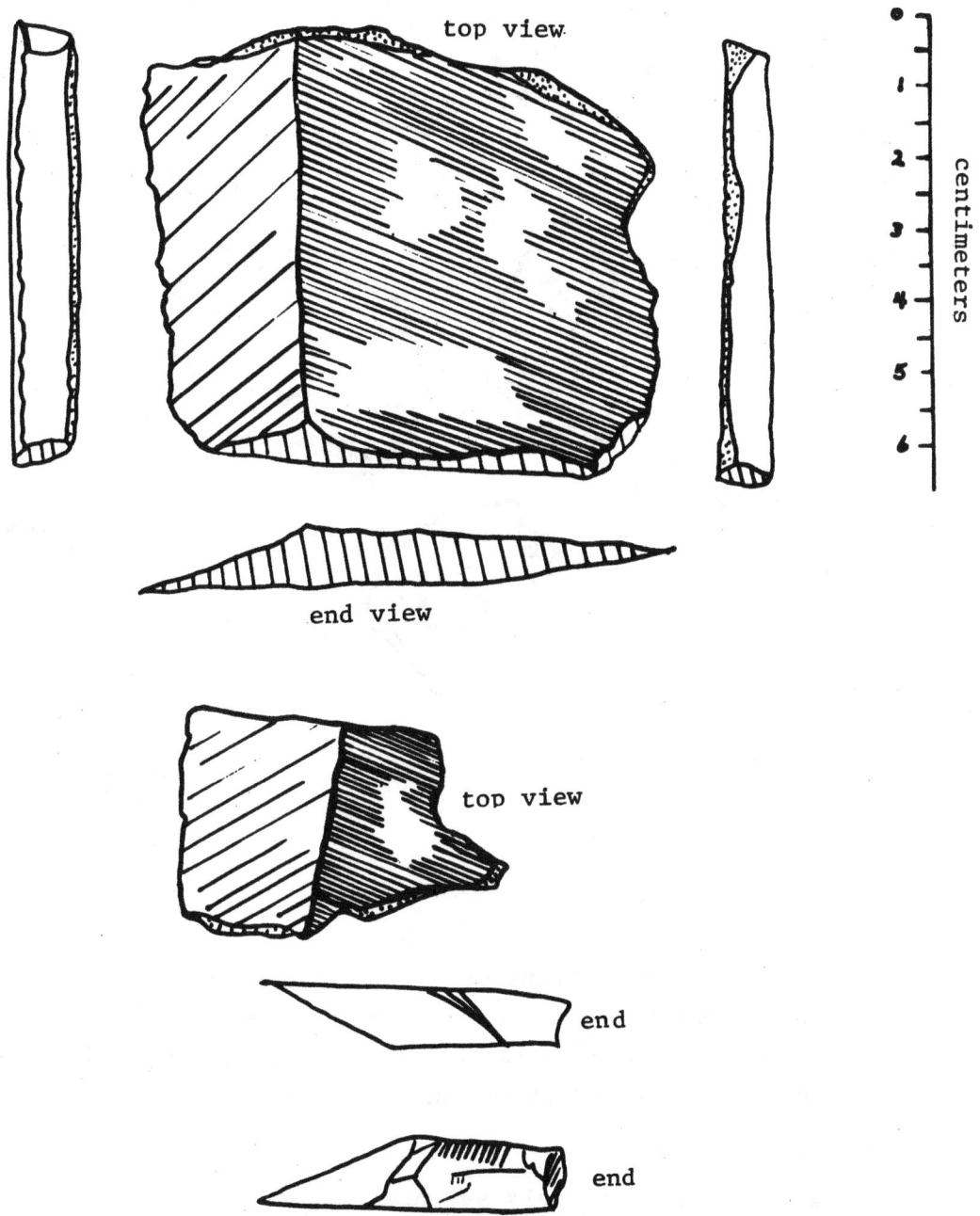

top view

end view

top view

end

end

centimeters

Figure 37

STONE ARTIFACTS

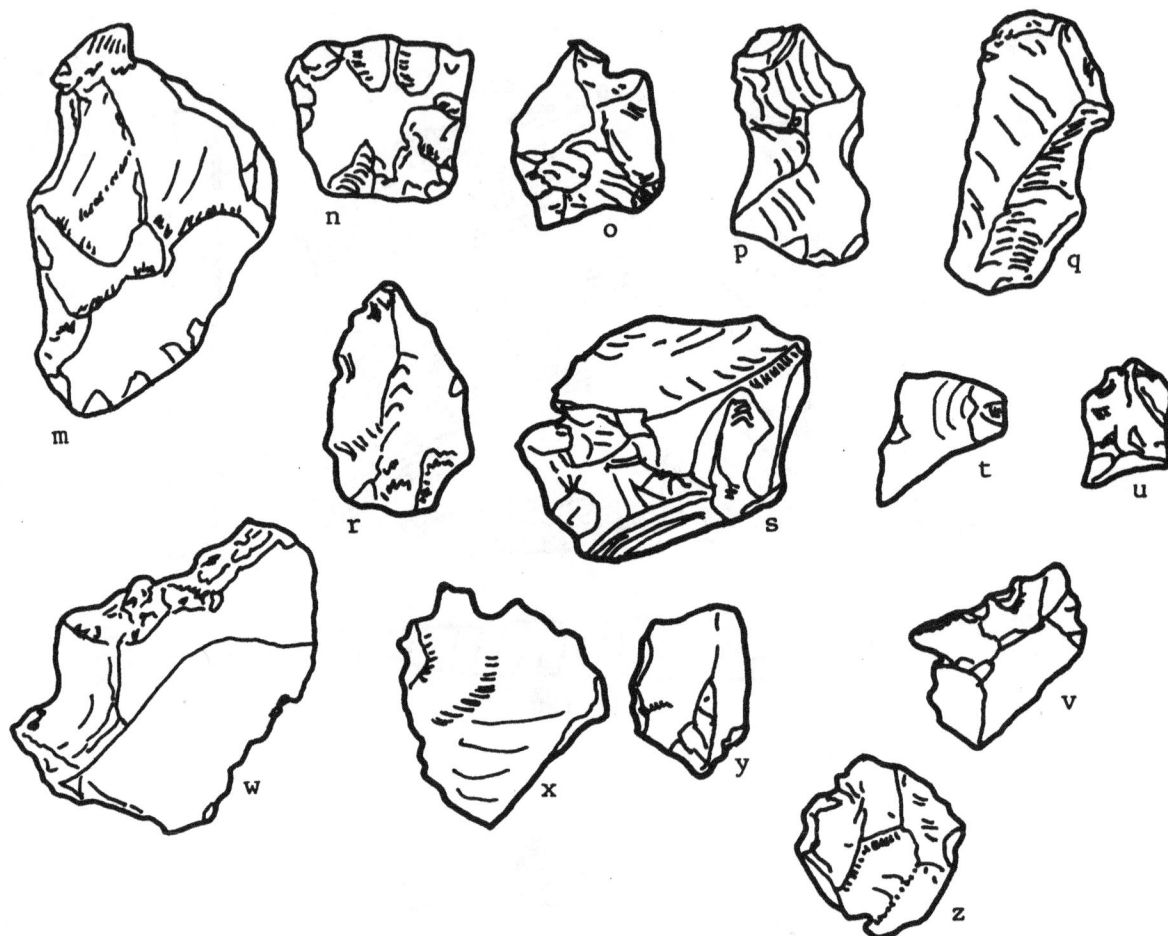

m.   Through v. - Obsidian

w., x., y., and z. - translucent whitish chert
     most appear to have been used as is or especially worked for
     a particular need; except for t, u, v, and y, which may be
     only unused waste chips and fragments.

m.   Knife for hafting

w.   Saw, showing purposely serrated edge

Figure 38

STONE ARTIFACTS

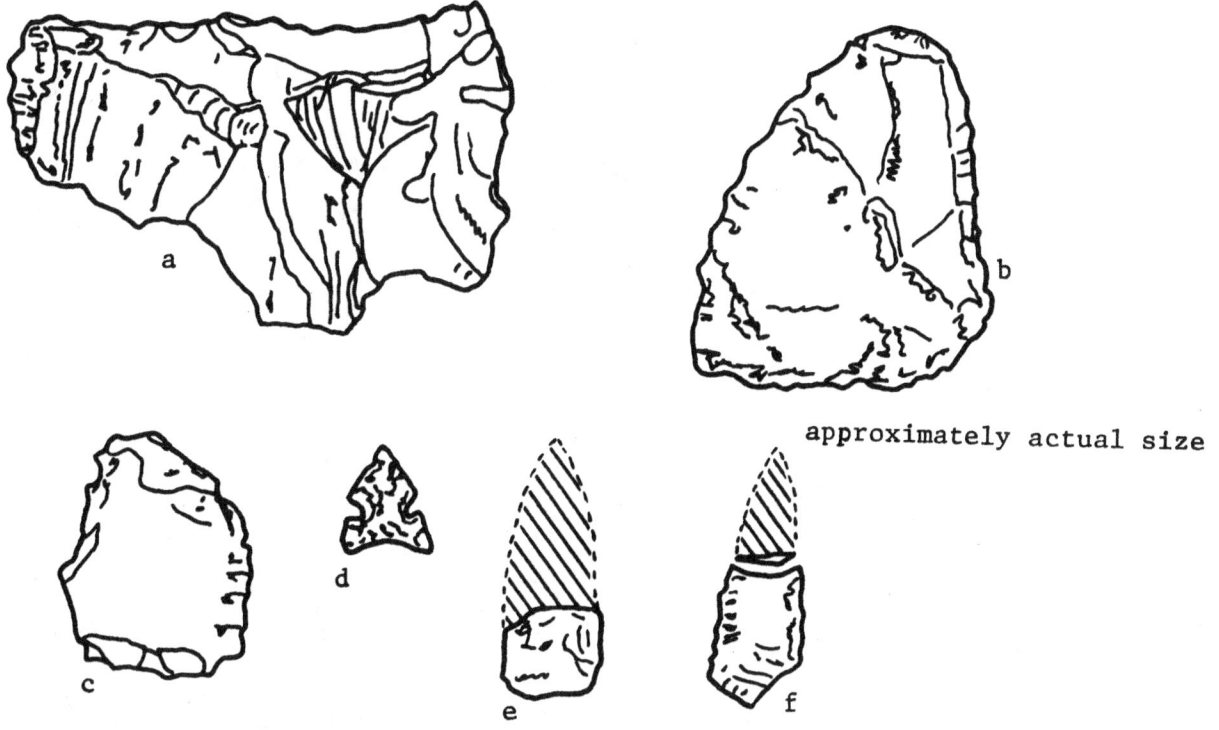

approximately actual size

a. scraper - obsidian

b. scraper - obsidian

c. scraper - chalcedony

d. point - quartz, white

e. partial point (?) chert, white

f. partial point (?) obsidian

Figure 39

STONE ARTIFACTS

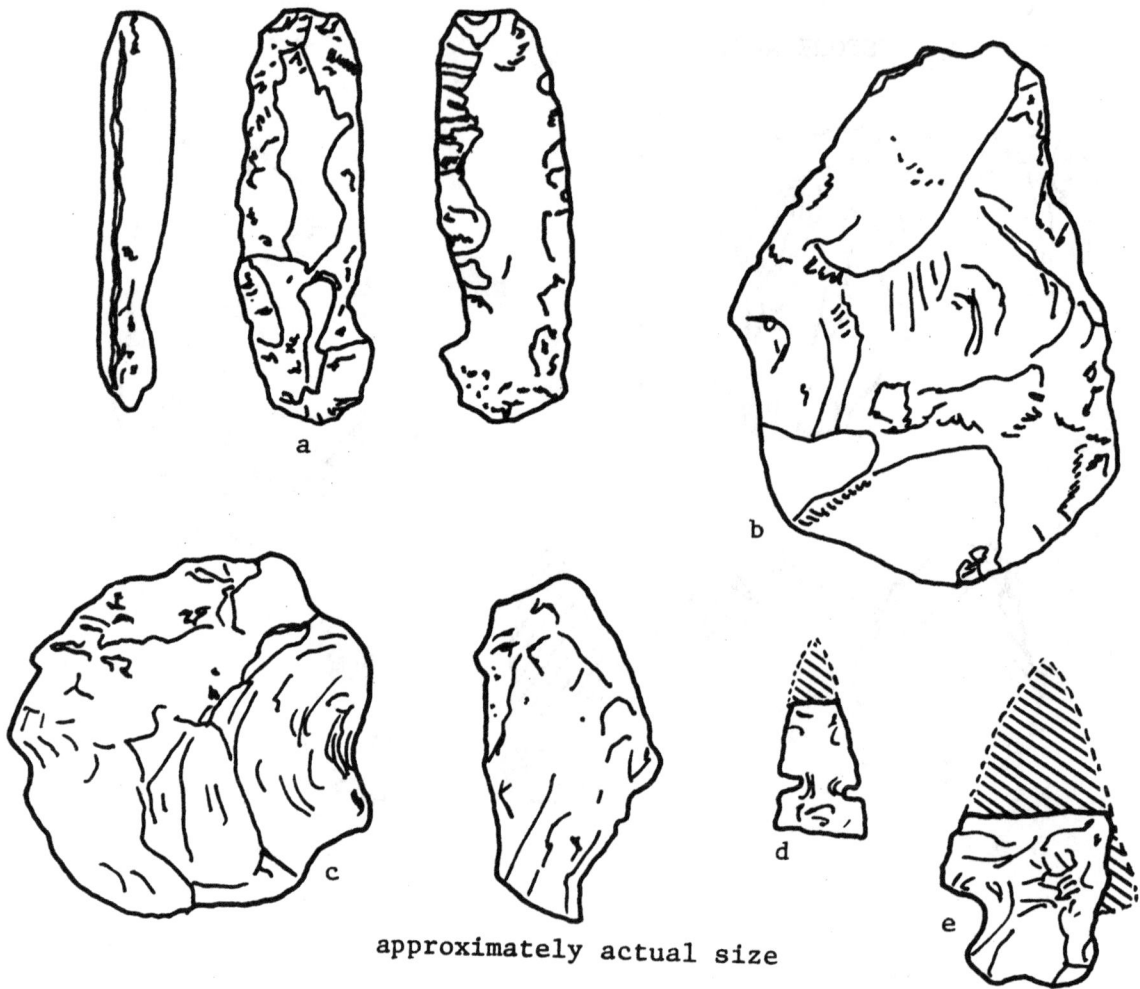

approximately actual size

a. side scraper? knife? - obsidian

b. scraper-grey welded silitic tuff

c. core scraper - chert

d. point, partial - obsidian

Above are best representatives found in cave 12.

Figure 40

196

STONE ARTIFACTS

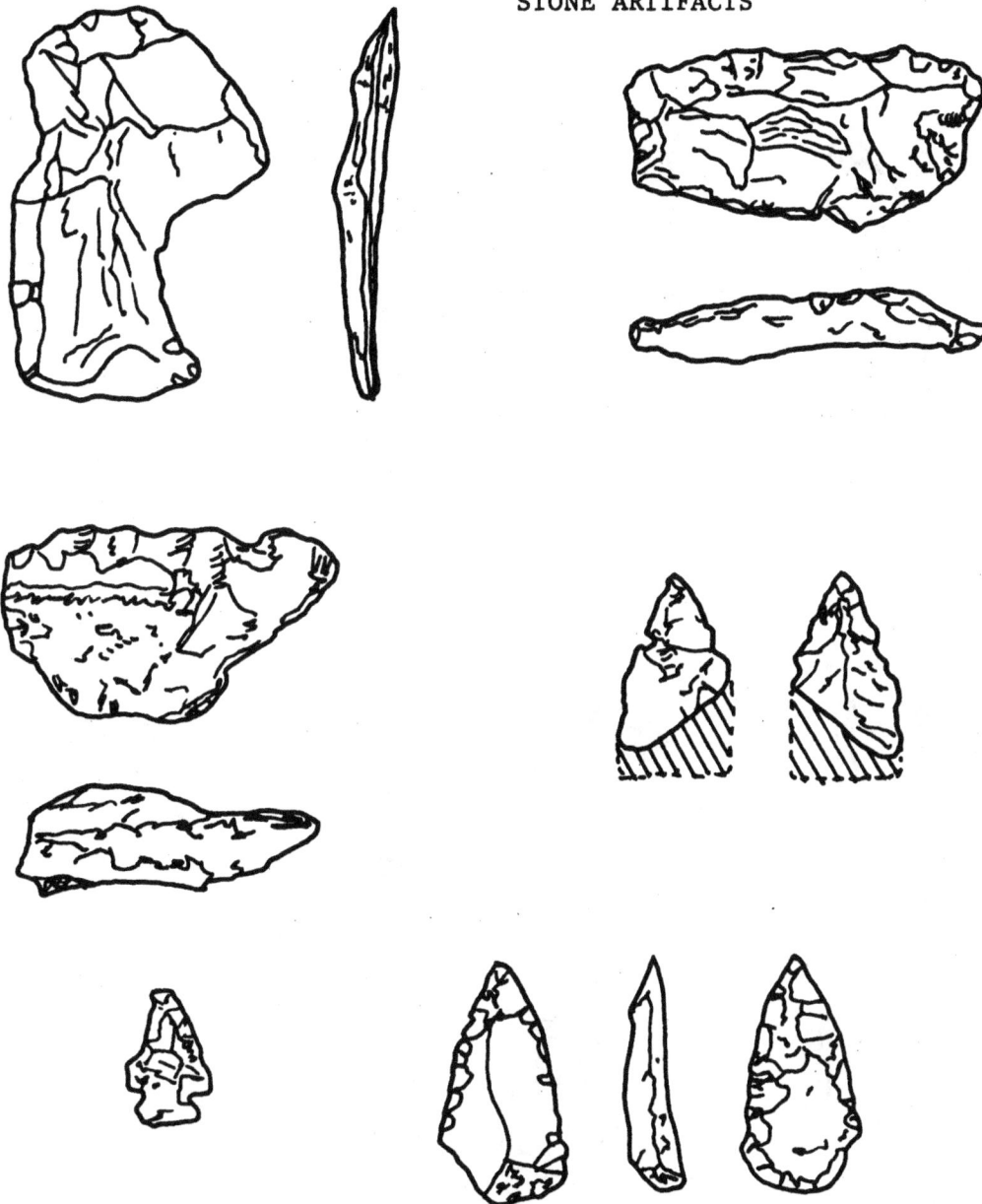

a. worked blade – chert, translucent, v. light brown

b. scraper – obsidian

c. scraper – chert – chalcedony, pinkish-white

d. point, partial – quartz, semi-translucent

e. point partial – obsidian

f. point-jasper, dark brown, opaque (actually qualifies as flint
   due to translucence along thinned edge. Therefore, probably
   not local.)

Figure 41

197

STONE ARTIFACTS

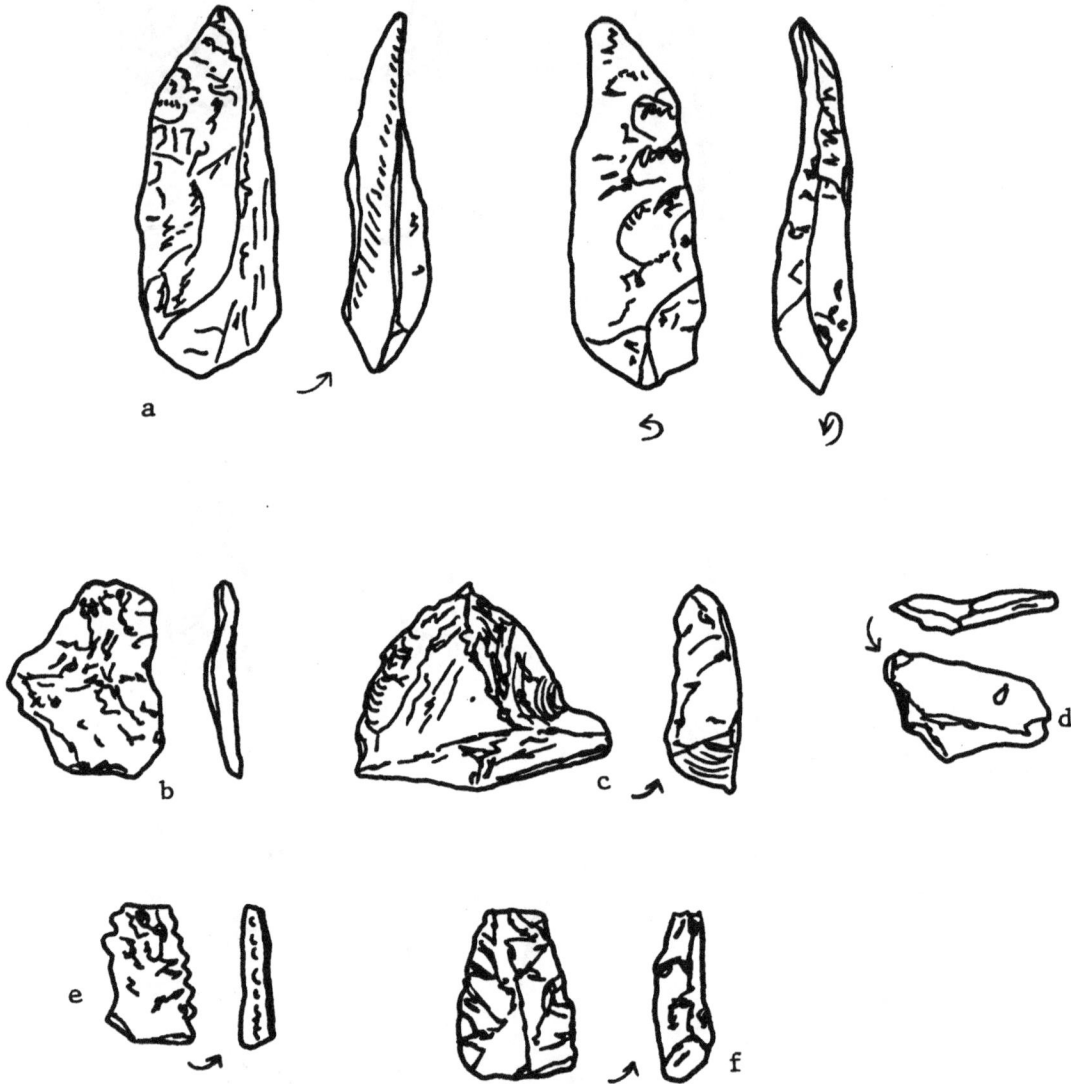

a. knife (scraper?) obsidian

b. worked flake - translucent chert with red inclusions.

c. worked flake (graver?) - obsidian

d. worked flake - obsidian

e. point, partial-grey, translucent obsidian; n.e. quad. at 6 in.

f. point (?) partial - obsidian

Figure 42

Alley II - feature No. 27 House

a. arrow point - obsidian
b. partial arrow point - obsidian
c. possible arrow point - obsidian
d. arrow point - obsidian
e. partial arrow point - white chert
f. partial arrow point - chalcedony

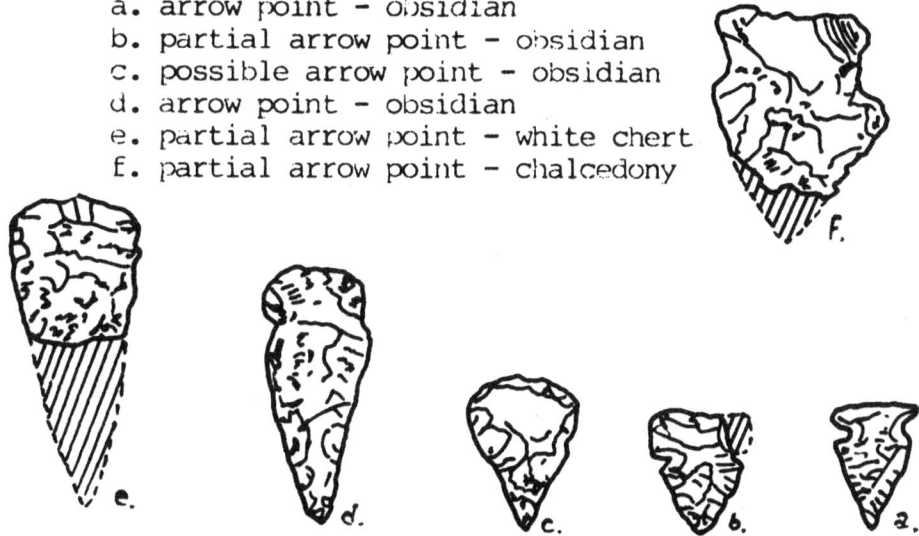

f.

e.   d.   c.   b.   a.

minutely
flaked point

combination
knife-scraper-graver tool
- whitish chert

very finely
serrated edge

Scale 1:1

Figure 43

VIII

The Use Of Bone And Antler

The use of antler tines for flaking instruments can be presumed, though none were found. In fact, only one antler piece was retrieved, and in its broken state we could not know that it had or had not been worked or used. Our single important find of an artifact of antler during our later work on Gallina home villages in the Llaves area was an implement which appears to have been a dagger made from a polished elk tine. This implement was found beneath the back of a youth who died in one of the houses attacked and burned in Rattlesnake Point village. Whether the young man was defending himself and family or was killed by one of the enemy who branished that weapon as he came through the roof entry and down the ladder we cannot say.

A single broken bone awl was found in House III-1, Dulce Springs, on Canjilon Mountain but it had been burned and broken into several pieces, three of which we have. It was somewhat larger than those we later uncovered in the home village sites and without their characteristic long and very slender tip for making coiled basketry. In an area with heavy winter snows and considerable summer rainfall, bone and antler do not last except when deeply covered or beneath some shelter.

APPENDIX

Comparison of Canjilon Mountain Sites and Artifacts to other High-Altitude Finds

Because so little is known of prehistoric Pueblo hunting and/or gathering sites in the Southwest, we need to examine the single report dealing with the few known for the upper Rio Grande.

In 1959 Wendorf and Miller published a small discussion on artifacts they had come across between 1955 and 1957 while doing some detailed geologic investigation in the southern end of the Sangre de Cristo Mountains, east of the Rio Grande and only a few miles north of Santa Fe. As there were no structural remains and even summer climate is strenuous at those altitudes, we may surmise that the campers remained only long enough to accomplish their missions.

Eight sites are described, but the statement is made that single occasional stone artifacts were found between and beyond those more condensed sites:

1. On the Rio Valdez Divide (altitude 11,500-12,000 ft) artifacts were found in "large grassy meadows above timberline." The only water source was a small pond on the divide. Access is thought to have been from the east, which would suggest that the hunters probably came from the Pecos area. Fourteen points were found.

2. Artifacts were picked up all along the high ridges between the Truchas Peaks and the Pecos Baldy Peak area (altitude 11,500-11,800 ft, much of it above timberline). Access for Tewa Pueblo people of the Upper Rio Grande Valley could have been via the Rio Medio and for peoples east of the mountains by way of tributaries of the Pecos River. Pecos Baldy Lake was the only water source. The authors suggest that the Pecos Baldy site may be the second youngest of the group, the basis for this opinion being 2 points which are said to "occur commonly in all late ceramic sites in the upper Rio Grande Valley area...." It was thought that some of these sites had been used intermittently through the centuries.

3. In an open meadow on Elk Mountain between the altitudes of 11,000 and 11,300 feet, artifacts were found, including two large but rather crude points or blades. Here access is easiest via the Pecos Valley from the east.

4. Slightly above timberline on the Pecos-Santa Barbara Divide (altitude about 11,800 ft) in a pass between the middle fork of the Rio Santa Barbara and a tributary of the upper Pecos River, large quantities of chipped flint and obsidian, other artifacts of the same materials, and "rude hearths" were found " over an area of several acres." This is interpreted by the authors as indicative of use of the

camp either by many people or use over a considerable time. Spring water is available within a mile. Mineral materials carried in by hunters and worked here indicate that some groups came from the Rio Grande Valley area by way of the Santa Barbara River which runs down into Tewa territory, and some came up the Pecos Valley east of the mountains. Thirty-two points, the largest number found at any of these Sangre de Cristo high-altitude sites, came from site 4.

5. At Horse Thief Meadow (altitudes 9,700 ft) along Horse Thief Creek, artifacts could be picked up where the grass cover of the meadow had been broken, but only 1 point was found.

6. The only site at which potsherds occurred was at the Horse Thief-Panchuela West Divide (altitude about 11,000 ft, close to timberline). Western drainage into the Rio Grande River runs past the area of Nambé's ancestral pueblos and into the center of Tewa territory. Drainage to the east runs into the Pecos River. I have picked up Nambé stories of use of this area for hunting and herding in the old days. A perpetual spring lies close by the site. "Flakes and artifacts were rare...."

The pottery classifies as Rio Grande Glaze type IV, produced between approximately 1490 and 1505, though never by the Tewa. As the authors state, the temper is andesite which at present is considered to indicate origin of the vessels in the Galisteo Basin where glaze wares predominate. According to Nambé tradition (Ellis 1962), some of the Nambé people did move to the Galisteo Basin. San Ildefonso (Ellis 1968) also tells of some of their people having left their earlier homes on the Pajarito plateau when drought forced abandonment of that entire plateau. The years between A.D.1470 and 1483 were bad. There was another dry period between A.D. 1560 and 1569, except for 1563 and 1565, and a worse one between 1579 and 1587. On the basis of the pottery, the authors consider this site to have been the latest of those they examined. Only 1 point was found here.

7. At the juncture of the Rio Medio and Rio Gallina (not the Gallina River of our Gallina culture area) at an altitude of 7,500 feet, artifacts were found in a small meadow. Nambé carries the tradition of hunting and herding here. Four points were found.

8. At Puerto Nambé (altitude 11,000 ft) approximately at timberline, artifacts were found over several acres. This again is in territory for which Nambé traditions of use are known. Water is available at a mile's distance. Four points were found.

At all these 8 mountain sites (other than Site 6) the preponderant type of point was characterized by "short leaf-shaped blades with deep diagonal notches removed from basal corners.... The bases are convex to straight and narrower than the shoulders." The authors believe them to have been typical of a period centering around the time of Christ as indicated by 2 fragments of points of this type retrieved from a site deeply buried in alluvium near Tesuque and given a Carbon 14 date of 2330 ± 250 years ago. Other Rio

Grande sites with similar points have been estimated to belong to the same period. The culture complex presumably would be late Archaic, a stage congruous with the circular one-hand manos also found in some of the Sangre de Cristo Mountain sites.

Other point types associated with the preponderant type in these sites were (1) small, with triangular blades, stems slightly expanding and ground, with notched base, and (2) the heavy and usually larger type point with thick triangular blades, often serrated, with shallow side notches, deep basal notches and expanding stems. Stems and bases often show grinding.

Two more point types found in these meadows are the Basketmaker II diagonally corner-notched long points without bifurcated base and the shorter but contemporary Lobo points dating from second to fourth centuries A.D.

Artifacts more or less similar to those of the Sangre de Cristo sites and apparently representing the pre-ceramic or late Archaic period have been reported from the La Sal Mountains in eastern Utah at comparable elevations, as well as at lower elevations in both Utah and Colorado and at Vail Pass, Colorado. None of the several "early types" of points have been found in our Canjilon Mountain sites.

BIBLIOGRAPHY

Ayer, Mrs. E.E., Jr.	1916	The Memorial of Fray Alonso de Benavides, 1630. Privately printed. Chicago.
Bahti, T.N.	1949	A Largo-Gallina Pit House and Two Surface Structures. El Palacio 56:2:52-59.
Bice, Richard A.	1980	An Instrument Survey of Gallina Sites on Rattlesnake Ridge. Collected Papers in Honor of Helen Greene Blumenshein. Papers of the Archaeological Society of New Mexico 5:141-164. Albuquerque Archaeological Society Press.
Bloom, L.B	1922	The West Jemez Culture Area. El Palacio XII:2:19-25. Museum of New Mexico, Santa Fe.
Bloom, L.B. and L.B. Mitchel	1938	The Chapter Elections in 1672. New Mexico Review XXIII:1:85-119
Bolton, H.S. (ed)	1916	Spanish Explorations in the Southwest, 1542-1706. Barnes and Noble, Inc., N.Y.
Bullard, Wm. R., Jr.	1962	The Cerro Colorado Site and Pithouse Architecture in the Southwestern United States Prior to A.D. 900. Papers of the Peabody Museum of American Archaeology and Ethnology. Harvard University. XLIV:2. Cambridge.
Castetter, Edward	1935	Ethnobotanical Studies in the American Southwest. Uncultivated Native Plants used as Sources of Food. University of New Mexico Biological Series 4:1. Albuquerque.
Chapman, Kenneth and Bruce T. Ellis	1951	The Line Break, Problem Child of Pueblo Pottery. El Palacio 58:9:257-269. Museum of New Mexico
Cushing, Frank Hamilton	1974	reprint. Zuni Breadstuff. Indian Notes and Monographs 8, Museum of the American Indian. Heye Foundation, N.Y.
Dick, Herbert	1980	Cohesive and Dispersive Configurations in Settlement Patterns of the Northern Anasazi: A Hypothesis. Collected Papers in Honor of Helen Greene Blumenschein. Papers of the Archaeological Society of New Mexico 5:57-82. Albuquerque Archaeological Society Press.
Dittert, Alfred E., Jr., Frank W. Eddy, and Beth L. Dickey	1963	Evidences of Early Ceramic Phases in the Navajo Reservoir District. El Palacio 70:1-2:5-12. Museum of New Mexico, Santa Fe.
Doney, Hugh H.	1968	Geology of the Cebolla Quadrangle, Rio Arriba County, New Mexico. Bulletin 92, New Mexico Institute of Mining and Technology, Socorro.
Eddy, Frank W.	1966	Prehistory in the Navajo Reservoir District, Northwestern New Mexico. Museum of New Mexico Papers in Anthropology 15, pt. II. Museum of New Mexico Press.

Ellis, Florence Hawley	1953	Authoritative Control and the Society System in Jemez Pueblo. Southwestern Journal of Anthropology 9:4:385-393.University of New Mexico.
—	1956	Anthropological Evidence Supporting the Land Claim of the Pueblos of Zia, Santa Ana, and Jemez. Ms. Indian Land Claim Commission. Washington, D.C.
—	1958	Archaeological Evidence Pertaining to the Land Claim of Nambé Pueblo. Ms. Indian Land Claim Commission, Washington, D.C.
—	1959	The Woman's Page: Laguna Pueblo. El Palacio 66:16-20.
—	1964	A Reconstruction of the Basic Jemez Pattern of Social Organization with Comparisons to Other Tanoan Social Structures. University of New Mexico Publications in Anthropology II. UNM Press.
—	1968	San Ildefonso's Ancestry and Their Water Use. Ms. Bureau of Indian Affairs, Albuquerque.
—	1976	Small Structures Used by Historic Pueblo Peoples and their Immediate Ancestors. In: Limited Activity and Occupation Sites (59-68). Contributions to Anthropological Studies I. Center for Anthropological Studies, Albuquerque.
Gifford, E.W.	1940	Culture Element Distributions XII. Apache-Pueblo. Anthropological Records 4:1. University of California Press, Berkeley.
Gooding, John D., (ed).	1980	The Durango South Project: Archaeological Salvage of Two Late Basketmaker III Sites in the Durango District. Anthropological Papers of the University of Arizona 34.
Green, Roger	1962	The Hormigas Site of the Largo-Gallina Phase. El Palacio 69:142-157. Museum of New Mexico, Santa Fe.
—	1964	The Carricito Community. El Palacio 71:2:27-39. Museum of New Mexico, Santa Fe
Green, Roger C., Maryanne A. Danfelser, and Gwinn Vivian	1958	Interpretation of Bg 91: A Specialized Largo-Gallina Surface Structure. El Palacio 65:2:41-60. Museum of New Mexico, Santa Fe.
Guernsey, Samuel James	1931	Explorations in Northeastern Arizona. Papers of the Peabody Museum of American Archaeology and Ethnology 12:1. Cambridge.
Guernsey, S.J. and A.V. Kidder	1921	Basket Maker Caves of Northeastern Arizona. Papers of the Peabody Museum of American Archaeology and Ethnolology 8:2. Cambridge.
Hackett, C.W.	1942	Revolt of the Pueblo Indians. Coronado Historical Series VIII. UNM Press.
Hall, E.T., Jr.	1944a	Early Stockaded Settlements in the Gobernador, New Mexico. Columbia Studies in Archaeology and Ethnology II:1. Columbia University Press.

Hall, E.T., Jr.   1944b   Recent Clues to Athapascan Prehistory in the Southwest. American Anthrpologist XLVI:1: pt. 1:98-105.

Harrington, H.D.   1976   Edible Native Plants of Rocky Mountains. UNM Press.

Hawley, Florence, M. Pijoan, and C.A. Elkin   1943   An Inquiry into Food Economy in Zia Pueblo. American Anthropologist 45:4: 547-556.

Hayes, Alden C. and Thomas C. Windes   1975   An Anasazi Shrine in Chaco Canyon. In Frisbie, T.E. (ed), Collected Papers in Honor of Florence Hawley Ellis. Papers of the Archaeological Society of New Mexico: 2. Hooper Publishing Co., Norman.

Hewett, Edgar L.   1906   Antiquities of the Jemez Plateau, New Mexico. Bureau of American Ethnology Bulletin 32. Washington, D.C.

Hibben, Frank C.   1948   The Gallina Architectural Forms. American Antiquity XIV:32-36.

—   1949   The Pottery of the Gallina Complex. American Antiquity 14:3:194-202.

Holbrook, Sally J. and James C. Mackey   1976   Prehistoric Environmental Change in Northern New Mexico: Evidence from a Gallina Phase Archaeological Site. The Kiva 41:309-317.

Ireland, Arthur K.   1982   A Potential Gallina Communications System. Ms. Paper prepared for the 55th Pecos Conference, Pecos National Monument, Pecos, N.M. August 12, 1982.

Jenness, D.   1934   The Indians of Canada. National Museum of Canada Anthropological Series 15, Bulletin 65 (2nd. ed.).

Kidder, A.V.   1924   An Introduction to the Study of Southwestern Archaeology. Phillips Academy, Yale Press. Andover.

Kidder, A.V. and J.C. Guernsey   1919   Archaeological Explorations in Northeastern Arizona. Bureau of American Ethnology Bulletin 65. Washington, D.C.

Kelly, Charles   1966   Mesoamerica and the Southwestern United States. Handbook of Middle American Indians 4:95-110. Smithsonian Institution. Washington, D.C.

Kubler, George   1940   The Religious Architecture of New Mexico. The Taylor Museum. Colorado Springs.

Linton, Ralph   1944   North American Cooking Pots. American Antiquity X:369-380.

Lister, Robert H. and Florence C. Lister   1981   Chaco Canyon Archaeology and Archaeologists. UNM Press.

Mackey, James   n.d.   Five Papers. Ms.

Mackey, James and Sally J. Holbrook   1978   Environmental Reconstruction and the Abandonment of the Largo-Gallina Area, New Mexico. Journal of Field Archaeology 5:29-49.

Mackey, James and R.C. Green   1979   Largo-Gallina Towers: An Explanation. American Antiquity 44:1:144-154.

Mera, H.P. 1935 Ceramic Clues to the Prehistory of North Central New Mexico. Laboratory of Anthropology Technical Series Bulletin 8, Santa Fe.

Morris, Earl H. 1939 Archaeological Studies in the La Plata District Publication 519. Carnegie Institution of Washington. Washington, D.C.

Morris, Earl H. and Robert F. Burgh 1954 Basket Maker II Sites Near Durango, Colorado. Publication 604. Carnegie Institution of Washington. Washington, D.C.

Pendelton, La Verna 1952 The Gallina Phase of Northern New Mexico. In Indian Tribes of Aboriginal America: Selected Papers of the Twenty ninth International Congress of Americanists, ed. S. Tax, pp. 145-152.

Prudden, T.M. 1914 The Circular Kivas of Small Ruins in the San Juan Watershed. American Anthropologist. n.s. 16:1:35-58. Lancaster.

— 1918 A Further Study of Prehistoric Small House Ruins in the San Juan Watershed. American Anthropological Association, V:1:3-50. Lancaster.

Reed, Erik 1963 An Early Gallina Burial from the Jicarilla Country (LA 6163). El Palacio 70:3:24-35.

Reiter, Paul 1938 The Jemez Pueblo of Unshagi, New Mexico, with Notes on the Earlier Excavations at "Amoxiumqua" and Guisewa, Pts. I, II. University of New Mexico Bulletin 326. University of New Mexico Monograph Series 1:4. Albuquerque.

Roberts, Frank H.H. 1930 Early Pueblo Ruins in the Piedra District, Southwestern Colorado. Bureau of American Ethnology Bulletin 96. Washington, D.C.

Robinson, Wm. J. and Richard Warren 1971 Tree Ring Dates from New Mexico and Northern Rio Grande Area. Laboratory of Tree Ring Ring Research University of Arizona. Tucson.

Rose, Martin R., Jeffrey S. Dean and William J. Robinson 1981 The Past Climate of Arroyo Hondo New Mexico Reconstructed from Tree Rings. School of American Research Press, Arroyo Hondo Archaeological Series, Vol. 4. Santa Fe, New Mexico.

Scholes, France 1929 Documents for the History of New Mexico Missions in the Seventeenth Century. New Mexico Historical Review IV:1:45-58.

Schulman, Edmond 1956 Dendroclimatic changes in semiarid America. Laboratory of Tree-Ring Research, University of Arizona. Tucson, Arizona.

Smiley, Terah, Stanley Stubbs, and Bryant Bannister 1953 A Foundation for the Dating of Some Late Archaeological Sites in the Rio Grande Area, New Mexico. University of Arizona Bulletin 6: XXIV:3, Laboratory of Tree Ring Research, Tucson.

Smith, C.T., A.J. Budding, and C.W. Pitrat 1961 Geology of the Southwestern Part of the Chama Basin. Bulletin 75, New Mexico Institute of Mining and Technology. Socorro.

Steen, Charles 1982 Pajarito Plateau Archaeological Survey and Excavations 2. LA 8860. Los Alamos National Laboratory, Los Alamos, N.M.

Strong, W.D. 1935 An Introduction to Nebraskan Archaeology Smithsonian Institution Miscellaneous Collections XCIII:10. Washington, D.C.

Streuver, Mollie 1976 Letter to Dr. Florence Ellis dated May 14,1976, reporting results of tests done on samples submitted from the Red Hill Site. Department of Biology, University of New Mexico. Albuquerque.

Stubbs, Stanley A. and W.S. Stallings Jr. 1953 The Excavation of Pindi Pueblo New Mexico. Monograph 18 of the School of American Research and Laboratory of Anthropology, Santa Fe, New Mexico.

— 1941 Yearbook of Agriculture: Climate and Man. Washington, D.C.

Vivian, R. Gwenn, Dulce N. Dodgen, and Gayle H. Hartmann 1978 Wooden Ritual Artifacts from Chaco Canyon, New Mexico: The Chetro Ketl Collection, Anthropological Papers of the University of Arizona 32, Tucson

Weltfish, Gene 1932 Preliminary Classification of Southwestern Basketry. Smithsonian Miscellanious Collections 87:7. Washington, D.C.

Wendorf, Fred and John P.Miller 1959 Artifacts from High Mountain Sites in the Sangre de Cristo Range, New Mexico. El Palacio 66:2:37-52.

Windship, G.P. 1896 The Coronado Expedition. 1540-42. Bureau of American Ethnology Annual Report 14, Pt 1. Washington, D.C.

Woodbury, Richard B. 1954 Prehistoric Stone Implements of Northeastern Arizona. Reports of the Awatovi Expedition 6. Papers of the Peabody Museum of American Archaeology and Ethnology XXIV. Harvard University. Cambridge.

Index